2009 SUN SIGN BOOK

Forecasts by
Kris Brandt Riske

Book Editing: Sharon Leah
Cover Design: Kevin R. Brown

Copyright 2008 Llewellyn Publications
ISBN: 978-0-7387-0721-1
A Division of Llewellyn Worldwide, Ltd.
Llewellyn is a registered trademark of Llewellyn Worldwide, Ltd.
2143 Wooddale Drive, Woodbury, MN 55125
Printed in the USA

2009

JANUARY

S	M	T	W	T	F	S
				1	2	3
4	5	6	7	8	9	10
11	12	13	14	15	16	17
18	19	20	21	22	23	24
25	26	27	28	29	30	31

FEBRUARY

S	M	T	W	T	F	S
1	2	3	4	5	6	7
8	9	10	11	12	13	14
15	16	17	18	19	20	21
22	23	24	25	26	27	28

MARCH

S	M	T	W	T	F	S
1	2	3	4	5	6	7
8	9	10	11	12	13	14
15	16	17	18	19	20	21
22	23	24	25	26	27	28
29	30	31				

APRIL

S	M	T	W	T	F	S
			1	2	3	4
5	6	7	8	9	10	11
12	13	14	15	16	17	18
19	20	21	22	23	24	25
26	27	28	29	30		

MAY

S	M	T	W	T	F	S
					1	2
3	4	5	6	7	8	9
10	11	12	13	14	15	16
17	18	19	20	21	22	23
24	25	26	27	28	29	30
31						

JUNE

S	M	T	W	T	F	S
	1	2	3	4	5	6
7	8	9	10	11	12	13
14	15	16	17	18	19	20
21	22	23	24	25	26	27
28	29	30				

JULY

S	M	T	W	T	F	S
			1	2	3	4
5	6	7	8	9	10	11
12	13	14	15	16	17	18
19	20	21	22	23	24	25
26	27	28	29	30	31	

AUGUST

S	M	T	W	T	F	S
						1
2	3	4	5	6	7	8
9	10	11	12	13	14	15
16	17	18	19	20	21	22
23	24	25	26	27	28	29
30	31					

SEPTEMBER

S	M	T	W	T	F	S
		1	2	3	4	5
6	7	8	9	10	11	12
13	14	15	16	17	18	19
20	21	22	23	24	25	26
27	28	29	30			

OCTOBER

S	M	T	W	T	F	S
				1	2	3
4	5	6	7	8	9	10
11	12	13	14	15	16	17
18	19	20	21	22	23	24
25	26	27	28	29	30	31

NOVEMBER

S	M	T	W	T	F	S
1	2	3	4	5	6	7
8	9	10	11	12	13	14
15	16	17	18	19	20	21
22	23	24	25	26	27	28
29	30					

DECEMBER

S	M	T	W	T	F	S
		1	2	3	4	5
6	7	8	9	10	11	12
13	14	15	16	17	18	19
20	21	22	23	24	25	26
27	28	29	30	31		

2010

JANUARY

S	M	T	W	T	F	S
					1	2
3	4	5	6	7	8	9
10	11	12	13	14	15	16
17	18	19	20	21	22	23
24	25	26	27	28	29	30
31						

FEBRUARY

S	M	T	W	T	F	S
	1	2	3	4	5	6
7	8	9	10	11	12	13
14	15	16	17	18	19	20
21	22	23	24	25	26	27
28						

MARCH

S	M	T	W	T	F	S
	1	2	3	4	5	6
7	8	9	10	11	12	13
14	15	16	17	18	19	20
21	22	23	24	25	26	27
28	29	30	31			

APRIL

S	M	T	W	T	F	S
				1	2	3
4	5	6	7	8	9	10
11	12	13	14	15	16	17
18	19	20	21	22	23	24
25	26	27	28	29	30	

MAY

S	M	T	W	T	F	S
						1
2	3	4	5	6	7	8
9	10	11	12	13	14	15
16	17	18	19	20	21	22
23	24	25	26	27	28	29
30	31					

JUNE

S	M	T	W	T	F	S
		1	2	3	4	5
6	7	8	9	10	11	12
13	14	15	16	17	18	19
20	21	22	23	24	25	26
27	28	29	30			

JULY

S	M	T	W	T	F	S
				1	2	3
4	5	6	7	8	9	10
11	12	13	14	15	16	17
18	19	20	21	22	23	24
25	26	27	28	29	30	31

AUGUST

S	M	T	W	T	F	S
1	2	3	4	5	6	7
8	9	10	11	12	13	14
15	16	17	18	19	20	21
22	23	24	25	26	27	28
29	30	31				

SEPTEMBER

S	M	T	W	T	F	S
			1	2	3	4
5	6	7	8	9	10	11
12	13	14	15	16	17	18
19	20	21	22	23	24	25
26	27	28	29	30		

OCTOBER

S	M	T	W	T	F	S
					1	2
3	4	5	6	7	8	9
10	11	12	13	14	15	16
17	18	19	20	21	22	23
24	25	26	27	28	29	30
31						

NOVEMBER

S	M	T	W	T	F	S
	1	2	3	4	5	6
7	8	9	10	11	12	13
14	15	16	17	18	19	20
21	22	23	24	25	26	27
28	29	30	31			

DECEMBER

S	M	T	W	T	F	S
			1	2	3	4
5	6	7	8	9	10	11
12	13	14	15	16	17	18
19	20	21	22	23	24	25
26	27	28	29	30	31	

Table of Contents

2009 Sun Sign Book Articles

Meet Kris Brandt Riske

Kris Brandt Riske holds professional certification from the American Federation of Astrologers (PMAFA). She has a master's degree in journalism and has authored several books, including: *Llewellyn's Complete Book of Astrology: The Easy Way to Learn Astrology* (2007); *Mapping Your Money* (Llewellyn, 2005); *Mapping Your Future* (Llewellyn, 2004); *Astrometeorology: Planetary Power in Weather Forecasting* (AFA); and she coauthored *Mapping Your Travels and Relocation* (Llewellyn, 2005).

Kris also writes for astrology publications, and does the annual weather forecast for *Llewellyn's Moon Sign Book*. She specializes in relationships, romance and forecasting. She's an avid auto racing fan; although NASCAR is her favorite and she'd rather be a driver than a spectator, she also has a pole-side seat at the Indianapolis 500 each May. She's an avid gardener, and recently transformed her yard into a flowering Arizona-style garden, complete with a fountain and two brick patios. She and her husband are parents to three cats.

New Concepts for Signs of the Zodiac

The signs of the zodiac represent characteristics and traits that indicate how energy operates within our lives. The signs tell the story of human evolution and development, and all are necessary to form the continuum of whole life experience. In fact, all twelve signs are represented within your astrological chart.

Although the traditional metaphors for the twelve signs (such as Aries, the Ram) are always functional, these alternative concepts for each of the twelve signs also describe the gradual unfolding of the human spirit.

Aries: The Initiator is the first sign of the zodiac and encompasses the primary concept of getting things started. This fiery ignition and bright beginning can prove to be the thrust necessary for new life, but the Initiator also can appear before a situation is ready for change and create disruption.

Taurus: The Maintainer sustains what Aries has begun and brings stability and focus into the picture, yet there also can be a tendency to try to maintain something in its current state without allowing for new growth.

Gemini: The Questioner seeks to determine whether alternatives are possible and offers diversity to the processes Taurus has brought into stability. Yet questioning can also lead to distraction, subsequently scattering energy and diffusing focus.

Cancer: The Nurturer provides the qualities necessary for growth and security, and encourages a deepening awareness of emotional needs. Yet this same nurturing can stifle individuation if it becomes too smothering.

Leo: The Loyalist directs and centralizes the experiences Cancer feeds. This quality is powerfully targeted toward self-awareness, but can be shortsighted. Hence, the Loyalist can hold steadfastly to viewpoints or feelings that inhibit new experiences.

Virgo: The Modifier analyzes the situations Leo brings to light and determines possibilities for change. Even though this change may be in the name of improvement, it can lead to dissatisfaction with the self if not directed in harmony with higher needs.

Libra: The Judge is constantly comparing everything to be sure that a certain level of rightness and perfection is presented. However, the Judge can also present possibilities that are harsh and seem to be cold or without feeling.

Scorpio: The Catalyst steps into the play of life to provide the quality of alchemical transformation. The Catalyst can stir the brew just enough to create a healing potion, or may get things going to such a powerful extent that they boil out of control.

Sagittarius: The Adventurer moves away from Scorpio's dimension to seek what lies beyond the horizon. The Adventurer continually looks for possibilities that answer the ultimate questions, but may forget the pathway back home.

Capricorn: The Pragmatist attempts to put everything into its rightful place and find ways to make life work out right. The Pragmatist can teach lessons of practicality and determination, but can become highly self-righteous when shortsighted.

Aquarius: The Reformer looks for ways to take what Capricorn has built and bring it up to date. Yet there is also a tendency to scrap the original in favor of a new plan that may not have the stable foundation necessary to operate effectively.

Pisces: The Visionary brings mysticism and imagination, and challenges the soul to move beyond the physical plane, into the realm of what might be. The Visionary can pierce the veil, returning enlightened to the physical world. The challenge is to avoid getting lost within the illusion of an alternate reality.

Understanding the Basics of Astrology

Astrology is an ancient and continually evolving system used to clarify your identity and your needs. An astrological chart—which is calculated using the date, time, and place of birth—contains many factors that symbolically represent the needs, expressions, and experiences that make up the whole person. A professional astrologer interprets this symbolic picture, offering you an accurate portrait of your personality.

The chart itself—the horoscope—is a portrait of an individual. Generally, a natal (or birth) horoscope is drawn on a circular wheel. The wheel is divided into twelve segments, called houses. Each of the twelve houses represents a different aspect of the individual, much like the facets of a brilliantly cut stone. The houses depict different environments, such as home, school, and work. The houses also represent roles and relationships: parents, friends, lovers, children, partners. In each environment, individuals show a different side of their personality. At home, you may represent yourself quite differently than you do on the job. Additionally, in each relationship you will project a different image of yourself. Your parents rarely see the side you show to intimate friends.

Symbols for the planets, the Sun, and the Moon are drawn inside the houses. Each planet represents a separate kind of energy. You experience and express that energy in specific ways. (For a complete list, refer to the table on the next page.) The way you use each of these energies is up to you. The planets in your chart do not make you do anything!

The twelve signs of the zodiac indicate characteristics and traits that further define your personality. Each sign can be expressed in positive and negative ways. (The basic meaning of each of the signs is explained in the corresponding sections ahead.) What's more, you have all twelve signs somewhere in your chart. Signs that are strongly emphasized by the planets have greater force. The Sun, Moon, and planets are placed on the chart according to their position at the time of birth. The qualities of a sign, combined with the energy of a planet, indicate how you might be most likely to use

Signs of the Zodiac

Aries	♈	The Initiator
Taurus	♉	The Maintainer
Gemini	♊	The Questioner
Cancer	♋	The Nurturer
Leo	♌	The Loyalist
Virgo	♍	The Modifier
Libra	♎	The Judge
Scorpio	♏	The Catalyst
Sagittarius	♐	The Adventurer
Capricorn	♑	The Pragmatist
Aquarius	♒	The Reformer
Pisces	♓	The Visionary

that energy and the best ways to develop that energy. The signs add color, emphasis, and dimension to the personality.

Signs are also placed at the cusps, or dividing lines, of each of the houses. The influence of the signs on the houses is much the same as their influence on the Sun, Moon, and planets. Each house is shaped by the sign on its cusp.

When you view a horoscope, you will notice that there appear to be four distinctive angles dividing the wheel of the chart. The line that divides the chart into a top and bottom half represents the horizon. In most cases, the left side of the horizon is called the Ascendant. The zodiac sign on the Ascendant is your rising sign. The Ascendant indicates the way others are likely to view you.

The Sun, Moon, or planet can be compared to an actor in a play. The sign shows how the energy works, like the role the actor plays in a drama. The house indicates where the energy operates, like the setting of a play. On a psychological level, the Sun represents who you think you are. The Ascendant describes who others think you are, and the Moon reflects your inner self.

The Planets

Sun	☉	The ego, self, willpower
Moon	☽	The subconscious self, habits
Mercury	☿	Communication, the intellect
Venus	♀	Emotional expression, love, appreciation, artistry
Mars	♂	Physical drive, assertiveness, anger
Jupiter	♃	Philosophy, ethics, generosity
Saturn	♄	Discipline, focus, responsibility
Uranus	♅	Individuality, rebelliousness
Neptune	♆	Imagination, sensitivity, compassion
Pluto	♇	Transformation, healing, regeneration

Astrologers also study the geometric relationships between the Sun, Moon, and planets. These geometric angles are called aspects. Aspects further define the strengths, weaknesses, and challenges within your physical, mental, emotional, and spiritual self. Sometimes, patterns also appear in an astrological chart. These patterns have meaning.

To understand cycles for any given point in time, astrologers study several factors. Many use transits, which refer to the movement and positions of the planets. When astrologers compare those positions to the birth horoscope, the transits indicate activity in particular areas of the chart. The *Sun Sign Book* uses transits.

As you can see, your Sun sign is just one of many factors that describes who you are—but it is a powerful one! As the symbol of the ego, the Sun in your chart reflects your drive to be noticed. Most people can easily relate to the concepts associated with their Sun sign, since it is tied to their sense of personal identity.

Using this Book

This book contains what is called "Sun sign astrology," that is, astrology based on the sign that your Sun was in at the time of your birth. The technique has its foundation in ancient Greek astrology, in which the Sun was one of five points in the chart that was used as a focal point for delineation.

The most effective way to use astrology, however, is through one-on-one work with a professional astrologer, who can integrate the eight or so other astrological bodies into the interpretation to provide you with guidance. There are factors related to the year and time of day you were born that are highly significant in the way you approach life and vital to making wise choices. In addition, there are ways of using astrology that aren't addressed here, such as compatibility between two specific individuals, discovering family patterns, or picking a day for a wedding or grand opening.

To best use the information in the monthly forecasts, you'll want to determine your Ascendant, or rising sign. If you don't know your Ascendant, the tables following this description will help you determine your rising sign. They are most accurate for those born in the continental United States. They're only an approximation, but they can be used as a good rule of thumb. Your exact Ascendant may vary from the tables according to your time and place of birth. Once you've approximated your ascending sign using the tables or determined your Ascendant by having your chart calculated, you'll know two significant factors in your chart. Read the monthly forecast sections for both your Sun and Ascendant to gain the most useful information. In addition, you can read the section about the sign your Moon is in. The Sun is the true, inner you; the Ascendant is your shell or appearance and the person you are becoming; the Moon is the person you were—or still are based on habits and memories.

I've also included information about the planets' retrogrades this year. Most people have heard of "Mercury retrograde." In fact, all the planets except the Sun and Moon appear to travel backward (retrograde) in their path periodically. This only appears to happen because we on the Earth are not seeing the other planets from the middle of the solar system. Rather, we are watching them from our own moving object. We are like a train that moves past cars on the freeway that are going at a slower speed. To us on the train, the cars look like they're going backward. Mercury turns retrograde about every four months for three weeks; Venus every eighteen months for six weeks; Mars every two years for two to three months. The rest of the planets each retrograde once a year for four to five months. During each retrograde, we have the opportunity to try something new, something we conceived of at the beginning of the planet's yearly cycle. The times when the planets change direction are significant, as are the beginning and midpoint (peak or culmination) of each cycle. These are noted in your forecast each month.

Your "Rewarding and Challenging Days" sections indicate times when you'll feel either more centered or more out of balance. The rewarding days are not the only times you can perform well, but the times you're likely to feel better integrated! During challenging days, take extra time to center yourself by meditating or using other techniques that help you feel more objective.

The Action Table found at the end of each sign's section offers general guidelines for the best time to take a particular action. Please note, however, that your whole chart will provide more accurate guidelines for the best time to do something. Therefore, use this table with a grain of salt, and never let it stop you from taking an action you feel compelled to take.

You can use this information for an objective awareness about the way the current cycles are affecting you. Realize that the power of astrology is even more useful when you have a complete chart and professional guidance.

2009 at a Glance

The outer planets—Jupiter, Saturn, Neptune, Uranus, and Pluto—are major players in 2009, just as they were in 2008. Whenever two (or more) of these planets join forces they influence world conditions and also individual lives to a greater or lesser extent, depending upon their zodiacal placement.

This year, Jupiter and Neptune share space in Aquarius, forming an exact alignment in May and December. Jupiter represents expansion and luck, but also overoptimism and false hope. Neptune is the planet of spirituality, faith, compassion, and creativity, but also illusion and confusion. So it can be tough to get the best of this duo while avoiding its less attractive side.

The tendency here is toward wishful thinking, and it's easy to tune out reality. As great as this influence can be for creative and humanitarian endeavors, it's one that urges maximum financial caution. That extends beyond the obvious risk of investments and games of chance to letting others win your sympathies. Unless you're independently wealthy, keep donations in proportion to income and steel yourself to requests from friends and relatives. All are a set-up for major regrets. Instead, use Jupiter-Neptune to find an outlet for positive self-expression, possibly one that might help others: tap into your creative energy, volunteer for a good cause, or discover (or re-discover) your inner faith and strength through a self-help group.

This year also brings two more exact alignments of Saturn in Virgo and Uranus in Pisces. (The first was in November 2008.) When restrictive Saturn meets unpredictable Uranus, the challenge is to break free from restriction in the pursuit of change and independence, while still managing to maintain the status quo. While this lineup will affect everything from business to politics to collective individual freedoms, real estate, and health care, on a personal level it will manifest as profound change or endings. For some people the focus will be money matters, a relationship or job, for example, while others will experience Saturn/Uranus on an internal level that results in new directions. Be cautious. Changes made during a Uranus transit are almost always irreversible.

A new outer planet phase begins October 29, when Saturn enters Libra and aligns with Pluto in Capricorn. (These two planets will contact each other three times between November 2009 and August 2010.) Frustration and an inability to control major forces of change are characteristic of this transit, which in some respects will continue what was begun by Saturn/Uranus. Jobs, finances, and real estate will be hotspots, and there could be an increasing demand for governmental and corporate change. This lineup can impact people's lives in any of these areas, while also encouraging a general desire to revamp and restructure life as part of an evolutionary process. Again, though, sudden decisions aren't the wisest choice because change associated with Pluto is also usually irreversible.

Ascendant Table

Your Time of Birth

Your Sun Sign	6–8 am	8–10 am	10 am–Noon	Noon–2 pm	2–4 pm	4–6 pm
Aries	Taurus	Gemini	Cancer	Leo	Virgo	Libra
Taurus	Gemini	Cancer	Leo	Virgo	Libra	Scorpio
Gemini	Cancer	Leo	Virgo	Libra	Scorpio	Sagittarius
Cancer	Leo	Virgo	Libra	Scorpio	Sagittarius	Capricorn
Leo	Virgo	Libra	Scorpio	Sagittarius	Capricorn	Aquarius
Virgo	Libra	Scorpio	Sagittarius	Capricorn	Aquarius	Pisces
Libra	Scorpio	Sagittarius	Capricorn	Aquarius	Pisces	Aries
Scorpio	Sagittarius	Capricorn	Aquarius	Pisces	Aries	Taurus
Sagittarius	Capricorn	Aquarius	Pisces	Aries	Taurus	Gemini
Capricorn	Aquarius	Pisces	Aries	Taurus	Gemini	Cancer
Aquarius	Pisces	Aries	Taurus	Gemini	Cancer	Leo
Pisces	Aries	Taurus	Gemini	Cancer	Leo	Virgo

Your Time of Birth

Your Sun Sign	6–8 pm	8–10 pm	10 pm–Midnight	Midnight–2 am	2–4 am	4–6 am
Aries	Scorpio	Sagittarius	Capricorn	Aquarius	Pisces	Aries
Taurus	Sagittarius	Capricorn	Aquarius	Pisces	Aries	Taurus
Gemini	Capricorn	Aquarius	Pisces	Aries	Taurus	Gemini
Cancer	Aquarius	Pisces	Aries	Taurus	Gemini	Cancer
Leo	Pisces	Aries	Taurus	Gemini	Cancer	Leo
Virgo	Aries	Taurus	Gemini	Cancer	Leo	Virgo
Libra	Taurus	Gemini	Cancer	Leo	Virgo	Libra
Scorpio	Gemini	Cancer	Leo	Virgo	Libra	Scorpio
Sagittarius	Cancer	Leo	Virgo	Libra	Scorpio	Sagittarius
Capricorn	Leo	Virgo	Libra	Scorpio	Sagittarius	Capricorn
Aquarius	Virgo	Libra	Scorpio	Sagittarius	Capricorn	Aquarius
Pisces	Libra	Scorpio	Sagittarius	Capricorn	Aquarius	Pisces

How to use this table: 1. Find your Sun sign in the left column.

2. Find your approximate birth time in a vertical column.

3. Line up your Sun sign and birth time to find your Ascendant.

This table will give you an approximation of your Ascendant. If you feel that the sign listed as your Ascendant is incorrect, try the one either before or after the listed sign. It is difficult to determine your exact Ascendant without a complete natal chart.

Astrological Glossary

Air: One of the four basic elements. The air signs are Gemini, Libra, and Aquarius.

Angles: The four points of the chart that divide it into quadrants. The angles are sensitive areas that lend emphasis to planets located near them. These points are located on the cusps of the First, Fourth, Seventh, and Tenth Houses in a chart.

Ascendant: Rising sign. The degree of the zodiac on the eastern horizon at the time and place for which the horoscope is calculated. It can indicate the image or physical appearance you project to the world. The cusp of the First House.

Aspect: The angular relationship between planets, sensitive points, or house cusps in a horoscope. Lines drawn between the two points and the center of the chart, representing the Earth, form the angle of the aspect. Astrological aspects include conjunction (two points that are 0 degrees apart), opposition (two points, 180 degrees apart), square (two points, 90 degrees apart), sextile (two points, 60 degrees apart), and trine (two points, 120 degrees apart). Aspects can indicate harmony or challenge.

Cardinal Sign: One of the three qualities, or categories, that describe how a sign expresses itself. Aries, Cancer, Libra, and Capricorn are the cardinal signs, believed to initiate activity.

Chiron: Chiron is a comet traveling in orbit between Saturn and Uranus. Although research on its effect on natal charts is not yet complete, it is believed to represent a key or doorway, healing, ecology, and a bridge between traditional and modern methods.

Conjunction: An aspect or angle between two points in a chart where the two points are close enough so that the energies join. Can be considered either harmonious or challenging, depending on the planets involved and their placement.

Cusp: A dividing line between signs or houses in a chart.

Degree: Degree of arc. One of 360 divisions of a circle. The circle of the zodiac is divided into twelve astrological signs of 30 degrees each. Each degree is made up of 60 minutes, and each minute is made up of 60 seconds of zodiacal longitude.

Earth: One of the four basic elements. The earth signs are Taurus, Virgo, and Capricorn.

Eclipse: A solar eclipse is the full or partial covering of the Sun by the Moon (as viewed from Earth), and a lunar eclipse is the full or partial covering of the Moon by the Earth's own shadow.

Ecliptic: The Sun's apparent path around the Earth, which is actually the plane of the Earth's orbit extended out into space. The ecliptic forms the center of the zodiac.

Electional Astrology: A branch of astrology concerned with choosing the best time to initiate an activity.

Elements: The signs of the zodiac are divided into four groups of three zodiacal signs, each symbolized by one of the four elements of the ancients: fire, earth, air, and water. The element of a sign is said to express its essential nature.

Ephemeris: A listing of the Sun, Moon, and planets' positions and related information for astrological purposes.

Equinox: Equal night. The point in the Earth's orbit around the Sun at which the day and night are equal in length.

Feminine Signs: Each zodiac sign is either masculine or feminine. Earth signs (Taurus, Virgo, and Capricorn) and water signs (Cancer, Scorpio, and Pisces) are feminine.

Fire: One of the four basic elements. The fire signs are Aries, Leo, and Sagittarius.

Fixed Signs: Fixed is one of the three qualities, or categories, that describe how a sign expresses itself. The fixed signs are Taurus, Leo, Scorpio, and Aquarius. Fixed signs are said to be predisposed to existing patterns and somewhat resistant to change.

Hard Aspects: Hard aspects are those aspects in a chart that astrologers believe to represent difficulty or challenges. Among the hard aspects are the square, the opposition, and the conjunction (depending on which planets are conjunct).

Horizon: The word "horizon" is used in astrology in a manner similar to its common usage, except that only the eastern and western horizons are considered useful. The eastern horizon at the point of birth is the Ascendant, or First House cusp, of a natal chart, and the western horizon at the point of birth is the Descendant, or Seventh House cusp.

Houses: Division of the horoscope into twelve segments, beginning with the Ascendant. The dividing line between the houses are called house cusps. Each house corresponds to certain aspects of daily living, and is ruled by the astrological sign that governs the cusp, or dividing line between the house and the one previous.

Ingress: The point of entry of a planet into a sign.

Lagna: A term used in Hindu or Vedic astrology for Ascendant, the degree of the zodiac on the eastern horizon at the time of birth.

Masculine Signs: Each of the twelve signs of the zodiac is either "masculine" or "feminine." The fire signs (Aries, Leo, and Sagittarius) and the air signs (Gemini, Libra, and Aquarius) are masculine.

Midheaven: The highest point on the ecliptic, where it intersects the meridian that passes directly above the place for which the horoscope is cast; the southern point of the horoscope.

Midpoint: A point equally distant to two planets or house cusps. Midpoints are considered by some astrologers to be sensitive points in a person's chart.

Mundane Astrology: Mundane astrology is the branch of astrology generally concerned with political and economic events, and the nations involved in these events.

Mutable Signs: Mutable is one of the three qualities, or categories, that describe how a sign expresses itself. Mutable signs are Gemini, Virgo, Sagittarius, and Pisces. Mutable signs are said to be very adaptable and sometimes changeable.

Natal Chart: A person's birth chart. A natal chart is essentially a "snapshot" showing the placement of each of the planets at the exact time of a person's birth.

Node: The point where the planets cross the ecliptic, or the Earth's apparent path around the Sun. The North Node is the point where a planet moves northward, from the Earth's perspective, as it crosses the ecliptic; the South Node is where it moves south.

Opposition: Two points in a chart that are 180 degrees apart.

Orb: A small degree of margin used when calculating aspects in a chart. For example, although 180 degrees form an exact opposition, an astrologer might consider an aspect within 3 or 4 degrees on either side of 180 degrees to be an opposition, as the impact of the aspect can still be felt within this range. The less orb on an aspect, the stronger the aspect. Astrologers' opinions vary on how many degrees of orb to allow for each aspect.

Outer Planet: Uranus, Neptune, and Pluto are known as the outer planets. Because of their distance from the Sun, they take a long time to complete a single rotation. Everyone born within a few years on either side of a given date will have similar placements of these planets.

Planet: The planets used in astrology are Mercury, Venus, Mars, Jupiter, Saturn, Uranus, Neptune, and Pluto. For astrological purposes, the Sun and Moon are also considered planets. A natal or birth chart lists planetary placement at the moment of birth.

Planetary Rulership: The sign in which a planet is most harmoniously placed. Examples are the Sun in Leo, Jupiter in Sagittarius, and the Moon in Cancer.

Precession of Equinoxes: The gradual movement of the point of the Spring Equinox, located at 0 degrees Aries. This point marks the beginning of the tropical zodiac. The point moves slowly backward through the constellations of the zodiac, so that about every 2,000 years the equinox begins in an earlier constellation.

Qualities: In addition to categorizing the signs by element, astrologers place the twelve signs of the zodiac into three additional categories, or qualities: cardinal, mutable, or fixed. Each sign is considered to be a combination of its element and quality. Where the element of a sign describes its basic nature, the quality describes its mode of expression.

Retrograde Motion: Apparent backward motion of a planet. This is an illusion caused by the relative motion of the Earth and other planets in their elliptical orbits.

Sextile: Two points in a chart that are 60 degrees apart.

Sidereal Zodiac: Generally used by Hindu or Vedic astrologers. The sidereal zodiac is located where the constellations are actually positioned in the sky.

Soft Aspects: Soft aspects indicate good fortune or an easy relationship in the chart. Among the soft aspects are the trine, the sextile, and the conjunction (depending on which planets are conjunct each other).

Square: Two points in a chart that are 90 degrees apart.

Sun Sign: The sign of the zodiac in which the Sun is located at any given time.

Synodic Cycle: The time between conjunctions of two planets.

Trine: Two points in a chart that are 120 degrees apart.

Tropical Zodiac: The tropical zodiac begins at 0 degrees Aries, where the Sun is located during the Spring Equinox. This system is used by most Western astrologers and throughout this book.

Void-of-Course: A planet is void-of-course after it has made its last aspect within a sign, but before it has entered a new sign.

Water: One of the four basic elements. Water signs are Cancer, Scorpio, and Pisces.

Meanings of the Planets

The Sun

The Sun indicates the psychological bias that will dominate your actions. What you see, and why, is told in the reading for your Sun. The Sun also shows the basic energy patterns of your body and psyche. In many ways, the Sun is the dominant force in your horoscope and your life. Other influences, especially that of the Moon, may modify the Sun's influence, but nothing will cause you to depart very far from the basic solar pattern. Always keep in mind the basic influence of the Sun and remember all other influences must be interpreted in terms of it, especially insofar as they play a visible role in your life. You may think, dream, imagine, and hope a thousand things, according to your Moon and your other planets, but the Sun is what you are. To be your best self in terms of your Sun is to cause your energies to work along the path in which they will have maximum help from planetary vibrations.

The Moon

The Moon tells the desire of your life. When you know what you mean but can't verbalize it, it is your Moon that knows it and your Sun that can't say it. The wordless ecstasy, the mute sorrow, the secret dream, the esoteric picture of yourself that you can't get across to the world, or that the world doesn't comprehend or value—these are the products of the Moon. When you are misunderstood, it is your Moon nature, expressed imperfectly through the Sun sign, that feels betrayed. Things you know without thought—intuitions, hunches, instincts—are the products of the Moon. Modes of expression that you feel truly reflect your deepest self belong to the Moon: art, letters, creative work of any kind; sometimes love; sometimes business. Whatever you feel to be most deeply yourself is the product of your Moon and of the sign your Moon occupies at birth.

Mercury

Mercury is the sensory antenna of your horoscope. Its position by sign indicates your reactions to sights, sounds, odors, tastes, and touch impressions, affording a key to the attitude you have toward the physical world around you. Mercury is the messenger through which your physical body and brain (ruled by the Sun) and your inner nature (ruled by the Moon) are kept in contact with the outer world, which will appear to you according to the index of Mercury's position by sign in the horoscope. Mercury rules your rational mind.

Venus

Venus is the emotional antenna of your horoscope. Through Venus, impressions come to you from the outer world, to which you react emotionally. The position of Venus by sign at the time of your birth determines your attitude toward these experiences. As Mercury is the messenger linking sense impressions (sight, smell, etc.) to the basic nature of your Sun and Moon, so Venus is the messenger linking emotional impressions. If Venus is found in the same sign as the Sun, emotions gain importance in your life, and have a direct bearing on your actions. If Venus is in the same sign as the Moon, emotions bear directly on your inner nature, add self-confidence, make you sensitive to emotional impressions, and frequently indicate that you have more love in your heart than you are able to express. If Venus is in the same sign as Mercury, emotional impressions and sense impressions work together; you tend to idealize the world of the senses and sensualize the world of the emotions to interpret emotionally what you see and hear.

Mars

Mars is the energy principle in the horoscope. Its position indicates the channels into which energy will most easily be directed. It is the planet through which the activities of the Sun and the desires of the Moon express themselves in action. In the same sign as the Sun, Mars gives abundant energy, sometimes misdirected in temper, temperament, and quarrels. In the same sign as the Moon, it gives a great capacity to make use of the innermost aims, and to make the inner desires articulate and practical. In the same sign as Venus, it quickens emotional reactions and causes you to act on them, makes for ardor and passion in love, and fosters an earthly awareness of emotional realities.

Jupiter

Jupiter is the feeler for opportunity that you have out in the world. It passes along chances of a lifetime for consideration according to the basic nature of your Sun and Moon. Jupiter's sign position indicates the places where you will look for opportunity, the uses to which you wish to put it, and the capacity you have to react and profit by it. Jupiter is ordinarily, and erroneously, called the planet of luck. It is "luck" insofar as it is the index of opportunity, but your luck depends less on what comes to you than on what you do with what comes to you. In the same sign as the Sun or Moon, Jupiter gives a direct, and generally effective, response to opportunity and is likely to show forth at its "luckiest." If Jupiter is in the same sign as Mercury, sense impressions are interpreted opportunistically. If Jupiter is in the same sign as Venus, you interpret emotions in such a way as to turn them to your advantage; your feelings work harmoniously with the chances for progress that the world has to offer. If Jupiter is in the same sign as Mars, you follow opportunity with energy, dash, enthusiasm, and courage; take long chances; and play your cards wide open.

Saturn

Saturn indicates the direction that will be taken in life by the self-preservative principle that, in its highest manifestation, ceases to be purely defensive and becomes ambitious and aspiring. Your defense or attack against the world is shown by the sign position of Saturn in the horoscope of birth. If Saturn is in the same sign as the Sun or Moon, defense predominates, and there is danger of introversion. The farther Saturn is from the Sun, Moon, and Ascendant, the better for objectivity and extroversion. If Saturn is in the same sign as Mercury, there is a profound and serious reaction to sense impressions; this position generally accompanies a deep and efficient mind. If Saturn is in the same sign as Venus, a defensive attitude toward emotional experience makes for apparent coolness in love and difficulty with the emotions and human relations. If Saturn is in the same sign as Mars, confusion between defensive and aggressive urges can make a person indecisive. On the other hand, if the Sun and Moon are strong and the total personality well developed, a balanced, peaceful, and calm individual of sober judgment and moderate actions may be indicated. If Saturn is in the same sign as Jupiter, the reaction to opportunity is sober and balanced.

Uranus

Uranus in a general way relates to creativity, originality, or individuality, and its position by sign in the horoscope tells the direction in which you will seek to express yourself. In the same sign as Mercury or the Moon, Uranus suggests acute awareness, a quick reaction to sense impressions and experiences, or a hair-trigger mind. In the same sign as the Sun, it points to great nervous activity, a high-strung nature, and an original, creative, or eccentric personality. In the same sign as Mars, Uranus indicates high-speed activity, love of swift motion, and perhaps love of danger. In the same sign as Venus, it suggests an unusual reaction to emotional experience, idealism, sensuality, and original ideas about love and human relations. In the same sign as Saturn, Uranus points to good sense; this can be a practical, creative position, but, more often than not, it sets up a destructive conflict between practicality and originality that can result in a stalemate. In the same sign as Jupiter, Uranus makes opportunity, creates wealth and the means of getting it, and is conducive to the inventive, executive, and daring.

Neptune

Neptune relates to the deepest wells of the subconscious, inherited mentality, and spirituality, indicating what you take for granted in life. Neptune in the same sign as the Sun or Moon indicates that intuitions and hunches—or delusions—dominate; there is a need for rigidly holding to reality. In the same sign as Mercury, Neptune indicates sharp sensory perceptions, a sensitive and perhaps creative mind, and a quivering intensity of reaction to sensory experience. In the same sign as Venus, it reveals idealistic and romantic (or sentimental) reactions to emotional experience, as well as the danger of sensationalism and a love of strange pleasures. In the same sign as Mars, Neptune indicates energy and intuition that work together to make mastery of life—one of the signs of having angels (or devils) on your side. When in the same sign as Jupiter, Neptune describes an intuitive response to opportunity along practical and money-making lines. In the same sign as Saturn, Neptune indicates intuitive defense and attack on the world, which is generally successful unless Saturn is polarized on the negative side; then there is danger of unhappiness.

Pluto

Pluto is a planet of extremes—from the lowest criminal and violent level of our society to the heights people can attain when they realize their significance in the collectivity of humanity. Pluto also rules three important mysteries of life—sex, death, and rebirth—and links them to each other. One level of death symbolized by Pluto is the physical death of an individual, which occurs so that a person can be reborn into another body to further his or her spiritual development. On another level, individuals can experience a "death" of their old self when they realize the deeper significance of life; thus they become one of the "second born." In a natal horoscope, Pluto signifies our perspective on the world, our conscious and subconscious. Since so many of Pluto's qualities are centered on the deeper mysteries of life, the house position of Pluto, and aspects to it, can show you how to attain a deeper understanding of the importance of the spiritual in your life.

Forecasts

By Kris Brandt Riske

ARIES

The Ram
March 20 to April 19

♈

Element: Fire

Quality: Cardinal

Polarity: Yang/Masculine

Planetary Ruler: Mars

Meditation: I build upon my strengths

Gemstone: Diamond

Power Stones: Bloodstone, carnelian, ruby

Key Phrase: I am

Glyph: Ram's head

Anatomy: Head, face, throat

Color: Red, white

Animal: Ram

Myths/Legends: Artemis, Jason and the Golden Fleece

House: First

Opposite Sign: Libra

Flower: Geranium

Key Word: Initiative

Your Strengths and Challenges

When it comes to pizzazz, you have it all—action, energy, and initiative. You're a whiz when you put these Aries qualities to good use. But you also can be impulsive and impatient, dashing through life almost at the speed of light. Used to advantage, however, these traits help you snap up the best of life's opportunities while other people are still debating the pros and cons.

Born under the first sign of the zodiac, you're a natural leader, almost always the first in line; and the one who jumps in, takes charge, and makes decisions. This infectious enthusiasm, fueled by fiery Mars, your ruling planet, is the spark that gets things moving. With it, however, comes a challenge—follow-through. You have a passion for new endeavors but your interest begins to wane when the newness wears off. Try to develop some staying power; you'll go further in life.

Noted for your quick mind, you can size up a situation in an instant, easily grasping most of the important points and players. Yet there are times when you jump to conclusions and make snap decisions you later regret. Learn from these experiences and teach yourself to think before you act; careful thought truly is sometimes the wisest option. Adopt a similar approach behind the wheel and in physical activities, where being a daredevil is likely to backfire.

Confident and outgoing, you greet each day with optimism and the freshness of your springtime sign, ready for life's latest adventure. This pioneering attitude sets you apart as someone who truly knows how to live each day to the fullest with all the zesty enthusiasm that can lead to great achievements.

Your Relationships

Although you delight in the company of others, only those who know you well realize the high value you place on relationships. Some see you as a mover-and-shaker who flies solo, interested only in your own agenda. That's true at times, but overall you want and need human companionship and have a knack for connecting with people. Just be sure to greet differing opinions with an open mind. Chances are, you'll learn something and might even change your views.

Your natural flair for romance gives you the instinctive know-how to wow a date, and later your partner, because you know how to keep the love alive. And that's very important to you because you feel incomplete until you link hearts with a soul mate—someone who can not only share your dreams but teach you the art of compromise. Libra, your opposite sign, could be your best match, and you also might be compatible with a Leo or Sagittarius, the other fire signs. Airy Gemini and Aquarius would stimulate your thinking, but conflict could be more the norm than the exception with a Cancer or Capricorn.

Domestic life is important to you, and most Aries people are actively involved in the lives of their children and extended family—parents, siblings, cousins, aunts, and uncles. These strong ties are a part of your emotional well-being and bring out your softer, nurturing side. Your children are a source of pride, although you can overindulge them. Remember, too, that sometimes it's better to let children learn life lessons the hard way rather than try to insulate them from reality.

You're a fabulous friend to those few in your inner circle, and also popular with your many acquaintances. Networking is your specialty, one of your keys to success, and you excel at teamwork when you feel it's in your best interests to join the crowd. Group activities, including clubs and organizations, bring out your best and maximize your leadership skills.

Your Career and Money

Your ambitions are centered on your career, where you have the potential to rise above the rest. Be aware, though, that it may take you longer than your peers to find your niche. Once you do, there's little that can deter you from your goal because you meet challenges head-on, knowing that with determination and effort you can succeed. So once you're on the right career path don't let impatience prompt you to move on, unless a new position can advance your aims.

You're good with details in your everyday work, although you also need the freedom to set your own pace. A hard worker, you expect coworkers to do the same and have little tolerance for those who don't perform up to their abilities or fulfill their responsibilities. Try to remember that not everyone has your drive.

You have wealth potential and a better chance of achieving it if you resist impulsive purchases. Think long term, let your practical side emerge, and live within a budget. You also have a knack for finding bargains if you take your time. Some people with an Aries Sun receive a sizable inheritance from a family member, and you also could do well in real estate. If you're a do-it-yourselfer, you might profit from remodeling houses or owning rental property.

Your Lighter Side

Because Aries is the first sign of the zodiac you have the unique ability to tap into the individual energy of all twelve signs in its purest form. This gives you an innate understanding of relationships, finances, communication, family, and all else that encompasses your life. It's your gift from the universe to use wisely and one that puts you a step ahead of the other eleven signs—just where you wish to be.

Affirmation for the Year

Patience!

The Year Ahead for Aries

Much of this year's outer planetary emphasis centers on your career and work life. But your 2009 agenda is definitely not all work and no play. The good news is you're well placed to achieve a satisfying balance between the two.

You may have experienced a shake-up at work in October or November 2008—or just an undercurrent of change on the horizon. It's also possible you felt a growing sense of dissatisfaction with your current job situation. That feeling—or a sudden change in your work life—will return in early February as stable Saturn in Virgo forms its second exact alignment with unpredictable Uranus in Pisces, your solar sixth-twelfth house axis. But it's likely to be early March before things reach a turning point. Even at that, it will be mid-September when the third and final Saturn-Uranus alignment occurs, that things will come full circle and you'll begin to feel more settled. You'll want to remember this and plan accordingly if you're searching for a new position. Unfortunately, it could take until September to land the right spot for you.

If your job sector is prone to layoffs (or even if it's not) you'll want to be alert for rumors and rumblings. Talk with people. Use your sixth sense to detect subtle shifts in the workplace environment, and look for opportunities to strengthen your position. You could just as easily and suddenly stake your claim to a fabulous new job opportunity. So be proactive, keep your options open and your resume updated.

Just as calm begins to return, however, you could be in for another bumpy career ride. Saturn enters Libra, your solar seventh house of close relationships, the end of October, where it will clash with Pluto in Capricorn, your career sector, for the rest of the year. You could have issues with a supervisor or someone else in authority during this time frame, when it would be wise to maintain a low profile and avoid being dragged into power plays. And with Mars, your ruler, turning retrograde in Leo about the same time, this could be a particularly frustrating time for you. Think happy thoughts, learn patience, fill your leisure-time hours with fun, and remember that nothing lasts forever.

On the positive side, with Pluto now firmly in Capricorn, you have a once-in-a-lifetime opportunity to make your career mark during the next fifteen years. This tiny but potent planet will challenge you to realign your ambitions and aim high, while remembering that people will be a key factor in your 2009–2010 achievements. More importantly, how you handle the Saturn/Pluto influence now could have a major influence on where you find yourself in seven years. Get to know the right people. Tame and channel your Martian energy so it can fuel your initiative, your drive, and new endeavors.

It takes Saturn twenty-eight years to move through the entire zodiac, spending about two-and-a-half years in each sign. As it moves through Libra, you'll experience ups and downs in relationships. But despite what you may have heard, Saturn in your relationship sector does not necessarily signal doom and gloom for a partnership. In fact, you and your mate could develop even stronger bonds of love or, if you're single, you could make a lifetime commitment. You can expect some people to exit your life, however. This could be because they (or you) relocate, but the most likely scenario is because you'll make a conscious decision to move on, such as simply deciding that certain friends are no longer good for you—for whatever reason. It also could indicate difficulties in a business partnership. (If you want to form a business alliance, it would be best to wait until at least 2010.)

With all this going on, you'll especially appreciate expansive Jupiter's year-long tour of Aquarius, your friendship sign. You'll remember 2009 as one of the best on the social scene, and welcome plenty of new faces to your circle of acquaintances. Some will become friends and you might even connect with a soul mate who offers you the wisest advice of your life.

If you're searching for a mate, you could meet the love of your life through a mutual friend. Or you might discover you have romantic feelings for a long-time pal.

Luck will come through other people, especially friends, and you'll polish your networking skills and make some valuable contacts. You might also want to get involved in a charitable organization, club, or professional group where you can meet people.

Also consider stepping into a leadership role, which will give you increased visibility and help you achieve your career goals.

But you'll want to be wary in May, June, and December, when Jupiter will join forces with Neptune. Someone you consider trustworthy could disappoint you or try to lead you astray. Take notes regarding the events that occur in early February, as well as people you meet; that information could give you a clue about what will happen later in the year. Above all, question everything and don't let wishful thinking color your judgment. What seems too good to be true probably is. And don't be surprised if you feel the need to explore your spiritual side in a quest for not just knowledge but wisdom.

What This Year's Eclipses Mean for You

Four eclipses occur most years; 2009 has six, some of which will bring gifts from the universe while others will challenge you.

This year's two eclipses in Aquarius—January 7 (solar) and August 8 (lunar)—boost the beneficial influence of Jupiter in the same sign. That's doubly positive for an active social life and memorable times with old friends and with new acquaintances. If you're involved in group activities at work or at play, you could effortlessly move into a top leadership role.

But these eclipses are about more than fun times. Aquarius is also your sign of hopes, wishes, goals, and objectives. Set a clear path for yourself and take action to create what you want to achieve—love, career, financial, or personal success. Keep Neptune in mind, however. The February 9 lunar eclipse in Leo will join forces with this planet of illusion and confusion, as well as spirituality and creativity. Dream big. Be realistic. Believe in yourself, although not necessarily in others, as you pursue excellence.

Two areas require the utmost caution: romance and speculation. It's okay to get serious if you're in a dating relationship. Just hold off on commitment until 2010. You might be in love, but there's an equal chance you could be in love with love and thus fail to see your paramour in a true light. If you're part of a couple, however, add some sizzle to your relationship and remember all the reasons you fell in love.

You'll want to be equally cautious with investments and games of chance. What seems like a sure thing may or may not be despite a friend's or someone else's assurances. That's not to say this person would intentionally try to mislead you; he or she could merely be misinformed. Rein yourself in and be conservative with money.

Of the other three eclipses this year, two are in Cancer, your sign of home and family. You'll be more interested and involved in family life, and have increased contact with relatives. Either of these eclipses, which occur July 22 (solar) and December 31 (lunar), could also trigger a move within the last six months of 2009 or the first six months of 2010. You also could begin or complete extensive renovations in order to create a more comfortable home. With this year's other influences, however, 2009 probably isn't the best to move in with someone you're dating.

If your birthday is within a few days of April 22, the time may be right to resolve long-standing family issues, even those that go back to childhood. You also could take on added responsibilities for your parents or other elderly relatives.

This year also features a July 7 lunar eclipse in Capricorn, which reinforces Pluto's career influence, and may open up an opportunity for advancement. Networking could be your best avenue so be alert when you talk with people at work and while socializing with friends and colleagues. You'll also want to plan ahead as much as possible because you'll be pushed for time with an increased workload and responsibilities through year's end. Managing that plus a busy domestic life will be a balancing act that tests your patience and stamina. This is especially true if your birthday is in the last few days of March or the first few days of April.

Saturn

If you were born between April 2 and 19, Saturn will contact your Sun from Virgo, your solar sixth house of daily work and health. One could impact the other, so you'll want to get plenty of rest and regularly de-stress through exercise, time with family, hobbies, and friends. You'll probably find yourself worrying more than usual, but try not to fall into the trap of borrowing trouble. Be your proactive best and take steps to resolve whatever weighs heavily on your mind. Also stay organized because it will be easy to get mired in details and to overload yourself at work. The latter will be to some extent unavoidable, which is where this year's Aquarius influence can come in handy: ask for help from friendly coworkers when you need it. By sharing the load you'll ease your own.

You'll experience these influences to a greater degree **if you were born between April 2 and 6**, with tension rising in May. **If you were born between April 7 and 11**, events will unfold more slowly from January through March, and conclude in July and August. However, **if you were born between April 12 and 19**, you'll have a few challenging weeks without the level of intensity experienced by others with an Aries Sun sign.

If you were born between March 20 and 24, you'll be among the first to have Saturn in Libra, your solar seventh house of close relationships, contact your Sun. You can expect one or more relationships to require attention. Some will be positive; others will be challenging. If you're married or in a serious romantic relationship, this transit will test your commitment as it also offers you the opportunity to strengthen ties. It's all about learning from and about each other. Some couples will draw closer together while others will question their future. Stop and think if your relationship is strained; the very behavior that suddenly upsets you may be more a reflection of your current mindset and actions. If you're contemplating lifetime commitment, however, it would be wise to wait until the fall of 2010, when Saturn will complete its final contact with your Sun. It's possible you and a long-time friend could part ways when you realize your values are out of sync. The same could be true of a business partner, and now is not the time to begin such an endeavor. Career conflict is likely with a coworker or supervisor, and you should be prepared to withstand increasing frustration the last two months of the year. At times you'll feel—and be—powerless to change the situation, and some days will test your patience and stamina to the max. Try to view it all as a learning experience in human nature and focus on rising above it. Exercise and hobbies are an excellent way to counteract the stress.

If you were born between April 8 and 16, Uranus in Pisces, your solar twelfth house, will subtly but firmly encourage you to look within for answers to life's puzzling questions. Your dreams are likely to be vivid and insightful, and this is a terrific time to tune in to your inner voice. If you've never considered yourself intuitive, now is the time to discover this other side of yourself. You'll benefit from the initially subtle messages that become stronger the more you listen to them.

If you were born between April 11 and 16, mystical Neptune in Aquarius could trigger your interest in humanitarian causes. Volunteer your time or take the lead in a fund-raising effort. More importantly, you can be an inspiration to many people this year by encouraging them to excel. You're also likely to develop a growing sense of spirituality, which motivates you to explore and define what you really want from life. Among all those with an Aries Sun, however, you need to be especially cautious about whom you trust. Some people will tell you only what you want to hear in the hope that you'll believe and act on what they say. Resist the pressure, be true to yourself, and do what's right for you even if that means disappointing someone else.

If you were born between March 20 and 24, Pluto will clash with your Sun from Capricorn, your solar tenth house of career, at the same time that Saturn contacts your Sun from Libra, your relationship sign. Although this is a difficult configuration, how it manifests in your life depends in part upon your outlook, your attitude, and your willingness to not only accept but embrace new personal and career directions. Granted, doing that may be easier said than done. However, if anyone can do it, you can. Focus on the bigger picture and try to position yourself earlier in the year for career growth and advancement. Be cautious, though, about whom you take into your confidence because someone could use this information for his or her gain and your loss. And, it's almost guaranteed that romantic relationship with a coworker (or supervisor) will lead to job and career difficulties. Think carefully before you go there and consider all the potential ramifications. This also is not the year to form a business partnership, even with your mate, a relative, or a close friend.

Aries/January

Planetary Hotspots

Your domestic life shines brightly under the January 10 lunar eclipse in Cancer. One question: what are you waiting for? Get cracking and finish all those projects you put on hold before the holidays. With Saturn in Virgo helping things along, all it takes is initiative. You'll have more success if you read directions first and act second, and keep friends out of the loop. You can do it on your own.

Planetary Lightspots

You are in luck. Expansive Jupiter enters Aquarius, your solar eleventh house, January 5, to launch a year of fun and friendship. Both really take off the week of the January 26 New Moon (and solar eclipse) in Aquarius. Host a get-together at your place for friends and colleagues, or organize a night out where you can meet new people. Just be sure to double-check times and places because Mercury will be retrograde in Aquarius from the 11th on.

Relationships

You have time with friends and an opportunity to get better acquainted with coworkers this month. Just be sure to keep confidences to yourself the third week of the month. If you're half of a couple, Venus in Pisces from the 3rd on is pure delight for romantic evenings and weekends designed for two. Surprise your partner around January 24, when Venus joins forces with Uranus.

Money and Success

Your career life is off and running this month, thanks to the Sun and Mars in Capricorn, your solar tenth-house. Both planets align favorably with Saturn in Virgo, which could trigger a new position or promotion. But don't be concerned if there's a delay until early next month. Patience will reward you.

Rewarding Days

1, 4, 5, 6, 12, 13, 17, 19, 20, 25, 26, 31

Challenging Days

2, 3, 9, 14, 22, 24, 29, 30

Aries/February

Planetary Hotspots

This month's exact Saturn/Uranus alignment in Virgo and Pisces is likely to trigger workplace turmoil and frustration. Sudden job changes are possible for you, coworkers, or both. At the least, you'll experience delays and changes in projects and responsibilities. Because these signs are also your health sectors, schedule a checkup if you haven't had one in a while. And don't ignore a lingering cold or flu.

Planetary Lightspots

You sparkle and shine with charisma, thanks to Venus, which enters your sign February 2. This terrific influence also boosts your powers of attraction, so share your wishes with the universe and then truly believe you deserve everything you desire. What you want can be yours. But act quickly because Venus will turn retrograde next month.

Relationships

With Venus in Aries and the February 9 Full Moon (and lunar eclipse) in Leo, it looks superb for love or reenergizing a committed relationship. Your social life moves into high gear February 4, when Mars, your ruler, dashes into Aquarius, your friendship sign, where it's joined by Mercury on Valentine's Day. Get out and meet people, but take no one at face value. With Neptune in Aquarius activated by the eclipse, first impressions can be misleading.

Money and Success

Mercury resumes direct motion in Capricorn, your career sign, February 1. Rather than help, it's likely to bring previous errors to light. Conflict with a superior is also possible that week so choose your written and spoken words with care. Say less rather than more, and try to maintain a low profile, especially around difficult, controlling people. Midmonth networking could yield a promising job lead or contact.

Rewarding Days

3, 4, 8, 10, 13, 17, 19, 22, 23, 27, 28

Challenging Days

5, 6, 7, 11, 12, 16, 18, 25

Aries/March

Planetary Hotspots

Venus, your personal relationship planet, turns retrograde in Aries, March 6, and you may notice fewer social and love opportunities come your way between now and mid-April. This is not the time for commitment or a wedding. If you meet a potential romantic interest, be patient; it might take until the end of April or May before you get together. Relationship misunderstandings are also more likely now, so pause to think before you say what's on your mind.

Planetary Lightspots

You are this month's planetary lightspot! Circle March 26 on your calendar. That's the date of the New Moon in Aries, and the symbolic start of your new solar year. Take some time that week to think about what you want to accomplish in the next twelve months, personally and professionally. Then put your goals in writing, get inspired, and set plans in motion.

Relationships

Although retrograde Venus can trigger relationship challenges, most are likely to be career-related. Month's end is the hotspot, so try not to let irritating people push your buttons. Even if you do know what's best regarding a career matter, be wise and go along with the boss's decisions. Anything else will be a no-win. Continue to see friends and network through March 13.

Money and Success

Keep your eyes and ears open at work the week of the March 10 Full Moon in Virgo. You could pick up some interesting information and undercurrents about continuing changes and possible opportunities. Expected payments could be delayed this month, and with Venus retrograde you should postpone major purchases, if possible.

Rewarding Days

3, 7, 8, 12, 13, 20, 21, 22, 26, 27, 29, 30

Challenging Days

2, 4, 5, 10, 11, 17, 25, 31

Aries/April

Planetary Hotspots
A values clash could trigger friendship difficulties this month, leaving you feeling disappointed and disillusioned. Consider it a tough lesson learned. It's also possible a friend could ask for a loan or want you to get involved in a business deal. Say no. Money and friendship are a poor mix now.

Planetary Lightspots
Your Aries pizzazz is at its finest beginning April 22, when Mars arrives in your sign. High energy and initiative are to your benefit, but you'll also be at your most impulsive. Take time to think things through before you act and try to refrain from snap decisions. That way you'll get the best of Mars and hopefully avoid the rest. Also be sure to tune out life before bedtime so you get restful sleep, night after night. Try light reading or meditation to calm your soul.

Relationships
Other people take center stage in your life this month as the April 9 Full Moon in Libra lights up your relationship sector. But there's still an increased chance for misunderstandings with Venus traveling retrograde in Pisces through April 16. Clear up any lingering difficulties after Venus returns to your sign, April 24.

Money and Success
Career frustration can get the best of you the first and last weeks of April. You'll be quick to find fault with others, so calm down and try to view the situation objectively before you speak. Do that and you lessen the chance for others to criticize you. Think cooperation and compromise even if you disagree. With luck you could see a bigger paycheck this month or next, thanks to the April 24 New Moon in Taurus, your personal financial sign.

Rewarding Days
4, 6, 9, 12, 16, 17, 18, 19, 23, 24

Challenging Days
1, 2, 3, 8, 14, 26, 27, 28

Aries/May

Planetary Hotspots

Life perks along this month with few exceptions. One is Mercury, which turns retrograde in Gemini, your solar third house of communication, May 7. Besides increasing the odds for mix-ups, you'll need to double-check what you write, especially e-mail. It would be all too easy to prematurely hit Send. You also could end up with a dead watch, car, or cell phone battery.

Planetary Lightspots

Combine fun with learning when the May 24 New Moon in Gemini triggers your curiosity. Visit a nearby historical spot, treat the family to a day at a zoo or amusement park, or load up at the library or bookstore. You might also find a leisure-time class that piques your interest, so check out what your community has to offer.

Relationships

Relationships, especially friendships, can inspire you , but you'll also want to be a little wary of anyone new who enters your life. And, like last month, friends and money are a poor mix, so don't let anyone convince you to part with your hard-earned cash. Workplace conflict is possible in early May, which is a good time to maintain a low profile, especially around the boss.

Money and Success

Retrograde Mercury in Taurus can impact money matters when it travels in your solar second house of personal resources May 13–29. Pay bills early, watch out for paycheck and credit card errors, and take extra precautions to safeguard financial information. The May 9 Full Moon in Scorpio could boost family funds, but the lunar energy could also trigger an extra expense. Plan ahead, and save any extra money that comes your way.

Rewarding Days

1, 6, 7, 10, 11, 14, 15, 16, 21, 24, 28

Challenging Days

4, 5, 13, 17, 18, 20, 25, 27

Aries/June

Planetary Hotspots

You'll be stretched thin the week of the June 22 New Moon in Cancer, your domestic sector. Normally this would be a positive influence, but this year the lunar energy forms an exact alignment with Pluto in Capricorn, your solar tenth house of career. This clash increases the potential for conflict and power plays at work. Rein yourself in and try to avoid difficult people and situations.

Planetary Lightspots

Give in and take a break from the routine when the June 7 Full Moon in Sagittarius triggers the urge for new scenery. A week or even a few days at a relaxing destination can do wonders to re-center you, body and soul. If time off is impossible, opt for a weekend at a local luxury hotel or spend the day touring museums to relieve stress and gain a new perspective.

Relationships

The first week of June is ideal for socializing, thanks to Venus's easy lineup with Jupiter and Neptune. If you're looking for a new relationship, a friend of a friend could be your link to love. Venus in Aries through June 5 also will draw other people into your orbit, at least one of whom will in some way bring you luck.

Money and Success

This month's financial picture is mostly positive with Mars, Venus, and Mercury traveling in Taurus, your personal finance house. You could see a nice raise, but don't spend it all in one place! The urge to splurge will be strong the fourth week of June, but be kind to your budget. If a new position is your goal, send out resumes that week to lay the groundwork. It could take until August or even September before you see much activity.

Rewarding Days

2, 6, 8, 10, 12, 17, 18, 19, 24, 29, 30

Challenging Days

1, 3, 5 7, 15, 21, 22, 27, 28

Aries/July

Planetary Hotspots

You'll encounter a wide variety of people this month. Some will be supportive, some will be difficult, and some will intentionally try to mislead you. So be cautious, keep personal and confidential information to yourself, and listen far more than you talk. Conflict with someone at work is possible; step away before it becomes heated.

Planetary Lightspots

You'll be on the go all month, especially after Mars arrives in Gemini, your solar third house, July 11. Take your car in for routine maintenance before then, and plan a family or romantic weekend getaway. But ease up on the gas and stay focused when you're behind the wheel. Mars increases the odds for an accident.

Relationships

June promises happy times with loved ones. You'll be on the same wavelength, which is a real plus for open, honest communication that can strengthen ties. If you have unresolved family issues, now is the time to clear the air. And although you might not totally agree you'll at least come to appreciate each other's viewpoints. Summer activities and socializing pick up after Mercury enters Leo July 17, followed by the Sun on the 22nd.

Money and Success

Your ambitions come alive under the July 7 Full Moon (and lunar eclipse) in Leo, your career sector. The influence will be in effect the next six months so plan now how to make the most of your talents throughout the rest of 2009. Finances require some caution the first ten days of July because first Venus, and then Mars, clash with Neptune. Tune out anyone who leans on you for money. But with luck you could net a small windfall.

Rewarding Days

7, 8, 9, 14, 18, 22, 23, 26, 27, 29

Challenging Days

2, 4, 6, 10, 13, 19, 25, 31

Aries/August

Planetary Hotspots
You're more susceptible to fast-talking friends this month, and your children could also try to mislead you. Be wise. Be alert. Ask questions and don't let anyone evade the answers. Your common sense and sixth sense are assets here so use them to give yourself the edge. Continue to drive with extra care; leave early so you don't have to rush.

Planetary Lightspots
Take a chance on the lottery the weekend of the 14th. You could win a small prize. But remember, it only takes one ticket to win so don't risk the grocery money. If you're looking for love, your big win could be a whirlwind romance around the time of the August 5 Full Moon (and lunar eclipse) or the New Moon in Leo on the 20th.

Relationships
You'll experience every facet of relationships this month as the Sun, Mercury, Venus, and Mars advance through several signs. Some people test your patience and others spark a flash of insight that clarifies a difficult personal or business relationship. Career-related ties are among the best and also the most challenging, as are family relationships. At times the wisest choice will be silence or tacit agreement, no matter how you feel. Nevertheless, with Venus in Cancer through the 25th, it's a terrific time to join forces with your partner on a domestic project.

Money and Success
Your thoughts are centered on work August 2–24, when Mercury transits your solar sixth house. With it will come some terrific opportunities to showcase your talents. But in order to succeed you'll need to follow the rules (no shortcuts!), focus on the details, and fulfill all your responsibilities.

Rewarding Days
3, 4, 6, 11, 12, 14, 17, 18, 20, 23, 27

Challenging Days
2, 8, 9, 10, 15, 16, 22, 26, 29

♈ Aries/September ♈

Planetary Hotspots

Expect to go another round with the relationship challenges you experienced in August. The culprit is Mercury, which turns retrograde in Libra, your solar seventh house, on September 7. It will be mid-October before the current issues are resolved. This means of course that you need to curb your temper and your frustrations and choose your words with care. Reread e-mail before you hit Send.

Planetary Lightspots

The universe offers you just the stress relief you need this month: the September 4 Full Moon in Pisces, your solar twelfth house. Surround yourself with calming energy every evening by tuning out the world with music and a good book, even for thirty minutes. Or, if energetic activity works better for you, ease tension with domestic projects as Mars advances in Cancer, your domestic sector.

Relationships

Friendship and socializing are in high focus the first three weeks of September. Venus in Leo, your solar fifth house, also brings romantic opportunities for singles and couples in love. But close personal ties are prone to misunderstandings because of retrograde Mercury. If you're unsure whether to take a relationship to the next level, put the decision on hold for now. October will bring clarity.

Money and Success

Saturn and Uranus align for the last time across your solar sixth-twelfth house axis the week of the September 18 New Moon in Virgo. You could be rewarded with a step up or be faced with a tough choice regarding your job. Change is a given, especially if your birthday is near April 14. Take some time off if you feel your job has run its course. You'll regret rash decisions made now.

Rewarding Days

1, 2, 7, 8, 9, 10, 11, 14, 20, 24, 28, 29

Challenging Days

3, 5, 6, 12, 13, 18, 23, 25

Aries/October

Planetary Hotspots

The effects of last month's Saturn/Uranus alignment continue the first two weeks of October. Your work life, although still unsettled, will even out and get back to normal as Mercury and Venus complete their Virgo transit. However, rather than just breathe a sigh of relief, reflect on recent events and what you've learned from them. The knowledge will serve you well for many years.

Planetary Lightspots

The October 4 Full Moon in Aries boosts energy and incentive, and gives you the initiative to take charge of your life. Include others in your plans, especially loved ones, who will back your efforts as Mars transits Cancer, your domestic sign, through October 15.

Relationships

You'll have a lot of people contact this month, some positive and some you'll wish you could avoid. Friendships and other close relationships are at their best, uplifting and laughter-filled, and you'll have plenty of opportunities to socialize after Mars moves into Leo, your solar fifth house, on October 16. Career relationships, however, are challenging. Unfortunately, you can expect more of the same because Saturn enters Libra, your solar seventh house, on the 29th, and Saturn will clash with Pluto through year's end. The second full week of October brings the first clue of how these planets might impact your life.

Money and Success

Money is on the horizon. It begins to flow your way when the Sun enters Scorpio, your solar eighth house, on October 22, followed by Mercury on the 28th. Plan ahead. Save more than you spend.

Rewarding Days

5, 7, 8, 12, 13, 17, 20, 21, 26, 27, 31

Challenging Days

2, 3, 9, 14, 15, 23, 30

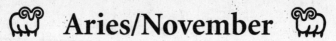 **Aries/November**

Planetary Hotspots

Saturn and Pluto form an exact alignment on November 15, although the effects of these two planets in your solar Seventh and tenth houses will be more apparent in December. Nevertheless, the second week of the month could bring a tense moment with a coworker or supervisor. You may initially perceive this person as friend, not foe. Be cautious about placing your trust in just anyone.

Planetary Lightspots

With the holidays fast approaching, this might be an odd time of year to begin an exercise program. Yet it's ideal because Mars is in Leo, your solar fifth house, all month. Besides that, it's a great stress reliever. Mars here also keeps your social life in active status, and it's great for passionate romance.

Relationships

Venus in Libra through the 6th enhances close relationships and acts like a magnet to attract helpful people into your life. You'll also be in touch with out-of-town friends and relatives during the last two weeks of October. If you have the time, visit a friend or travel with one, even for a long weekend.

Money and Success

Finances are a major theme this month as the Sun, Mercury, and Venus move through Scorpio, your solar eighth house. The New Moon in the same sign on November 24 could trigger a small windfall, as could the November 2 Full Moon in Taurus, your solar second house. With luck and this strong influence in your financial sectors, you (or your partner) could profit from a raise. But be cautious about mixing money with friendship. Protect your resources, and safeguard valuables when you're out socializing.

Rewarding Days

4, 5, 7, 8, 10, 13, 14, 17, 20, 22, 28

Challenging Days

2, 6, 9, 12, 15, 19, 27

♈ Aries/December ♈

Planetary Hotspots

Mars turns retrograde in Leo on the 20th. Although this might slow your social life somewhat, the retrograde period is most important for another reason: Mars is your ruling planet. This means you'll at times feel as though your life is on hold. Consider it a lesson in patience and find a constructive outlet for your frustration. With that, a smile, and a positive outlook you'll weather this phase, which lasts until early March, in style.

Planetary Lightspots

If you didn't manage a getaway last month (or even if you did), take a break from the hectic holidays. Or, give yourself and your partner or family the gift of a winter or spring trip. You can also satisfy your desire for new horizons by taking a fun class in gourmet cooking or stocking up on reading material at the library or bookstore.

Relationships

December's Jupiter-Neptune merger in Aquarius, your solar eleventh house, promises lively and inspirational moments with friends. Some bring you luck and others motivate you to set high goals for the new year. Much of this you'll realize upon reflection in the weeks ahead as your sixth sense and dreams offer insights.

Money and Success

Career stress rises with several planets in Capricorn, your solar tenth house, contacting both Pluto in Capricorn and Saturn in Libra. Tread softly around the boss and keep controversial opinions to yourself. This is not the time to take a stand or to push your own agenda, no matter your beliefs. Be a team player. The Saturn/Pluto influence can also strain personal relationships, so you'll want to avoid spending the holidays with difficult relatives if at all possible.

Rewarding Days
5, 6, 11, 12, 14, 15, 18, 21, 27, 30, 19

Challenging Days
3, 7, 8, 9, 10, 13, 24, 31

Aries Action Table

These dates reflect the best—but not the only—times for success and ease in these activities, according to your Sun sign.

	JAN	FEB	MAR	APR	MAY	JUN	JUL	AUG	SEPT	OCT	NOV	DEC
Move							4-29	16-17				
Start a class			3-4			16-17, 20-21, 25, 29-30	13-14, 18-19					
Join a club	8-9	5-28	1-7									
Ask for a raise	6									26-27		
Look for work						9-10, 18		20-24		6-7		
Get pro advice							27			5-7, 14		
Get a loan										16, 21-22, 26-27		
See a doctor		26	19, 25	21						28	11	
Start a diet		10-11	11							14-15	10-11	
End relationship		12-13									10-11	
Buy clothes		8			1-2					16-17	13	10-11
Get a makeover		27		23-24	1, 20-21		22-23					6
New romance	8				1-2, 29		22					
Vacation							31	27-28			17-30	1-4

The Bull
April 19 to May 20

♉

Element: Earth	Glyph: Bull's head
Quality: Fixed	Anatomy: Throat, neck
Polarity: Yin/feminine	Color: Green
Planetary Ruler: Venus	Animal: Cattle
Meditation: I trust myself and others	Myths/Legends: Isis and Osiris, Cerridwen, Bull of Minos
Gemstone: Emerald	House: Second
Power Stones: Diamond, blue lace agate, rose quartz	Opposite Sign: Scorpio
	Flower: Violet
Key Phrase: I have	Key Word: Conservation

Your Strengths and Challenges

Thorough, practical, and dependable, your follow-through is the envy of many, so people know they can count on you to deliver what you promise. That's your fixed-sign determination in action; but there are times when the flip side—stubbornness—emerges. Learn the art of give-and-take.

Born under the ultimate comfort-loving sign, you dislike being rushed and covet your routine. Your need for security and stability and your dislike of change means you can get stuck in a rut, which can diminish your success. Accept change and occasionally be the one to initiate it.

As a Taurus, you're especially attuned to the sense of touch. You unconsciously feel clothing and other objects when shopping, and a hug renews your spirit. Your voice may be distinctive, and you could be a talented amateur or professional singer or speaker.

Venus, your ruling planet, gives you an eye for beauty and many people with a Taurus Sun surround themselves with artwork and collectibles. The homes of some, however, are cluttered, from basement to attic, with every closet stuffed to the max. If this describes your space, ask yourself why it's so tough to let go.

Your Relationships

Warm and affectionate, you cherish passionate moments. You also take matters of the heart seriously. Although lifetime commitment is your goal, it can be a challenge to achieve because you're highly selective about whom you date. That's admirable, but remember that first impressions aren't always accurate. Take a chance and you could meet the soul mate you desire. Possessive by nature, your partnership lesson is to develop trust and confidence in love. Face your fears realistically rather than let jealousy become a relationship issue. You could make a sizzling match with Scorpio, your polar opposite, and you have much in common with the other earth signs, Virgo and Capricorn. Cancer and Pisces are in sync with your solar energy, but life with Leo or Aquarius could have you feeling insecure.

You take great pride in your home, and are loyal and devoted to those you love. They're a source of confidence for you, as you are for them, and when in your own space you feel at one with the universe. Your home is also an expression of your ego and you strive to make it a reflection of yourself and your worldly achievements.

Taurus parents expect a lot from their children—often to the point of perfection. Even though you have their best interests at heart, this can undermine their self-esteem. So rather than be critical, aim for constructive, supportive encouragement and praise their best efforts as you grant them the freedom to explore their own interests, which may or may not be your own.

You're a caring, compassionate friend who goes to the "nth" degree for those in your inner circle. Most are worthy of your largesse, but there will always be those few who take advantage of your kind heart. Be selective and trust only those you know well, who also benefit from your talent for inspiring others to do and be their best.

Your Career and Money

Your choice is stability and security. But this area of your life is prone to sudden changes. In today's world it's to your benefit to be aware of trends so you can take action before it becomes a necessity. And by doing that you can make your own luck and seize the best opportunities available. In your day-to-day work life, you're happiest in an upscale environment with congenial coworkers. Conflict and controversy are not for you, and you need daily people contact in your work in order to feel fulfilled at day's end.

Your financial instincts are among the best. Although you're thrifty, value is of the utmost importance. No matter the price, you rarely spend unless you get your money's worth. You also attract bargains and have a sixth sense about where to shop when. Many people with a Taurus Sun gain through a family inheritance or careful, long-term investments. Budgeting, however, is also important, because you can be overly optimistic and spend on a whim.

Your Lighter Side

Others might see your leisure-time pursuits as work, but you don't. You get great satisfaction from the tangible results of practical hobbies such as gardening. Woodworking, refinishing furniture, and home improvements are popular evening and weekend activities for many born under your sign, and it's possible you could turn your interest and mechanical ability into a profitable second income.

Affirmation for the Year

I have the strength and determination to realize my dreams.

The Year Ahead for Taurus

You'll have plenty of opportunities to make your mark in the world during 2009, as the planetary energy spotlights your career and work life. You'll also discover new facets of yourself along with an increasing desire for knowledge. Much of this will develop the last six months of the year so you'll want to take advantage of the relatively easygoing winter and spring seasons to enjoy the status quo. Change will be the norm as summer becomes fall and 2010 is on the horizon.

Jupiter will shine brightly from Aquarius, your career sector, the sign it enters January 5. You'll reap the benefits of this expansive planet, which can trigger lucky breaks and have you among the favored few. Although it might be tempting to sit back and enjoy this bountiful career ride, Jupiter's other face will soon begin to nudge you to do more. The future beckons. Jupiter is your portal. Make the most of it; twelve years will pass before Jupiter again visits this sign.

As the year unfolds and Jupiter draws closer to Neptune, which entered Aquarius in 1995, you'll begin to see many possibilities. In fact, the first subtle hints of what your future could hold will occur in February. Take note of your career experiences that month and, more importantly, your idle thoughts and dreams. You'll find hints in what drifts through your mind as the stage is set for what's to come later in the year.

Neptune's influence is complex, more subtle and difficult to define than Jupiter. Both are planets of hope, faith, and spirituality—concepts somewhat foreign to your down-to-earth sign. Take a risk this year and tune in to their message. Both planets will encourage you to look beyond what is to what might be and to believe in yourself and the many possibilities open to you in the universe.

Jupiter promises a lot; it often delivers, but sometimes it doesn't. Neptune masks reality with illusion. But it also inspires. Getting only the best of this duo can thus be a challenge. That's okay. You have a decided advantage: your innate practicality. Rely on it to balance and weigh the realities of your career prospects against your hopes and wishes for more.

Saturn will enter Libra, your solar sixth house of daily work, October 29. Saturn in this life sector indicates two-and-a-half years of hard work with, unfortunately, scant recognition. Although Jupiter will to some extent offset this influence this year, its influence will begin to wane as Saturn's increases.

Enter Pluto, planet of transformation—also defined as major change. This tiny planet does everything on a grand scale, but its roots run deep and its influence is slow and steady, eroding the past to make way for the future. That's familiar energy to you, and with Pluto in Capricorn, a fellow earth sign and your solar ninth house of knowledge, you can more easily handle the changes in your world even if you can't control them to the extent you wish.

Saturn in Libra will square off with Pluto during the final two months of the year to push you to step outside your current life and take action. But this duo also indicates frustration in moving forward. You'll get farther and faster if you allow events to unfold at their own pace and accept that much of it will be out of your control.

The bottom line? The planetary scenario may develop like this as 2009 progresses: Your ambition will come alive, prompting you to aim for bigger and better as Jupiter and Neptune work their magic. And you may have some initial success and even earn a promotion, but the wind will shift later in the year. Then you could be disappointed to discover that education or training separate you from your goal. You might also become disillusioned with your current career path and decide to return to school to pursue your new dream. Even if your career life is on an even keel, you should consider broadening your knowledge, whether you gain practical skills, pursue a degree, or explore yourself—your motivations, desires, and reason for being—and resolve any issues that hold you back.

Saturn in Virgo (through October 28) and Uranus in Pisces, your solar fifth/eleventh house axis, will continue to influence your social life and your love life, a trend that began in late October 2008. If you're involved in a major group activity such as a club or organization, or even a team project at work, you can expect last year's events to reach a turning point in February and to conclude in September, the months when this planetary alignment will be at its peak. Be prepared, however, for the unexpected and for carefully laid plans to suddenly switch direction in February. If this is career-related, it could trigger initial thoughts about moving on that come full circle this fall.

Saturn may have restricted your love life and your social life since it entered Virgo in 2007. But it's equally possible that the emphasis has been on quality rather than quantity. You can expect the pattern to be much the same through the end of October when Saturn enters Libra. If you're in a serious dating relationship, or enter one, it might not have the pizzazz of previous liaisons, but it will feel stable and solid, bringing you much pleasure and a feeling of security. If, however, things aren't working out as you hoped they would, September's Saturn/Uranus alignment could prompt you to cut ties, possibly because you see someone more exciting on the horizon. Love-at-first-sight with a soul mate is not out of the question.

You'll want to be especially cautious about investments and putting funds at risk. Maintain your conservative financial attitude and don't let the lure of high profits tempt you. Chances are, you'll end up wiser but poorer.

If you're a parent, especially of teens, be aware of what your children are doing, get involved in their activities, and get to know their friends even if your kids think you're meddling. Whatever age your children are, they'll benefit from your wisdom, guidance, care, and concern.

What This Year's Eclipses Mean for You

This year features six eclipses, two solar and four lunar. With one exception, each reinforces this year's planetary emphasis on your solar sectors of knowledge and career.

The January 7 solar eclipse in Aquarius, just two days after Jupiter enters the same sign, will highlight your career and fuel your ambitions. This influence could trigger a promotion, especially if you were born near April 25. At the least you'll see your prospects for advancement rise along with renewed enthusiasm for worldly success. Make the most of it and claim your share of the spotlight because your focus will begin to shift away from career interests around the time of the August 6 lunar eclipse, also in Aquarius, when you'll transition into a new phase.

This new phase will actually begin to take root with the July eclipses—July 7 in Capricorn and July 22 in Cancer—which occur in your solar third and ninth houses of learning, information, and knowledge. Read, talk with people, surf the Net, take a class for fun or profit, or make reservations for the trip of a lifetime. Better yet, do it all! Because Cancer and Capricorn are compatible with your sign, you can easily access this eclipse energy and put it to practical use. Choose wisely. What you learn now will serve you well about ten years from now when you'll reach the career pinnacle of a lifetime.

Your Taurus energy may encourage you to take things slowly. That actually could work to your advantage because December 31 brings a lunar eclipse in Cancer—and just the impetus you need to embrace the future with all the excitement and enthusiasm that accompanies a new endeavor and personal growth. Think big. The possibilities are almost limitless once you make the commitment.

This year also brings a February 7 lunar eclipse in Leo, your domestic sign. Remind yourself—when you're wrapped up in your career—that loved ones also need your time and attention. Above all, this influence will challenge you to find a balance between work and the important people in your life. The bonus is that you'll cherish the moments and the memories.

It's also possible the lunar eclipse could trigger a desire for a new or renovated home, or possibly the opportunity to relocate to pursue your dreams. But because this eclipse activates Neptune, you'll want to remember that this planet can mask reality. And that makes it wise to proceed with caution where money and mortgages and leases are involved. Get several estimates before remodeling, or thoroughly research a potential new location, including schools and the community as a whole, before you sign on the dotted line.

Saturn

If you were born between May 4 and 20, stable Saturn in Virgo, your solar fifth house, will contact your Sun between January and the end of October, which makes 2009 one of the best for concentration and sustained effort.

Now would be a good time to begin an exercise program as a first step toward building an overall healthier lifestyle. You'll have more stamina and establish a healthy habit that can pay off for years to come. Find the right sport or program that works for you and, most importantly, one that's fun and makes you feel great. You'll also want to explore your creativity. Do something such as learning a new hobby that relaxes you and yields a concrete result. You could refinish furniture, acquire the do-it-yourself skills for a domestic project, or possibly turn a leisure-time interest into a second income.

You'll be more involved in your children's lives this year, and will learn as much and possibly more from them than they will from you. Get involved in their activities and teach them by example. If you're a step-parent, make the effort and you can strengthen these ties. Long-term romantic relationships will be stable, thanks to Saturn's easy contact with your Sun, and if you're searching for a soul mate you could find him or her.

If you were born between May 4 and 7, you'll have easy access to Saturn's energy in April and May, while **those among you born between May 8 and 12** will have two Saturn periods—January through March, and July and August. **If you were born between May 13 and 20,** you'll benefit from Saturn's stabilizing effects in September or October.

Saturn and Pluto

If you were born between April 19 and 24, you'll be among the first of your sign to experience Saturn's influence on your work life after it enters Libra, your solar sixth house, October 29. You can expect an increased workload and pressure to perform. Libra is also your health sign, so it's important to counteract job tension and frustration with a daily stress reliever—reading, vigorous exercise, walking, music, or meditation. It would also be wise to schedule a check-up at that time and to do your own research regarding the latest health trends.

Because Pluto will contact your Sun during the same time frame, you'll have the willpower to get in shape, change your diet, or transform yourself and your life. Pluto also will give you the strength to say less rather than more with anyone in authority should you be faced with a power struggle at work or difficulties involving in-laws. You, more than most who share your Sun sign, may feel the urge to return to school in order to advance in your current career or to prepare for an entirely different one. With Pluto involved, what you do now is likely to dramatically change your life, so think carefully and make wise choices.

If you're involved in a legal matter (which you should try to avoid at this time), it will be lengthy and may not conclude until 2011, and then only after considerable effort. It's also a good idea to avoid travel in November and December, if possible.

Uranus

Friendship and new experiences are only the beginning of an exciting year **if you were born between May 10 and 17**. With Uranus in Pisces, your solar eleventh house, contacting your Sun, you'll have abundant opportunities. It's up to you, however, to seize them and profit from them. Get out of the house, get involved in a like-minded group, go where you can meet people, and become active on the social scene. You'll be rewarded with many new friends and networking contacts, some of whom will enlighten you in surprising ways. They'll also be invaluable to your career in the future.

Because Uranus is a psychic planet and Pisces is a psychic sign, you'll probably experience everything from gentle intuitive nudges to flashes of insight. Listen and learn to trust both. They can give you the edge in many situations, and whatever you do to develop your sixth sense now is likely to stay with you for a lifetime.

Neptune

If you were born between May 12 and 17, Neptune will contact your Sun from Aquarius, your solar tenth house of career. The effect of this planet can manifest in one of two ways, or possibly both: disillusionment or inspiration. Finding the balance will be easier because of your practical nature, but it's just as possible that this strong influence can encourage you to chase not a realistic dream but a pot of gold. Your best path here may be to enlist the support of someone who can be a sounding board—someone whose common sense, values, and confidentiality are ultimately trustworthy, and who has no connection with your career. Colleagues may appear to back you, but in actuality try to undermine your position. If you're truly disillusioned with your career and feel it has run its course, take your time rather than make a sudden move. That's better left until next year when this influence is past.

Inspiration to soar above the rest is the best possible outcome of this Neptune transit. Go for it if that's what you want, always keeping your practical side within reach. You'll have all the charm and charisma necessary to gain the support of those who count, and if you work with the public you'll have a magical quality that many will find irresistible.

Taurus/January

Planetary Hotspots

Learn all you can this month, both formally and informally, as the January 10 Full Moon (and lunar eclipse) in Cancer, your solar third house, motivates you to seek information. Renew your library card, enroll in a class, talk with people, and polish your presentation skills. All will pay off in some way during the next six months, most likely in your career, as would joining a professional organization.

Planetary Lightspots

Pack your bags and go do something fun this month. With the Sun and Mars in Capricorn, your travel sector is where the action is. If a business trip is on your agenda, try to schedule a few extra days for romance or sightseeing. Or splurge a little and escape winter in a sunny locale.

Relationships

Looking for a new romance? Tell your friends. One of them could be your link to love at first sight the third week of January as Venus meets Uranus in Pisces, your solar eleventh house. But because the love planet will also clash with Saturn, a rocky dating relationship could come to an end. You also could reconnect with someone from the past at a reunion or while traveling. For couples in love, it's a great time to plan for the future and to discuss priorities, hopes, and wishes.

Money and Success

You have the career luck factor this year, thanks to Jupiter, which enters Aquarius, your solar tenth house, January 5. Cross your fingers for great things around January 20, when the Sun, Mercury, and Jupiter join forces in Aquarius. The result could be a promotion or job offer. It could be mid-February before all is said and done, though, because Mercury, which travels retrograde from January 11 on, slips out of Aquarius and back into Capricorn January 21.

Rewarding Days

1, 5, 6, 13, 18, 19, 20, 23, 25, 28

Challenging Days

2, 3, 8, 9, 16, 22, 29, 30

Taurus/February

Planetary Hotspots

The February 9 Full Moon (and lunar eclipse) in Leo could trigger a leak or another mechanical problem in your home. Check appliances and take necessary precautions if you live in an area prone to flooding or severe winter weather. If you're looking for a roommate, someone who appears to be a promising candidate may or may not be the right match for you. Be cautious.

Planetary Lightspots

Venus in Leo provides the ideal balance during this busy career month. With your ruling planet in your solar twelfth house you'll find it easy to unwind at day's end and get the restful sleep you need. You'll also value time alone to pursue your own interests. Enjoy cozy evenings with your partner.

Relationships

A close friendship or dating relationship is stressful this month as Saturn and Uranus form an exact alignment across your solar fifth/eleventh house axis. The relationship could reach the breaking point, as could your involvement in a club or organization. Used positively, however, you can be an agent for change for other people or a humanitarian effort. Give your children extra time and attention if you're a parent, and get to know their friends. Teens will exert their independence.

Money and Success

You're in the career spotlight this month, thanks to a beautiful planetary lineup in Aquarius, your solar tenth house. Go for it if your sights are set on a promotion, but be sure you have all the facts because all may not be as it seems on the surface. You also have behind-the-scenes supporters on your side this month, and your superiors will be impressed with you the last week of February.

Rewarding Days

2, 3, 10, 14, 15, 16, 17, 19, 24

Challenging Days

1, 5, 6, 11, 18, 25, 26

Taurus/March

Planetary Hotspots

Life will frustrate you at times this month. Venus, your ruling planet, turns retrograde in Aries, your solar twelfth house, March 6. It will be mid-April before it turns direct. Keep this in mind when personal plans stall, and think of it as an opportunity to refine your goals prior to the Sun's arrival in your sign next month.

Planetary Lightspots

Listen to your inner voice around the time of the March 26 New Moon in Aries. It could reveal new insights regarding your love life, your job, and your values. Meditation can also be effective now as both a stress-reliever and a way to calm your mind and open it to fresh insights.

Relationships

Last month's relationship challenges will resurface under the March 10 Full Moon in Virgo. The positive news is the matter should be resolved, at least to the point where you can begin to move forward. Group activities associated with business or an organization are also impacted by the lunar energy and are best postponed until April, if possible. With the Sun, Mercury, and Mars in Pisces at various times this month you'll have plenty of chances to see friends and meet new people. Among them could be someone who will prove to be a valuable future contact.

Money and Success

Mars completes its dash through Aquarius, your solar tenth house, on March 13. Use the first two weeks of the month to reinforce your position with decision-makers, and aim for the first week of March if you plan to schedule an interview or presentation. With Venus retrograde, however, there could be delays in important job-related matters, so be prepared to rely on your notable patience.

Rewarding Days

1, 12, 13, 14, 15, 20, 24, 28, 29

Challenging Days

2, 4, 5, 11, 17, 23, 25, 31

Taurus/April

Planetary Hotspots

Sleep could elude you some nights as Mars transits Aries, your solar twelfth house, from April 22 on. So set aside time every evening to relax and unwind and, most importantly, tune out the day's activities. Light reading or television will help calm your mind, as could herbal tea and a light, healthy dinner.

Planetary Lightspots

Circle April 24 on your calendar. That's the date of the New Moon in your sign, which signals the symbolic start of your solar year. It will trigger your curiosity and push you to explore new horizons through study or travel. If you're set to go in April, though, try to plan your trip for mid-month when planetary alignments are more favorable.

Relationships

Your social life continues to be active this month, including the opportunity to get better acquainted with colleagues in after-work get-togethers where you could pick up some interesting confidential information. Mars in Pisces, your friendship sector, through April 21 has you in touch with pals, but the best news is Venus, which turns direct in Pisces on April 17, the sign it transits through the 23rd. A romance could bloom with a friend of a friend.

Money and Success

Work will be hectic this month once the April 9 Full Moon in Libra activates your solar sixth house. Try not to push yourself too hard, though, because you can easily overdo it, get run down, and catch a cold. The lunar energy will also boost your esteem with superiors, which could be the first step toward a promotion later this year. But you'll want to be somewhat cautious about what you say to whom. Keep your ambitious plans to yourself for now.

Rewarding Days

6, 9, 10, 11, 16, 19, 20, 24, 25

Challenging Days

1, 3, 8, 13, 22, 27, 28

Taurus/May

Planetary Hotspots

Your innate patience serves you well again this month, although it will be a challenge at times to keep from pushing forward with all the determination your sign is noted for. This will begin to change by month's end. Action-oriented Mars will arrive in Taurus on May 31, just a day after Mercury turns direct, also in your sign. Both planets will fuel your drive in June, when you'll feel as though your life is finally moving forward.

Planetary Lightspots

Venus is an asset as it continues its slow transit through Aries, your solar twelfth house. It's a good antidote for frustratingly slow progress in other areas of your life because it encourages you to take it easy and enjoy the moment. If you're part of couple, Venus here is ideal for togetherness time.

Relationships

Relationships are in positive focus the week of the May 9 Full Moon in Scorpio, your solar seventh house. The lunar energy is a plus for both romantic liaisons and business contacts. You'll also learn a few things about human nature and the importance of cooperation and compromise—if you're open to other opinions and perspectives and willing to listen to the other person's viewpoint.

Money and Success

The May 24 New Moon in Gemini has all the potential to trigger a nice raise either at month's end or in early June. But with Mercury turning retrograde in the same sign on the 7th, you'll want to carefully check bills and pay them early. Mix-ups are not only possible but likely. Career matters require finesse. Don't push even though you can see the big picture that others miss. You'll get the support you need the last week of May.

Rewarding Days

3, 7, 8, 14, 15, 19, 21, 22, 31

Challenging Days

1, 2, 5, 13, 18, 27, 29

Taurus/June

Planetary Hotspots

The June 22 New Moon in Cancer, your solar third house, encourages you to get out of town for a change of scenery. That's not the best timing, however, because the lunar energy will activate powerful Pluto in Capricorn. The trip would be far from relaxing and there's an increased chance for a delay or cancellation as well as car trouble. Drive with extra care that week, and also try to avoid legal matters and discussions with difficult neighbors or relatives.

Planetary Lightspots

Alluring charm, charisma, and magnetism! You'll have it all this month after Venus enters your sign on June 6. Make the most of it in your career to win supporters and in your personal life to attract admirers. That's not all you can attract this month. Think about what you want and what's realistic and then visualize success.

Relationships

You'll want to choose your words with care throughout April. Planetary alignments prime conditions for misunderstandings, and it would be easy to unintentionally say the wrong thing at the wrong time. You also should clarify instructions, whether you're giving or receiving them, especially at work.

Money and Success

Finances shine brightly under the June 7 Full Moon in Sagittarius. The lunar influence plus Mercury's arrival in Gemini on June 13 make this an excellent month to organize financial records, comparison shop for insurance and interest rates, and to negotiate (or renegotiate) loan and consumer credit terms. Also check with your employer to be sure you have all the latest information on available benefits.

Rewarding Days

2, 4, 6, 8, 9, 14, 18, 19, 23, 24, 30

Challenging Days

1, 3, 5, 11, 16, 21, 22, 25, 27, 28

Taurus/July

Planetary Hotspots

You're highly motivated to succeed in the wider world this month. That's great! But try to curb your Taurus determination (stubbornness?) just a little. A big push will backfire. A more easygoing approach, logical reasoning, and tactful words yield success, as does getting key supporters to back your plans and ideas. Do all of this and you'll be a winner the first week of July.

Planetary Lightspots

Give in to the urge when this month's Capricorn Full Moon and lunar eclipse (July 7) and Cancer New Moon and solar eclipse (July 21) activate your solar third/ninth house axis. Take a vacation, a romantic cruise, or a couple of long weekends at a luxury destination. It might be even more fun if you travel with friends or share a beach cottage. You'll benefit from the time off now because August will be hectic.

Relationships

Family time becomes a higher priority when Mercury enters Leo, your domestic sector, July 17, followed by the Sun on July 22. Give loved ones quality and quantity time and you'll be rewarded with more of the same in return. Also make plans to see long-time friends earlier in the month when planetary alignments enhance get-togethers. Consider carefully, however, if a former romantic interest wants to resume a relationship.

Money and Success

You'll be money-motivated with Venus in Gemini, your solar second house, July 5–30, and Mars there after July 10. Although you could gain through a windfall or raise, extra expenses and an urge to splurge are also likely. Save by using your sixth sense for bargains. Your month-end goal: more in your bank account than you had July 1.

Rewarding Days

1, 7, 8, 12, 15, 16, 17, 21, 27, 29

Challenging Days

2, 4, 6, 10, 13, 19, 25, 30

Taurus/August

Planetary Hotspots

You'll encounter controlling people in early and late August whose mission seems to be to make your life difficult. Although there might be some truth to that, much depends upon your perspective as several planets clash with Pluto. Sometimes the best choice is to accept what is and that others do indeed have the final word. You should also try to avoid major decisions during the same time frames because it will be tough to be objective. Speak and also drive with care.

Planetary Lightspots

A close friend is your best sounding board this month. Talk can be enlightening and motivational, and shared experiences will inspire and empower you to do and be your best. Do the same for someone else.

Relationships

Summer socializing is at its best with Mercury in Virgo, your solar fifth house, August 2–24, where it will be joined by the Sun on the August 22. Line up events but remember to either catch a ride or name someone as designated driver. If you're single, take the initiative to meet new people and ask friends to introduce you to a potential match. You could connect with a soul mate.

Money and Success

Mars spends much of the month (through August 24) in Gemini, continuing July's emphasis on money matters. Its favorable alignment with Jupiter and Neptune in Aquarius, your solar tenth house of career, could bring news of a raise. At the least you'll claim some fame sparked by the August 5 Full Moon (and lunar eclipse) in Aquarius. This is powerful energy you can build on the rest of the year.

Rewarding Days

3, 4, 6, 7, 11, 12, 13, 17, 23, 30, 31

Challenging Days

1, 2, 8, 9, 15, 16, 22, 26, 29

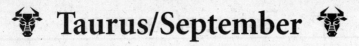 Taurus/September

Planetary Hotspots

Saturn and Uranus form their last exact alignment this month in Virgo and Pisces, your solar fifth/eleventh house axis. You'll experience its effects the week of the September 18 New Moon in Virgo, especially if your birthday is within a few days of May 16. A dating relationship or friendship may end, if not now, then in early October. Change also surrounds group activities just as it did in February. If you're a parent you'll need to again be aware of what's going on in your children's lives. Compromise is the way to resolve challenges.

Planetary Lightspots

With Mars advancing in Cancer, your solar third house, your mind is quick and your thinking clear and on target. This is a plus for decision-making, important talks, and meetings, as well as information gathering. Reading is an excellent September stress-reliever.

Relationships

Family relations are a bright spot with Venus in Leo, your domestic sector, through September 19. You'll also enjoy upbeat times with friends the week of the September 4 Full Moon in Pisces. Work relationships, however, are more stressful than not, in part because Mercury turns retrograde in Libra, your solar sixth house, on September 7. Mix-ups, misunderstandings, and disagreements are likely, and you'll encounter manipulative, controlling people. Keep your cool and focus on the knowledge that nothing lasts forever.

Money and Success

At times you'll feel like work progress is not only stalled but that you're moving backwards. That's retrograde Mercury's other effect this month and it's sure to trigger frustration. But the more you try to move things forward the worse it will become. Accept what is and be patient.

Rewarding Days

2, 7, 8, 14, 20, 21, 26, 28, 29, 30

Challenging Days

3, 5, 6, 12, 18, 23, 25

Taurus/October

Planetary Hotspots

Listen to the message of this month's Full Moon, October 4 in Aries, your solar twelfth house. It will encourage you to treat yourself well—to eat healthy, make relaxation a part of every day, and refresh your body and soul with sound sleep night after night. This is particularly important now because you'll be more than usually prone to colds and other viruses. Think healthy and energetic!

Planetary Lightspots

Much of the October action outside of work is centered on the domestic scene. Go with the urge when Mars, which arrives in Leo on October 16, pushes you to zip through household repairs and projects and get your place in top shape. If you feel especially ambitious, dive into a home improvement project. But set a deadline. Otherwise you might not finish it until next year.

Relationships

Relationship issues that occurred at the time of September's New Moon continue to unfold the first two weeks of October. For the most part, you can reach final resolution and move on. You'll also have the chance to enjoy friends in a relaxed atmosphere as three planets advance in Virgo. Cupid's arrows zing the hearts of some singles with a love-at-first-sight romance.

Money and Success

Work takes center stage this month as four planets and the October 18 New Moon in Libra energize your solar sixth house. But the big news is Saturn, which enters Libra October 29. You may be asked to take on additional responsibilities in the next few years, and although praise may be slim, your efforts will bring rewards seven years from now. Your star shines brightly now.

Rewarding Days

5, 6, 7, 8, 14, 17, 20, 27, 28

Challenging Days

2, 3, 9, 15, 23, 25, 30

 **Taurus/November**

Planetary Hotspots

You probably won't experience the full effect of this month's Saturn/Pluto clash until December, but you will feel rumblings and undercurrents. These two planets, placed in Libra and Capricorn, are active in your solar sixth and ninth houses, so your job may be involved. Take action if it becomes apparent that education is necessary to future success; investigate school options. Avoid legal matters if at all possible. Relationships with in-laws could be difficult and spark resentment.

Planetary Lightspots

Get set to shine as the November 2 Full Moon aims its bright beams in your sign. You'll attract the attention and interest of many and have added determination to achieve almost anything to which you're truly committed. Be sure to include other people in your plans; they're vital to your success.

Relationships

It's opportunity month! And your opportunity from the universe is to take your people skills to a new level of understanding. Most will be positive experiences, although some will test your ability to win supporters. Someone may try to mislead you around the time of the November 16 New Moon in Scorpio, your solar seventh house, so be skeptical and ask pointed questions, especially regarding career matters.

Money and Success

Finances are in positive territory, thanks to Mercury, which enters Sagittarius, your solar eighth house, on November 15, followed by the Sun on the 21st. You could net some extra cash from your employer or a family member just in time for the holidays.

Rewarding Days

3, 5, 7, 10, 11, 13, 16, 20, 21, 24, 29

Challenging Days

2, 6, 9, 12, 15, 19, 27, 30

 Taurus/December

Planetary Hotspots

Think carefully if you want to travel during the holidays. Mercury turns retrograde on December 26 in Capricorn, your solar ninth house. That's almost a guarantee for delays and cancellations. But it's only the start. The December 31 Full Moon (and lunar eclipse) in Cancer, your solar third house, aligns with Mercury, Venus, and Pluto in Capricorn. So you could be stranded as a result of weather or mechanical problems. This lineup also increases the potential for a clash with relatives.

Planetary Lightspots

December has plenty of positive planetary alignments that promise an active social season. Why not host a get-together of your own? All but the third weekend of December are good choices, with the fourth being the best.

Relationships

Mars turns retrograde in Leo, your domestic sector, December 20 through early April 2010. Sooner or later it will spark tension on the home front, which is all the more reason to think carefully before you commit to a holiday trip to visit relatives.

Money and Success

Money! It's one of your favorite topics, and chances are, you'll cash in this month. The December 2 Full Moon in Gemini and the New Moon in Sagittarius on December 16 occur in your solar second and eighth houses of money. Venus in Sagittarius through the December 24 magnifies the influence. Cross your fingers for a nice company year-end bonus and the same from a family member. Even better, the odds favor a pleasant surprise with your name on it. You can also make a valuable contact the week of the Full Moon who will in some way benefit your career early next year.

Rewarding Days

4, 5, 6, 8, 11, 12, 18, 21, 23, 26, 27

Challenging Days

3, 7, 9, 10, 17, 24, 28, 29, 31

Taurus Action Table

These dates reflect the best—but not the only—times for success and ease in these activities, according to your Sun sign.

	JAN	FEB	MAR	APR	MAY	JUN	JUL	AUG	SEPT	OCT	NOV	DEC
Move		8			1-2		22-23			12-13		5-6
Start a class		24-25	15-19	29-30		23-24	6-11				6-7	
Join a club				20-21			11			28-29		
Ask for a raise		4-5				18-19	18				5	
Look for work		12-13					26-27			16-27		
Get pro advice								25			10-14	
Get a loan		17						1		21	17-18	14-16
See a doctor		27-28		24		16-17	27	10-11		16	27	10-11
Start a diet										16-17	13	10-11
End relationship		14-15									15-16	
Buy clothes		11				28		21			10-11	
Get a makeover				25		19	17			6-7		
New romance						27	25	20-21				
Vacation	1-4	1-3					6-7				19-20	22-31

GEMINI

The Twins
May 20 to June 21

Ⅱ

Element: Air

Quality: Mutable

Polarity: Yang/masculine

Planetary Ruler: Mercury

Meditation: I explore my inner worlds

Gemstone: Tourmaline

Power Stones: Ametrine, citrine, emerald, spectrolite, agate

Key Phrase: I think

Glyph: Pillars of duality, the Twins

Anatomy: Shoulders, arms, hands, lungs, nervous system

Color: Bright colors, orange, yellow, magenta

Animal: Monkeys, talking birds, flying insects

Myths/Legends: Peter Pan, Castor and Pollux

House: Third

Opposite Sign: Sagittarius

Flower: Lily of the valley

Key Word: Versatility

Your Strengths and Challenges

Gemini has a talent for being here, there, and everywhere, seemingly all at the same time. While that's not physically possible (at least for most Geminis!), you have the mental agility to quickly switch topics and thought patterns and also to think about two things at once. That's the nature of your mutable air sign, which also excels at multi-tasking. In fact, the more things you can juggle at once the happier you are. But that also makes it easy to spread yourself too thin.

Lively, witty, and fun-loving, you have a youthful spirit, whatever your age. Your notable curiosity is part of your charm, and you know a little about a lot of things—just enough so people perceive you as an expert in many subjects. Depth, however, is not your strength because your interests are wide and varied.

Mercury-ruled Gemini is the sign of communication. A master information-gatherer, you enjoy learning and sharing what you know. But some Geminis forget to listen, and thus dominate conversations. And that can frustrate other people to the max. If you're among them, you'll get further if you say less rather than more and give others your full attention. You'll also gain a lot of information that you can use to your advantage.

You're restless and easily bored, yet agreeable and adaptable—an ideal combination for circulating on the social scene, where you're well-liked. In other areas of life, however, such as your career, follow-through is essential for success. Try to complete important projects before beginning new ones, which will ultimately reduce your stress level.

Your Relationships

Gemini is the consummate flirt of the Zodiac, which makes you popular on the social scene, and in touch with many potential mates during your dating years. But as much as you enjoy playing the field, you prefer a single dating relationship at a time—even if that means only one or two dates before moving on to the next person who catches your eye. It's togetherness you crave, that special feeling of one-on-one that prompts some Geminis to mistake infatuation for true love.

Your soul mate is likely to be someone at least as carefree as you are and even more adventuresome. In fact, the two of you should set aside designated togetherness time every week. Otherwise you could find yourselves passing in the night as you each dash off to the next adventure. A match with another air sign—Libra or Aquarius—would fulfill your need for intellectual stimulation, but the relationship might be too easygoing and lack passion. An Aries or Leo would keep things lively, but earthy Virgo or watery Pisces probably isn't your style. Your best match might be enthusiastic Sagittarius, your opposite sign.

Family communication is a high priority for most Geminis, and you encourage your children to share their thoughts and lives with you, even when they're adults. Your home probably has bookcases, games, and the latest technology and is either messy or neat—nothing in between—but still organized, even if you're the only one who can find anything! Geminis usually have a friendly, if somewhat distant, relationship with in-laws, but some develop a solid friendship with them.

Your friends are few, your acquaintances many, and people move in and out of your ever-evolving circle. That's just the way you like it; new people stimulate your active mind and you especially enjoy the getting-to-know-you phase. In a best friend you want a strong mental rapport as well as someone who's as active and spontaneous as you are.

Your Career and Money

Many Geminis seek a career in the communications field or one that requires strong communication skills. Creative expression is a must for career success, whether it takes the form of ideas, design or artistic talent, or finding the right approach in sales or promotional activities. But be patient with yourself if it takes you longer than most to find your ideal career niche. Because so many things interest you, it can be tough to settle on a single endeavor. That's why some Geminis have dual careers—one to pay the bills and another to satisfy their emotional needs. In your day-to-day work environment you're happiest when in charge. So look for positions that allow you the freedom to structure your daily work. You also like privacy in the workplace and prefer to keep your work and home lives separate.

Although you have a periodic spending streak, overall you're more conservative about money than about a lot of things. You also understand the value of thinking long-term, especially with savings and investments. Some Geminis, however, shop when they're feeling low and end up with a closet full of unworn clothing. If this describes you, find an alternative to boost your spirits, such as exercise or a creative hobby. Your bank account will benefit from it. You're also likely to see your net worth increase more rapidly later in life, and could receive an inheritance from a male relative.

Your Lighter Side

Your lighter side is, in a word, you! People find you fascinating and a bit of a puzzle. You can blend in or stand out, speak on almost any topic, out-charm the best of them, and adapt to fit into almost any situation and group. It's rare that you're exactly the same two days in a row, or sometimes from one hour to the next. And that keeps people guessing and wondering as they try to identify the many facets of the real, lively you!

Affirmation for the Year

I seek knowledge and wisdom.

The Year Ahead for Gemini

Life is about change. Embrace this concept and 2009 will bring you exciting adventures and new opportunities for personal and career growth.

Get ready, get set, go! That's the message of Jupiter, which will arrive in Aquarius, your solar ninth house, January 5. It's almost guaranteed you'll pack your bags at some time this year and probably more than once as adventuresome Jupiter triggers a desire for new spaces and places. Plan a dream trip to an exotic location or somewhere you've always wanted to see, or an extended trip to multiple destinations. You could even substitute with a series of long weekends to nearby locations.

Jupiter's influence goes beyond travel. It will boost your curiosity to the max and motivate you to seek knowledge and to explore other cultures and ways of life. Experience and learn all you can this year by expanding your mental horizons. Consider taking a class for fun or profit, learn another language, see museum exhibits, talk with people, read, and open your mind to different viewpoints. As you do it all, go beyond information into the realm of knowledge. What you gain from these experiences will in some way benefit your career and your ambitions in 2010.

You'll discover (or rediscover) your spiritual side as Jupiter moves closer to and eventually meets Neptune (also in Aquarius) in May and December. This planetary duo could also motivate you to return to school for a degree or certification in order to fulfill your dreams.

But the Jupiter-Neptune union can indicate unrealistic goals and wishful thinking as often as it can trigger inspiration and faith in yourself and the universe. So you'll want to objectively weigh the pros and cons of any major decision before you proceed. Also be cautious about taking anyone new at face value, especially a potential business or romantic partner. Be equally careful if you're involved in a legal situation this year. Check references if you need to hire an attorney and keep all discussions to yourself. Trusting the wrong person could cost you money.

Saturn almost completes its time in Virgo, your solar fourth house of home and family, this year. (It will briefly return to Virgo in 2010.) As has been true since 2007, when this serious planet entered Virgo, you'll experience domestic ups and downs, rewards and challenges. And it will continue to be a learning experience in everything from relationships to relatives to the physical space you call your own. The difference this year is you'll almost complete the journey in preparation for moving on to a new area of focus.

Saturn could prompt you to remodel your home or acquire a new one. Be cautious if you want to purchase a home of your own or are considering a roommate. If you have a home to sell, do that first, and then buy less rather than more in order to keep mortgage payments in the lowest possible range. Do the same if you need a home equity loan to fund improvements. Then acquire the necessary do-it-yourself skills in order to do much of the work yourself; it will cut costs.

Elderly relatives may need your help this year and you could find yourself handling many daily tasks for them, including managing their financial affairs. This could of course put a strain on your own family, so search for viable alternatives to minimize the impact on all of you.

This Saturn transit can challenge the flexibility of even an ultra-flexible Gemini. But Saturn is only half the story this year. The rest of the chapters will be written by Uranus in Pisces, your solar tenth house, which forms an exact alignment with Saturn in February and September.

You can expect everything from last-minute projects to a sudden job change when Uranus, the ultimate planet of change, is in your career sector. As it aligns with Saturn, you'll feel stretched thin at times trying to balance domestic and career responsibilities. Be sure to keep your boss informed and ask coworkers to lend a hand when necessary. Above all, though, try not to let your home life interfere with job performance, and vice versa. Your employer will understand—to a point.

You also could relocate for a job, either of your own choosing or at your company's request. If a promotion or new position is your target, February is possible and September more likely. Before you make any move, however—physical or a job change—be sure it will contribute to your long-term goals, not just your immediate ones. Also thoroughly investigate the desirability and affordability of any new area before you agree to relocate.

Saturn will enter Libra, your solar fifth house, October 29. Although this planet could limit socializing and romance the next few years, it doesn't have to. It's really your choice whether to get out and about or not. Chances are, you'll enjoy seeing old friends more than making new ones and opt for get-togethers that promote conversation and give you the opportunity to really get to know people. Among them could be the soul mate you've been searching for, and a romantic relationship could bloom with someone who's much older or younger than you.

You'll also want to nurture your creativity in practical ways, such as beautifying your home or garden, or delving into a new hobby that produces concrete results. Because Libra is your sign of recreation, you could begin an exercise program and actually stick with it, or get involved in your children's sports and other after-school activities. Your children will also be a focal point, and what you teach them now can form a firm foundation for the future.

But your children, entertainment, and leisure-time activities could be an expensive item at year's end when Saturn will clash with Pluto in Sagittarius, your financial sector. Keep close track of expenses and try to save earlier in the year. Also think carefully before you spend big bucks on electronics and other high-end items, and be especially cautious about investments and games of chance.

Now is a good time to get in the habit of saving far more than you spend because Pluto will spend the next fifteen years in Sagittarius. Although this powerful planet could multiply your wealth during that period, it can also negatively impact your financial health. If you're the parent of young children, you also should begin saving regularly for their college educations.

What This Year's Eclipses Mean for You

Most years feature four eclipses; 2009 has six, each of which reinforces the year's planetary alignments. Eclipses are in effect for six to twelve months.

The January 6 solar eclipse and the August 6 lunar eclipse will be in Aquarius, your solar ninth house, activating the influence of Jupiter and Neptune. The timing is ideal if you want to return to school, take an online or community class, or schedule a vacation. It's also possible you could travel on business or attend a seminar or conference, where networking and your presentation skills will be invaluable assets to impress clients, colleagues, or a potential employer.

The February 9 lunar eclipse in Leo, Aquarius' polar opposite, will motivate you to do much the same. Leo, your solar third house, emphasizes learning, communication, and quick trips so you can expect to be on the go, juggling all the many details of a fast-paced life. Because this eclipse will activate Neptune, there's an increased chance for mix-ups and miscommunication, especially **if your birthday is around June 11**. This makes organization your best ally to keep up with it all. Make lists and update and review your calendar daily.

This year's other three eclipses will be in Cancer and Capricorn, your solar second and eighth houses of money: July 22 (solar eclipse) and December 31 (lunar eclipse) in Cancer, and July 7 (lunar eclipse) in Capricorn.

With this extra emphasis on finances you'll want to plan ahead and live within a budget. Both income and expenses can rise and you'll have a tendency to spend more than usual. Think security instead, be conservative, and build resources. **If your birthday is within a few days of June 20**, you could gain through a major windfall—or realize a significant loss. Keep this in mind if you plan to invest, and always read all the fine print before you sign any document. Some Geminis will benefit from an inheritance, although there may be difficulties associated with it.

Saturn

If you were born between June 4 and 20, Saturn will contact your Sun from Virgo, your domestic sector. But only **if you were born between June 4 and 12** will you experience Saturn's transit to the greatest extent. For Geminis born after that date, the influence will be minor, probably a week or two, in September or October.

Family or other domestic issues will reach a turning point in April, May, and June **for Geminis born between June 4 and 7**, while events will take longer to unfold **for those with birthdays between June 8 and 11**—January through March, and July and August. Your parents or other relatives may require your assistance, your home may need a major repair, or you might decide to renovate your place. If you want to sell your home, however, it could take longer than you expect.

This year isn't the best if you want a roommate. It's even less so if you and your paramour are talking about moving in together. That's better left for 2010, as is purchasing property with anyone but a legal partner.

You'll want to set aside time each day for rest and relaxation. Make this a priority along with getting enough sleep, because this Saturn contact can lower your immune system and you'll probably tire more easily. Get yourself a comfy chair and stock up on books to fill your evening hours.

Saturn and Pluto

If you were born between May 21 and 25, Saturn will contact your Sun from Libra as Pluto does the same from Capricorn. You'll want to be especially cautious with money matters, and try to avoid loans and other major credit commitments. You also might want to protect yourself (and family members) with fraud and identity theft insurance. At the least you should periodically check your credit, which you can do at no cost. Also be sure your home and property are adequately covered by insurance, and that you and yours have health coverage.

Despite the potential downside of this configuration, it's a terrific time to put yourself on a budget, pay off debt, and plan for retirement even if it's far in the future. You might also want to check your closets and storage spaces for potential collectibles. A childhood or family treasure could be worth a lot, and you could even stumble across something valuable at a yard sale or thrift store.

Uranus

If you were born between June 9 and 17, you could get an irresistible urge to change jobs or even your career. Boredom might be the chief reason, but it's also possible that family responsibilities will prompt that decision. The energy will be strongest in June, July, November, and December. You also could earn a sudden and very unexpected promotion or see major changes occur in your workplace.

This is also a year of personal change and in many ways it can be one of the most exciting of your life. You'll rediscover yourself and might even develop a previously untapped skill or talent. Most of all you'll experience an increasing desire to explore new personal directions. Think before you act, however. The changes you make now, including those involving close relationships, will be irreversible, and by 2010 you'll have an entirely new perspective on life, love, and yourself.

Neptune

If you were born between June 12 and 17, you'll be inspired and motivated as Neptune favorably contacts your Sun from Aquarius, your solar ninth house. The possibilities are nearly limitless and this mystical planet will boost your sixth sense and your creativity, and motivate you to achieve worldly success. Neptune's energy will peak in June, when you may decide to pursue your career dreams elsewhere. Be a little cautious; sometimes what appears to be ideal is not nearly so.

You'll connect with many people this year and be in the mood for romance, whether it's a new relationship or rekindling a long-term one. Some people, however, may tell you only what you want to hear and, because you'll want to see the best in everyone, it would be easy to misplace your trust. Anything or anyone that sounds too good to be true probably is. Don't risk your future, your heart, or your money.

Gemini/January

Planetary Hotspots

Finances are both positive and negative this month. Without question, they'll command your attention as the January 10 lunar eclipse in Cancer highlights your solar second house of personal resources. Limit spending, especially if your birthday is within a few days of June 12. Although unexpected expenses could arise, you might also gain through a windfall—a raise or bonus, an inheritance, or a lucky win. Even so, play it safe and don't bust your budget.

Planetary Lightspots

Your renowned curiosity takes on a life of its own this month as Jupiter begins its year-long transit of Aquarius, January 5. With the New Moon (and solar eclipse) in the same sign January 26, it's time to plan the vacation of your dreams. If your home turf is more appealing, enroll in a class for fun or profit, and consider distance learning. Keep in mind, though, that Mercury will be retrograde from January 11 on, so delays and mix-ups are possible.

Relationships

Travelers and students could make a terrific romantic or business connection this month, and you'll be in sync with most everyone, thanks to several planets in fellow air sign Aquarius. The third week of January offers some of the month's best days to meet new people and to get a positive reception from the boss and coworkers. But family members will need extra TLC at that time.

Money and Success

The positive alignment of the Sun and Mars in Capricorn with Saturn in Virgo could motivate you to buy or rent a home, begin improvements, or purchase furnishings. Be somewhat cautious if you need a mortgage or loan, however. Read the fine print and opt for less to keep payments down. The urge to splurge will be strong.

Rewarding Days

1, 4, 7, 11, 17, 20, 25, 26, 27, 31

Challenging Days

2, 3, 9, 14, 21, 22, 29

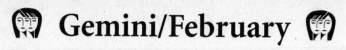 Gemini/February

Planetary Hotspots

This month's exact Saturn/Uranus alignment triggers career, family, and domestic changes for many Geminis, especially those born within a few days of June 11. You could be faced with a tough choice about whether to relocate or find yourself in the midst of a company reorganization or downsizing. This is not the month (or year) to purchase property; if you want to sell your home, be prepared for a lengthy process. A parent or another relative may need your assistance now.

Planetary Lightspots

Little pleases a Gemini more than being in the know, and that's exactly where you'll be this month, thanks to the February 9 Full Moon (and lunar eclipse) in Leo, your solar third house. There's an added plus: Mercury, Venus, and Mars connect with Jupiter, in Aquarius, your knowledge sector. The planetary combination is great for travel and even better for learning. Begin a course of study now and you could complete it within a year to open up new career avenues.

Relationships

You're among the most popular on the social scene as Venus advances in Aries, your solar eleventh house of friendship and groups. This is also a terrific influence for networking, and you could make a lucky love or career connection the third week of February.

Money and Success

The career picture brightens around the time of the February 24 New Moon in Pisces, your career sector, when you'll have an opportunity to impress decision-makers. If you're job-hunting, try to schedule interviews for the 27th or 28th. Finances benefit from Mercury, which turns direct in Capricorn on the 1st.

Rewarding Days

4, 8, 13, 17, 22, 23, 24, 27, 28

Challenging Days

1, 5, 6, 11, 12, 18, 25, 26

Gemini/March

Planetary Hotspots

Last month's Saturn/Uranus influence continues to be a hotspot the first three weeks of March. Both planets are activated by the March 10 Full Moon in Virgo, which at least will put you a step closer to resolution. Don't expect the process to be challenge-free, however. More than ever it will be a balancing act and a test of how willing you are to accept necessary changes in your career or domestic life, or both.

Planetary Lightspots

Planetary lineups give you another opportunity for travel this month. For some Geminis that means relocation or a business trip. If neither one is in your plans, try for a long weekend at a nearby luxury destination where you can party safely.

Relationships

Some friendships are rocky, while others are at their best, especially around the March 26 New Moon in Aries, your solar eleventh house. Even so, your social life won't be as active as usual because Venus turns retrograde in Aries on the 6th. Be patient if a potential romantic liaison doesn't immediately take off. It may be mid-May before you really have a chance to get to know each other.

Money and Success

Take a close look at your financial goals—or get busy and set them—including savings, debt reduction, and how best to maximize your earnings. It's possible you could net a raise or cost-cutting perk to get yourself started on the path to financial freedom. Skip all but the most conservative, long-term investments even if someone close encourages you to do otherwise, and don't mix money and friendship.

Rewarding Days

3, 7, 8, 12, 13, 21, 22, 27, 30

Challenging Days

4, 5, 9, 10, 11, 17, 25, 31

Gemini/April

Planetary Hotspots

Retrograde Venus slips back into Pisces, your career sector, April 11 before turning direct on the 17th. With Mars in the same sign through the 21st, work relationships will be tense at times. Frustration is the root cause, and any attempt to push others to perform is likely to backfire. Go easy on yourself and coworkers and stop before you make snap decisions and smart comebacks.

Planetary Lightspots

Your thoughts turn inward this month with Mercury in Taurus, your solar twelfth house, April 9–29. It's joined by the Sun on the 20th, four days before the New Moon in the same sign. This combined influence boosts your sixth sense as it also encourages you to reflect upon what you've achieved in the past twelve months. Pamper yourself, get a massage, enjoy some rare quiet time.

Relationships

The April 9 Full Moon in Libra activates your solar fifth house of romance and recreation. That's as great for your social life as is Mars moving into Aries, your friendship sector, on the 22nd, followed by Venus on the 24th. The lunar energy triggers a new romance for some Geminis, and others celebrate an addition to the family. If you're a parent, this is a terrific time to get involved in your children's sports and other after-school activities.

Money and Success

Money won't fall into your hands this month, but you can still get ahead. Get busy and clean out closets, drawers, and cupboards. Take the best to a consignment shop, and get together with neighbors to host a yard sale. Altogether you could make a nice profit. Also be alert for hidden treasure. Check pockets for cash and research the value of potential collectibles.

Rewarding Days

4, 5, 8, 9, 10, 12, 17, 18, 19, 30

Challenging Days

1, 2, 3, 7, 13, 14, 22, 27, 28

Gemini/May

Planetary Hotspots

You're hot to launch new personal directions now that Mercury is in Gemini. But it's not quite that easy. Your ruling planet turns retrograde in your sign on May 7 and slips back into Taurus on the 13th before turning direct on the 30th. Rather than let it frustrate you, consider it bonus time to think about new personal goals. You might surprise yourself. What you think you want to achieve may change by month's end.

Planetary Lightspots

The May 24 New Moon in Gemini has you in the spotlight, with all the attention-getting charm you're noted for. Use it to attract fascinating people, to promote yourself and your ideas, and to plan a summer trip with friends to an exotic destination. Consider a cruise; the idea might appeal to you with Jupiter and Neptune in Aquarius, your solar ninth house. But try to avoid travel the third week of the month. Delays are likely; a cancellation is possible.

Relationships

Plan a get-together with friends the last week of May, when Mars in Aries, your solar eleventh house, is beautifully aligned. But skip the first weekend of the month. It would be pricey, and besides, you'll simply enjoy time at home with loved ones, yourself, and your own interests.

Money and Success

Your workload increases the week of the May 19 Full Moon in Scorpio, your solar sixth house. But with it comes an opportunity to impress those who count. Share your clever, innovative ideas and snap up any chance to make a presentation or take the lead in a project. With Mars in Aries you can be an especially effective leader now and motivate others by example.

Rewarding Days

6, 7, 8, 10, 11, 15, 16, 20, 24, 28

Challenging Days

4, 5, 12, 13, 18, 25, 26, 30

Gemini/June

Planetary Hotspots

Mars is in Taurus, your solar twelfth house, throughout June. For someone as active as a Gemini this can be a particularly frustrating time. You can manage that if you want to. But this influence can keep your mind going when you should be sleeping. Make it a policy to calm yourself in the evening with light reading, a casual walk, or whatever will relax you.

Planetary Lightspots

Mercury, your ruling planet, zips into your sign on June 13. You'll feel right at home with this influence, and people will be receptive to your views and ideas. This is an overall positive time, but the end of June could bring a domestic clash if you're unwilling to listen to loved ones and give in to their wishes. Listen more than you talk. You'll learn a lot if you do.

Relationships

The June 7 Full Moon in Sagittarius spotlights your solar seventh house. You'll be drawn to people and they to you, and some singles will take a relationship to the next level. But it also can further strain already difficult ties. If you feel the stress, take the initiative to talk out what's on your mind. You might discover that your assumptions are just that and very far from the truth. For couples, romance is pure delight as Venus travels in Taurus from June 6 on.

Money and Success

This month's New Moon (June 22) is in Cancer. Usually a positive influence (and it may ultimately be this year as well), there's a good reason to be cautious and conservative. It's closely aligned with Pluto in Capricorn. With the emphasis on both of your financial sectors, and Pluto involved, the wise choice is to save and take no chances. Unexpected expenses are possible.

Rewarding Days

2, 6, 12, 14, 17, 19, 20, 24, 29, 30

Challenging Days

1, 5, 7, 15, 21, 22, 26, 27, 28

Gemini/July

Planetary Hotspots

Much of the action is centered behind the scenes the first two weeks of July as Venus and Mars complete their solar twelfth house transit. Listen to rumors and observe what's going on around you. You might pick up a clue about what's in the works regarding your career. Be especially cautious about what you put in writing. E-mail can find its way to people who shouldn't read what you're thinking. Keep confidences and personal matters to yourself.

Planetary Lightspots

You symbolically emerge into the light when Mars zips into your sign on July 11. This high-energy influence will be with you through the end of August, enhancing initiative but also the potential for mishaps. Slow down, and also fuel your body with nutritious foods and plenty of sleep so you're at your best day after day.

Relationships

Mercury in Leo, your solar third house, from July 17 on is a plus for communication. Share your thoughts and feelings with those closest to you and then listen closely. Mixed in between the lines may be clues that spark ideas and prompt you to look to the future. With Venus in your sign during the same time frame, some of what you hear may not exactly make you smile. But the objective perspective is on target. Learn from it.

Money and Success

Your solar second house of money sees a lot of action this month. The Sun is there through July 21, the date of the New Moon (and solar eclipse) in the same sign. It's joined by Mercury from the 3rd to the 17th. Although these influences are overall more positive than negative, including the chance for a nice raise, unexpected expenses could arise, possibly involving a home repair.

Rewarding Days

3, 8, 9, 12, 14 ,18, 21, 22, 26, 27

Challenging Days

1, 2, 4, 5, 6, 13, 19, 24, 25

Gemini/August

Planetary Hotspots

Finances continue in the forecast this month. The potential for a raise is again in your favor, but investments and major purchases are unwise in early and late August. Take the time to check your (and the family's) credit reports for errors, and be sure to safeguard valuables when you're out and about. With first Venus and then Mars clashing with Pluto in your solar eighth house, caution is needed.

Planetary Lightspots

Your travel houses are activated by the August 5 Full Moon (and lunar eclipse) in Aquarius and the New Moon in Leo on the 20th. Plan a vacation if you have time available, or opt for a long weekend to relax and unwind. If you've been thinking about returning to school or even taking a single course, get started now. It will pay off in your career in 2010. Online learning might be a good choice to fit your busy lifestyle.

Relationships

Mercury enhances family communication as it dashes through Virgo, your domestic sector, August 2–24. It's joined by the Sun on the 22nd. Important domestic decisions should be avoided mid-month, however, when Mercury clashes with Saturn and Uranus. If you want to host a get-together, next month is a better choice. Month's end brings Mercury in Libra, your solar fifth house—a terrific influence for your social life that continues into the fall.

Money and Success

Mars in your sign unleashes your ambitions. Go for it, but be cautious as you could alienate a decision-maker. Also make a point of sharing your knowledge with coworkers and, if you have the opportunity, offer to conduct a formal or informal company training seminar.

Rewarding Days

3, 4, 6, 11, 14, 18, 19, 23, 24, 27, 30, 31

Challenging Days

1, 2, 8, 9, 13, 15, 16, 17, 21, 22, 28, 29

Gemini/September

Planetary Hotspots

Saturn and Uranus make their final contact across your solar fourth/tenth house axis this month. With retrograde Mercury and the September 18 New Moon in Virgo in the mix, you can expect changes in your domestic and family life, especially if your birthday is within a few days of June 15. You could relocate, a relative could move in or out, or you might need a major home repair. Be sure your home has adequate insurance coverage.

Planetary Lightspots

Venus gives you a way with words through September 19. Combine charm with tact to get the supporters and information you need. Also listen closely and use your common sense because Venus's alignment with Jupiter and Neptune could cloud the facts.

Relationships

Family and work relationships are stressful at times because of Saturn/Uranus, so think before you speak. Just when it looks like your social life is becoming active, the trend reverses as Mercury turns retrograde in Libra, your solar fifth house, on September 7. The Sun arrives in Libra on the 22nd, but it will be next month before you get the full benefit of the solar energy.

Money and Success

This is not the month to purchase property, establish a business (especially a home-based one), or to welcome a new roommate. It will be tough enough to maintain the status quo without initiating such changes, which also could be costly. The September 4 Full Moon in Pisces, your career sign, could trigger a sudden promotion or difficult career decisions. If possible, wait until next month to make a career move.

Rewarding Days

1, 2, 7, 11, 19, 20, 24, 28, 29

Challenging Days

5, 6, 12, 14, 17, 18, 23, 25

Gemini/October

Planetary Hotspots

The lingering effects of September's Saturn/Uranus alignment continue the first two weeks of the month as first Mercury and then Venus, both in Virgo, contact these planets. The positive news is you can resolve the associated issues and move on. If you're selling property or plan to refinance, success is more likely the second and third weeks of October.

Planetary Lightspots

The daily pace picks up as Mars enters Leo, your solar third house, on October 16. Take your car in for routine service before then so you're set to go when curiosity motivates you to get out of the house. A relaxing weekend getaway is a great stress reliever if you can manage a few days off later this month.

Relationships

This is a great month for socializing and meeting new people. Watch expenses, though, because the Sun, Mercury, and Venus will clash with Pluto in Capricorn, your solar eighth house. Also keep a close eye on valuables. This month's big news, however, is Saturn, which enters Libra on the October 29 for a three-year tour. Although it could dampen your social prospects at times, you may form lasting ties, and it could link you with a soul mate.

Money and Success

Finances benefit from Mars in Cancer, your solar second house, through the 15th. The red planet could trigger an opportunity to earn some extra money around the time of the Full Moon. Your workload begins to pick up after the Sun enters Scorpio, your solar sixth house, on October 22, followed by Mercury on the 28th. If you're job-hunting, do your networking and pass out resumes that week.

Rewarding Days

8, 11, 12, 17, 20, 21, 26, 27, 31

Challenging Days

2, 9, 15, 16, 22, 23, 25, 30

Gemini/November

Planetary Hotspots

Saturn (in Libra) and Pluto (in Capricorn) clash this month in your solar fifth and eighth houses of speculation and money. Although it will be December before you experience the strong influence of this lineup, now is the time to take some precautions. Be especially careful with all but the most conservative long-term investments, including your retirement account, and avoid any financial risk. Even what you're sure is safe could backfire next month.

Planetary Lightspots

The universe offers you a chance to take a breather. Take time for yourself to relax and unwind at the end of every day, even for thirty minutes, to calm your mind before bedtime. Also take note of your dreams, which may offer clues about how best to achieve your deepest desires.

Relationships

Talk strengthens ties after Mercury enters Sagittarius, your solar seventh house, on November 15, followed by the Sun on the 21st. You can benefit from the influence in your personal life and at work, where some people will try to overstep their bounds. The first week is the month's best for socializing, with Venus in Libra, your solar fifth house, through November 6. Join friends for an evening out, or make it a romantic one designed for two.

Money and Success

Action centers on your solar sixth house of daily work throughout November. You'll be pushed to the max at times, but it's a terrific opportunity to showcase your skills and talents. And that could lead to a step up, if not this year, then next. The energy peaks at the November 16 New Moon in Scorpio, after which the pace will begin to ease. Work-related travel is possible midmonth.

Rewarding Days

4, 5, 13, 14, 17, 18, 21, 22, 28

Challenging Days

1, 2, 6, 9, 12, 15, 19, 27, 30

Gemini/December

Planetary Hotspots

Mars begins its retrograde period in Leo on the 20th. This can trigger mechanical problems in the next few months because it will be early March before Mars turns direct. So don't ignore telltale signs and sounds in your car or appliances. If you can possibly wait, postpone major purchases, including electronic equipment, until April. If not, consider an extended warranty.

Planetary Lightspots

December begins with a bright spot: the Full Moon in Gemini on the 2nd. That makes you an attention-getter with all the charming words and charisma to attract people into your circle. The lunar energy also fuels you with high energy to dash through this busy holiday social season where you'll be one of the most popular guests.

Relationships

December is a great month for relationships, especially with your partner and other loved ones. Close ties become more so with the New Moon in Sagittarius, your solar seventh house, on the 16th. Even better is Venus in Sagittarius through the 24th. The combination sparks a new romantic relationship for some Geminis, and for others it's lifetime commitment. The only potential challenge is with a coworker or supervisor, but even that will be minor. Enjoy the people in your life.

Money and Success

The Sun, Mercury, and later, Venus activate Saturn and Pluto at various times this month. This can put a strain on finances, so go easy on holiday shopping. Compounding the influence is Mercury, which turns retrograde in Capricorn, your solar eighth house, on December 26. The clash will be more prominent if you were born near May 22. Budget and plan ahead.

Rewarding Days

5, 6, 11, 12, 14, 15, 18, 19, 21, 23, 25, 30

Challenging Days

3, 7, 9, 10, 13, 20, 24, 26, 28, 29, 31

Gemini Action Table

These dates reflect the best—but not the only—times for success and ease in these activities, according to your Sun sign.

	JAN	FEB	MAR	APR	MAY	JUN	JUL	AUG	SEPT	OCT	NOV	DEC
Move		10-11			3-4			20-21			10-12	
Start a class		9		4			22-23	18-19		12-13		
Join a club		27-28			20-21						27-28	
Ask for a raise				10		23	21	17		10		
Look for work			14					25-26	21-22	28-29	11-16	3-4, 14-15
Get pro advice		17-18					3	27-28		21-22	17-18	17-18
Get a loan		2				9-10	7				20	
See a doctor			14-15			18-19	16-17	25		6	16	12
Start a diet		17-18		11							15	
End relationship					10	8						14-15
Buy clothes		13					26-27		1-2	16-17, 21-22, 26-27		10
Get a makeover						21	18, 22				4-5	
New romance						1-3, 29-30	26-27			16-17, 26-27		
Vacation	1-2, 20-31	5-28	1-7							26-27		

CANCER

The Crab
June 21 to July 22

Element: Water

Quality: Cardinal

Polarity: Yin/feminine

Planetary Ruler: The Moon

Meditation: I have faith in the promptings of my heart

Gemstone: Pearl

Power Stones: Moonstone, chrysocolla

Key Phrase: I feel

Glyph: Crab's claws

Anatomy: Stomach, breasts

Color: Silver, pearl white

Animal: Crustaceans, cows, chickens

Myths/Legends: Hercules and the Crab, Asherah, Hecate

House: Fourth

Opposite Sign: Capricorn

Flower: Larkspur

Key Word: Receptivity

Your Strengths and Challenges

You're sensitive, caring, and sympathetic, and when you get close to people you want to fulfill their every need and desire. It's this nurturing quality that draws others into the warmth of your aura. You're also intuitive and easily sense how others feel, but you need to be cautious about becoming too emotionally involved in their lives and problems.

Because you're so responsive to others, some people underestimate your inner strength, believing you're a pushover. Far from it! Cancer is a cardinal water sign, which gives you two major assets— dynamic action and the ability to win people's loyalty. And when someone pushes you too far, you're more than capable of holding your own.

Your Moon-ruled sign is super-sensitive to the environment. When entering a room you pick up on the vibrations, both positive and negative. It's partly your sixth sense and partly your receptive nature. This can be a real plus when you need to know how to present your ideas, for example. But it's also wise to mentally surround yourself with a protective shield rather than take the chance of absorbing unwanted energy.

You're happiest when life is predictable, safe, and secure. But with the Moon as your ruling planet, your life and your emotions are in a continual state of flux. That gives you a reputation for moodiness and others find it difficult to understand why you're up one minute and down the next. This is especially true when someone hurts your feelings, whether that's reality or only your perception.

Traditional and patriotic to the core, you value the past, might collect or refinish antiques, and probably have a large collection of family photos and memorabilia. Most Cancers are excellent cooks and enjoy entertaining friends and family in their tastefully decorated homes.

Your Relationships

Because Cancer is the universal sign of family, most people with the Sun in this sign have strong ties to loved ones—parents, grandparents, children, siblings, cousins, aunts and uncles. Most also want children to cherish and nurture. But as a parent you can be overly protective and try to shield your children from the hurts and realities that are good learning experiences. Give them room to grow and to explore their own personalities and talents while they have the safety and security of a supportive, loving home life. They'll thank you later as they become adults.

In love, your feelings run deep and at times you can be possessive, and even jealous, hanging on to a dating relationship when you know in your heart it's time to move on. You also experience the ultimate in passionate, romantic moments when you're with the right person. Although it might take you longer than your peers to find a soul mate (and Cancers truly do have soul mates), when you find your ideal match he or she is likely to share your desire for financial security and a stable family life. You could find happiness with one of the earth signs, Taurus, Virgo, and especially Capricorn, your polar opposite. The other water signs, Scorpio and Pisces, are in sync with your energy, but it could be difficult to satisfy your emotional needs with an Aries or Libra.

As a friend you're one of the best—loyal and supportive. Your circle, whether large or small, is filled with people around whom you can be yourself, and you most enjoy time with them one-on-one or in small groups. Generous with your time and resources, you treasure your friendships and have many life-long associations. Some of these people become members of your extended family.

In all relationships Cancers have a tendency to sacrifice their needs for others. Although compromise is necessary when two people come together, being too accommodating is unhealthy for both parties. Strive for a fifty-fifty average, sometimes giving more, sometimes less, in order to satisfy both your and your mate's needs, hopes, and wishes.

Your Career and Money

You have excellent financial instincts and a talent for making money. That's a plus to fulfill your security needs. But some Cancers take things to the "nth" degree and never achieve that goal because enough never seems to be enough—even when assets run into the millions. And that can encourage a fearful mind set as well as a miserly one. Learn to keep finances in perspective and be thrifty and wise, investing for the long term and saving to cover the inevitable unexpected expenses that are a normal part of life. Periodically reward you and yours with the luxury items you have an eye for.

Your cardinal-sign initiative is especially evident in your career life where you invest maximum energy to achieve your goals. A career with growth potential is a must, as is one where you can use your leadership skills. But therein lies a possible challenge. If promotions don't come as fast as you wish, your thoughts soon turn elsewhere. This can lead to job-hopping, which could slow your progress even more. Patience can pay off handsomely. In your daily work you need an upbeat, enthusiastic environment with a high level of activity and freedom, or at least limited supervision. For this reason many Cancers steer clear of desk jobs. You also need a job in which you can learn or teach others, formally or informally, along with open-minded coworkers and a free exchange of ideas.

Your Lighter Side

It's a well-kept secret that Cancer's powers of observation are among the best. Little escapes your notice, thanks to intuition and your excellent eye for detail. That and your tenacity make you an outstanding researcher. Once on the trail of information you persist until you find the answers. It's also difficult, if not impossible, for your children and others close to you to get away with much of anything; you're nearly always a step ahead of them.

Affirmation for the Year

I have confidence in myself, my talents, and my abilities.

The Year Ahead for Cancer

Money! It's one of your favorite topics and this year has the potential to be one of the financially best. For that you can thank Jupiter, planet of expansion, which enters Aquarius, your solar eighth house, January 5. You or your partner could earn a sizable raise or bonus or cash in on a windfall triggered by anything from an investment to the lottery. The goal here of course is to begin 2010 with a larger net worth than you had at the start of 2009. Save more than you spend and build assets that will grow into the future.

There is, however, one potential wrinkle in this otherwise glowing scenario: Neptune. This planet is also in Aquarius and, in May and December, it will join forces with Jupiter. That has its pros and cons. Neptune is illusion and confusion, but also intuition, creativity, faith, and inspiration. Your challenge is to use the best of Neptune to fatten your bank account while dodging its less positive aspects.

Be sure to get the facts before you make major financial decisions. If you have the slightest doubt, don't, no matter what anyone tells you. Read all the fine print even if you trust your banker and be especially cautious with consumer credit. It would be easy, for example, to overlook or misunderstand the due date on a limited-time, no-interest purchase.

Serious Saturn spends much of the year in Virgo, the sign it will revisit next spring (2010). Placed in your solar third house of communication, learning, and quick trips, all these activities will be emphasized as they have been since Saturn entered Virgo in September 2007.

On a practical level you could need a new vehicle or major appliance this year. If you think that's a possibility, research options before it becomes a necessity. That way you won't be rushed and risk the chance of making the wrong purchase. Stay on top of routine vehicle maintenance and if you sense a problem get it checked right away. Doing this could save you money.

Learning is in the spotlight with Saturn in Virgo and you can thoroughly grasp any subject you study now partly because of your increased ability to concentrate and absorb information. Get the practical how-to skills you need for your career or a leisure-time pursuit. Details will come easily, but the big picture could get lost, so periodically take a step back and see how everything fits together.

Communication will be equally important, especially in close relationships, both business and personal. Saturn's lesson here presents a quandary. On the one hand Saturn will encourage you to open up, while on the other it will discourage the same. So the true lesson is more one of confidence in your thoughts, ideas, and feelings. Think things through first so you're comfortable saying what you want to say.

If you've ever wanted to polish your public speaking and presentation skills, now is the time. You might also want to tutor students, teach a community class, or volunteer at the library or your children's school.

Saturn will operate in tandem with Uranus throughout much of 2009. These two planets will form an exact alignment in February and September across your solar third/ninth house axis.

Uranus represents change and the unexpected, while Saturn is the planet of stability and caution. The two are obviously at odds so your challenge is to blend their energies in the areas of information, knowledge, travel, and spirituality.

Try to avoid travel during February and September when you could experience delays, cancellations, and mechanical problems. Also be careful about what you put in writing during the same time frame, and resist the urge to make snap decisions and comebacks, which you may later regret.

Education may be the single most positive use of the Saturn/Uranus alignment. Take a class for fun or to boost your career prospects, read, ask questions, talk with people. And don't be surprised if you suddenly realize some long-held beliefs are changing. At the least it will be to your advantage this year to listen to and contemplate divergent opinions as a way to expand your mental horizons.

Saturn will enter Libra October 29 to begin a three-year emphasis on your domestic life. You may relocate or extensively remodel your home between then and 2012, or purchase your first home. This will be a period of establishing roots, when home and family take on added importance. Your parents or elderly relatives may require more of your time and attention and you could take on more responsibility for their daily care.

From the time Saturn enters Libra through year's end it will contact Pluto in Capricorn, your solar seventh house of close relationships. You'll experience the effects of this lineup as conflict, frustration, or both, when your values clash or you begin to see yourself and your identity in a different light. This is also a good time to resolve childhood issues so you can move into the future with renewed confidence.

What This Year's Eclipses Mean for You

This is an important year for you from another perspective. Of the six eclipses that occur this year, two are in your sign.

The July 22 solar eclipse in Cancer will motivate you to invest your time, energy, and resources in yourself. As you begin to identify new personal directions you'll discover more about what inspires you and what holds you back. You'll complete the first phase of this personal project about the time of the December 31 lunar eclipse, also in your sign. Its influence will continue into 2010, when you'll emerge with a renewed sense of yourself and fresh goals.

This year's eclipses in your sign are complemented by another—the July 7 lunar eclipse in Capricorn, your solar seventh house of relationships. As you learn more about yourself, you'll do the same with others, and what you see in them will be partly a reflection of yourself. The lessons involve compromise and cooperation and maintaining your individuality within a personal or business relationship.

A close relationship (or maybe several) will reach a turning point around the time of the Capricorn eclipse. That can be positive or negative, or possibly both. But you should try to hold off on making any related life decisions until later in 2010, when you'll have a much clearer perspective.

This year's other three eclipses will be in Leo and Aquarius. The Leo lunar eclipse, February 9, will highlight your solar second house of personal resources, income, and spending. It could trigger a raise but also prompt you to temporarily become a big spender. Indulge yourself in what you can realistically afford and stop there. In December, when Mars turns retrograde in Leo, you'll be glad to have some extra cash for unexpected expenses. And, if you're not careful, money can slip through your fingers and disappear as if into thin air this year.

The January 7 solar eclipse and the August 6 lunar eclipse will be in Aquarius, your solar eighth house of joint resources, insurance, loans, retirement funds, and your partner's finances. With Jupiter also in Aquarius your overall assets could see a nice increase, but the same is true of debt. And with illusive Neptune also here, the eclipses make it doubly important to safeguard financial information, monitor investments and interest rates, and trust your conservative instincts.

Saturn

If you were born between July 5 and 22, Saturn will contact your Sun from Virgo, your solar third house. You'll find yourself lost in thought more often than usual, along with a greater tendency to worry about anything and everything. Try to stop yourself before you slip into "what-if" thinking. Borrowing trouble is non-productive and only creates stress. Be realistic instead, put your imagination on hold, and look at the facts. If necessary, ask someone you trust for an objective opinion.

You'll be on the same wavelength with just about everyone, especially close friends, family, and partner. Open communication can add depth to these relationships and you'll be drawn to people who can broaden your views. Take their words to heart; you'll learn from them.

Formal education can be equally valuable now, and it will begin to pay off in your career as soon as 2010. If you need only a few classes to complete a degree or training program, now is the time to go for it.

You'll experience all of this to a greater extent **if you were born between July 5 and 13**. Travel cautions, however, apply to all Cancers. Try to schedule necessary, or vacation, trips for late spring or early summer in order to avoid the exact Saturn/Uranus alignment in February and September, which could be particularly troublesome **if your birthday is between July 11 and 19.**

Uranus

Although Uranus will form a favorable contact with your Sun **if you were born between July 11 and 19**, this planet of the unexpected will undoubtedly surprise you in many ways.

Uranus is all about change. But because it's in Pisces, a fellow water sign, you'll be able to initiate many of the year's changes and more easily adapt to others. This planetary influence is a perfect match for the two eclipses in your sign as it will give you added incentive to redesign yourself in whatever way you choose.

Saturn will of course firmly push you to do the same, especially when the two line up exactly across your solar third/ninth house axis. You, more than others born under the Cancer Sun, can get the best from this duo if you're willing to embrace new ideas and concepts. Focus on possibilities and seize opportunities that come your way. They'll appear as if by magic and from any imaginable source: someone from the past, a relative, a neighbor, a friend, a new acquaintance, or an organization. And each will encourage you to step out of the present and into the future. But be prepared to be patient and let things evolve because Saturn will slow the fast pace of Uranus.

Saturn-Pluto

If you were born between June 21 and 25, Saturn will contact your Sun after it enters Libra, your solar fourth house, October 29. Pluto will do the same from Capricorn all year.

Relationship difficulties are likely as Pluto, planet of transformation, applies pressure from your solar seventh house. Plain and simple, this can be a difficult transit. Fortunately it will occur only once in your lifetime. Coming as it does from your relationship sector you can expect tension with those closest to you as this planet can trigger power plays and control issues.

But it's important to understand that this is as much about you as it is about other people. Even the best relationship will feel the strain, primarily because your perspective of yourself, your place in the world, and how you relate to others is changing. Weathering it will be a challenge, and the outcome is mostly up to you. Be careful. Actions taken under a Pluto transit are almost always irreversible.

Saturn in Libra is an integral part of this process. It too will clash with your Sun, but from your solar fourth house of home and family. This means family relationships will be involved and thus you may experience major changes there, including the need to care for parents or elderly relatives, which can in turn disrupt your own family life.

Above all this is not the year to move in or purchase property with a romantic partner, or to plan a wedding. Put it on hold until later in 2010.

On another level your home could need a major repair or be prone to termite or other damage. Be sure all your property is fully covered by insurance. If you need to hire a contractor, check and double-check references and also the registrar of contractors for your state. Take no chances.

You can also put this Saturn/Pluto energy to positive use. Clean out your house! Get rid of clutter, junk, and anything you haven't looked at or used in years. Not only will the process feel great but you'll fill your space with fresh energy. And that alone will do wonders for your soul.

Neptune

If you were born between July 14 and 19, Neptune in Aquarius will encourage you to have faith in yourself and the universe. This inspirational planet can open new, albeit indefinable, vistas as it challenges you to act on trust and instinct. In the process you'll discover an entirely new dimension of yourself and the strength of your inner voice.

But you'll need to be wary of major financial decisions, including credit, loans, and anything that could put funds at risk. Read every word of every contract and get an expert opinion if necessary. Better yet, try to avoid anything that will commit you or your resources to short- or long-term indebtedness. Also be sure to carefully review insurance policies, especially for water damage. If you plan to travel, consider purchasing trip and baggage insurance.

On another level Neptune will motivate you to define what you value most in other people, your life, and your spirituality. Take your time. Read, ask questions, and think rather than let others push you into accepting their beliefs.

Cancer/January

Planetary Hotspots

Mercury turns retrograde in Aquarius, your solar eighth house of money, on the 11th. This increases the chance for delayed payments and deposits, and you also should verify paycheck amounts and deductions. Pay bills early, and try to postpone major purchases, especially electronics and appliances, until late February.

Planetary Lightspots

Chances are, you'll be ready to dash out of town around the 23rd, when Venus connects with Uranus, Mars, and Saturn. This alignment is great for a romantic getaway or a business trip, and some traveling singles reconnect with a former love or someone new. The planetary lineup also favors learning, but give yourself time to adjust if you're returning to school or taking your first online class.

Relationships

Relationships sizzle as Mars advances in Capricorn. But the fiery planet also increases the odds for conflict, especially at month's end when Mars joins forces with retrograde Mercury, which slips back into Capricorn on January 21. Pause and think before you speak, choose your words with care, and try to avoid snap decisions. Someone fascinating could open doors for you the week of the January 10 Full Moon in Cancer.

Money and Success

Here comes Jupiter! This fortunate, expansive planet enters Aquarius January 5 to begin its year-long lucky-money influence. You could get news of a bonus, raise, or windfall within a few days of the January 26 New Moon (and lunar eclipse) in Aquarius. But don't spend just yet because it could be February before you actually see the cash.

Rewarding Days

1, 6, 10, 13, 19, 20, 23, 24, 28

Challenging Days

2, 3, 8, 9, 14, 16, 22, 29

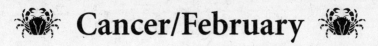 Cancer/February

Planetary Hotspots

Frustration can get the best of you throughout February but especially the first week when Saturn and Uranus align across your solar third/ninth house axis. Avoid travel if at all possible because the odds are you'll encounter delays and changes. Legal matters are unlikely to be resolved, and you may have challenges with in-laws or other relatives. If you're a student, Saturn-Uranus will test your determination to the point that you might consider dropping out. Think again. Ask for help.

Planetary Lightspots

All eyes are on you this month as Venus advances in Aries, your solar tenth house of career and status. Use this favorable influence to connect with decision-makers and to tactfully promote your skills, talents, and know-how with those who count.

Relationships

Resolve any recent relationship difficulties triggered by retrograde Mercury, which turns direct in Capricorn, your solar seventh house, on the 1st. You'll also find it easy to talk with almost anyone, and couples will be on the same wavelength. Despite all these positives, however, Saturn/Uranus will strain some relationships. You'll especially want to steer clear of difficult neighbors.

Money and Success

With a little luck, which you'll definitely have, you could realize a nice financial gain later this month when three planets connect with Jupiter in Aquarius. But the February 9 Full Moon (and lunar eclipse) could trigger an extra expense. More importantly, its alignment with Neptune makes it wise to be financially cautious and conservative. Take nothing for granted in money matters, even the word of someone you trust.

Rewarding Days

2, 3, 10, 11, 15, 16, 17, 21, 22, 24

Challenging Days

1, 5, 6, 12, 18, 26

Cancer/March

Planetary Hotspots

Lingering effects of last month's Saturn/Uranus alignment continue to advise against travel and legal matters, especially the week of the March 10 Full Moon in Virgo. Be extra cautious on the road this month and consider public transportation or car-pooling if those options are available. Learning, whether in class or on your own, stimulates your mind and, although it may frustrate you at times, success comes with persistence.

Planetary Lightspots

Laughter is a great antidote for this month's stresses and strains. With several planets in positive contact with Jupiter, you'll also benefit from an upbeat attitude and positive thinking. Spread this good cheer wherever you go and many people will brighten your day.

Relationships

You'll be faced with challenging workplace relationships around the time of the March 26 New Moon in Aries, your career sector. Power plays are possible and controlling people almost a given. Stay on the sidelines as much as possible, and protect your position. Part of this is the effect of Venus, which turns retrograde in Aries on the 6th. Be very cautious if you want to pursue a workplace romance. Get acquainted on your own time. Anything else could put your job at risk.

Money and Success

Despite the difficult relationships you'll experience in your career life, now is the time to lay the groundwork for success. Apply for a promotion if that's your goal, or send out resumes if you're ready for a new opportunity. What you do now will bring results in late April. Finances are mostly status quo this month, but double-check that all bills are paid on time.

Rewarding Days

1, 7, 9, 12, 13, 14, 15, 22, 24, 28

Challenging Days

2, 4, 5, 10, 11, 17, 23, 25, 31

Cancer/April

Planetary Hotspots

Spring arrives and with it comes the desire to connect with the world at large. Travel, however, isn't the best choice because Venus in Pisces is retrograde through the 16th in your solar ninth house, and Mars transits the same sign before moving on to Aries on the 22nd. Both of these planets and their contacts can spark challenges with travel so seek an alternative. See your own city and the surrounding area, visit historic sites and museums, or get involved in a community project.

Planetary Lightspots

The time is right to launch that home improvement project you've been thinking about. Incentive comes with the April 9 Full Moon in Libra, your domestic sign. And because it's beautifully aligned with Jupiter and Neptune, you can easily tap your creativity to cut expenses.

Relationships

April brings an active social life, thanks to the Sun, Mercury, and April 12 New Moon in Taurus, your friendship sector. Line up dates and outings throughout the month and consider hosting a get-together the second weekend. You'll connect with some fascinating people as April unfolds, and some Cancers launch a romantic relationship with a friend of a friend. Ask a pal to arrange a date.

Money and Success

Look for further developments in career matters that occurred in March, most likely at month's end. Before then you have plenty of opportunities to shine and might gain through a raise or bonus. Some workplace relationships are difficult, however. Do your best to minimize contact with these people, especially one-on-one.

Rewarding Days

6, 10, 11, 12, 16, 17, 20, 24, 29, 30

Challenging Days

1, 3, 7, 8, 13, 14, 22, 27, 28

Cancer/May

Planetary Hotspots

May features the first Jupiter-Neptune merger in Aquarius in 2009, your solar eighth house. This does have some potential to put more money in your pocket, but the odds for loss are much greater. The good news is the outcome depends mostly upon your decisions. Be conservative and wary because someone may try to separate you from your money as the Sun and Mercury clash with Jupiter and Neptune. If it sounds too good to be true, it probably is. A loan to a friend or relative is unlikely to be repaid.

Planetary Lightspots

Take a brief step out of your hectic life around the time of the May 24 New Moon in Gemini, your solar twelfth house. You'll enjoy some time alone with your own thoughts and a good book, and the opportunity to relax a little. Take it. You deserve a break.

Relationships

Socializing and romance are on your May agenda that features the Full Moon in Scorpio, your solar fifth house, on May 9. Use the lunar energy for a day or weekend trip with friends and, if you're single, take advantage of the chance to meet new people. You could encounter a soul mate. But with Mercury traveling retrograde, first in Gemini and then in Taurus, May 7–30, be sure to confirm times and places. One cautionary note: welcome new people but don't take them totally at face value.

Money and Success

Your career is in high focus with Venus and Mars in Aries, your solar tenth house. The pace is fast and the potential to make your mark one of the best, especially the last week of May. Give it your all and aim for high achievements. May could set the stage for a promotion later this year.

Rewarding Days

3, 6, 7, 8, 10, 13, 14, 19, 21, 22

Challenging Days

4, 5, 12, 17, 18, 25, 27

Cancer/June

Planetary Hotspots

Try not to push yourself too hard this month. And even though summer is here, cool evening temperatures and air conditioning make it smart to wear a sweater or light jacket. Otherwise you could suffer several miserable days with a cold in early or late June. Make sleep and healthy food your priorities.

Planetary Lightspots

The June 22 New Moon in Cancer is all about you. Set ambitious personal goals for the next twelve months and then measure them in September, December, and March to check your progress. It's important, however, to include your partner in your plans and to explain your current needs and desires because this New Moon clashes with Pluto in your solar seventh house.

Relationships

Summer socializing is at its best with Mercury, Venus, and Mars moving through Taurus, your solar eleventh house. Great times, great people, and great get-togethers are in the forecast, but like last month, you need to be somewhat cautious about new people and mixing friendship with money. You could, however, be successful in raising money for an organization or another good cause in your community.

Money and Success

Venus in Aries, your career sector, through June 5 gives you added incentive to succeed in the world at large and, even better, you're among the favored few. That gives you an advantage as you head into the week of the June 7 Full Moon in Sagittarius, your solar sixth house, when your workload picks up. Take the lead in a project and give close attention to details. Also keep the boss informed about progress.

Rewarding Days

2, 6, 9, 10, 14, 18, 19, 23, 29, 30

Challenging Days

1, 3, 7, 8, 11,, 15, 21, 22, 27, 28

Cancer/July

Planetary Hotspots

Celebrate Independence Day at home with friends rather than go away for the weekend. Both Venus and Mars in Taurus, your solar eleventh house, clash with several planets the first week of July. And that makes travel inadvisable. You could experience anything from lost luggage to sub-par accommodations to a delay or cancellation. Aim for next month if you want to visit or travel with friends.

Planetary Lightspots

You have everything going for you this month, thanks to the Sun in your sign, where it's joined by Mercury, July 3–16. Even better is the July 21 New Moon (and solar eclipse) in Cancer, which signals the symbolic start of your new solar year. Set new personal directions for the next twelve months and give yourself every advantage to achieve them.

Relationships

Close relationships are just as important this month, with the Full Moon (and lunar eclipse) in Capricorn, your solar seventh house, on the 7th. They'll be generally positive, although at times you'll feel like you're drifting away from someone. That might or might not be true. Look first to yourself, and then talk about your changing needs and goals. Open communication also strengthens ties.

Money and Success

Your interest begins to shift to money matters when Mercury enters Leo, your solar second house, on the 17th. That's a plus for income, but Mercury also encourages you to splurge, especially at month's end when it contacts Jupiter and Neptune in Aquarius, your solar eighth house. The combination could bring you or your partner a raise, bonus, or added perk, or set the stage for that next month.

Rewarding Days
1, 8, 12, 14, 16, 20, 21, 26, 27, 29

Challenging Days
4, 6, 13, 19, 23, 24, 25, 30, 31

Cancer/August

Planetary Hotspots

Mars travels in Gemini, your solar twelfth house, through August 24. With this action-packed energy working behind the scenes, you could find it difficult to sleep at night because your mind will work overtime. This position can also trigger worries—even if you realistically have nothing to worry about. Develop a new habit. Relax before bedtime with herbal tea, light reading, or music to calm yourself.

Planetary Lightspots

Venus in Cancer through August 25 boosts your powers of attraction. Think positive, share your wish with the universe, and make it happen! Other people are key to your success as you'll discover early and late in the month. Don't tune out someone who tells it like it is. The objective perspective can help you succeed.

Relationships

Neighbors and relatives are in this month's forecast with Mercury in Virgo, your solar third house, August 2–24, and the Sun in the same sign from the 22nd on. Most contacts are positive, and at least one of these people can be an excellent source of knowledge and information. You also could make a valuable networking contact, so consider hosting a get-together for neighbors. Among them could be just the person you've been searching for.

Money and Success

Much of your attention focuses on finances, where the prospects are good for a bigger bank balance by month's end. Nevertheless, with the August 5 Full Moon (and lunar eclipse) in Aquarius and the August 20 New Moon in Leo, your money signs, it's still wise to budget and plan for extra expenses. If you apply for a loan, even consumer credit, be sure to read all the fine print.

Rewarding Days

3, 4, 7, 9, 11, 12, 17, 23, 25, 30, 31

Challenging Days

1, 2, 8, 15, 16, 22, 26, 28, 29

Cancer/September

Planetary Hotspots

Saturn and Uranus align for the last time in Virgo-Pisces, your solar third/ninth house axis. If you're in school, stick with it. If not and you feel your career could benefit from more education, get started now. One or two classes might be all you need to position yourself for new career directions in a year or two. Travel is prone to delays and cancellations this month, which also is unfavorable for legal matters.

Planetary Lightspots

You have all the energy you need to do just about anything as Mars advances in your sign. This position is great for physical activity, but keep it in moderation because you're prone to mishaps now. Also take care in the kitchen and when working with equipment on the job or around the house. Get the best of Mars without the risk, and benefit from the stress relief.

Relationships

Expect family relationships to be a bit strained at times this month. Not only do Mercury and the Sun clash with Mars and Pluto but Mercury turns retrograde in Libra, your domestic sector, on the 7th. And that can easily spark misunderstandings. Ask before you assume, and do a daily update of everyone's plans to help avoid mix-ups. Also make it a priority to avoid difficult neighbors. If your community sponsors a neighborhood watch program, now would be a good time to get one organized in your area.

Money and Success

Money matters benefit from Venus in Leo, your solar second house, through the 19th. But it's still a good idea to be somewhat cautious because Venus contacts both Jupiter and Neptune in Aquarius. What sounds like a great deal may or may not be, so protect your resources.

Rewarding Days

2, 7, 8, 9, 10, 13, 20, 21, 24, 26, 30

Challenging Days

3, 5, 6, 12, 17, 18, 22, 23, 25

Cancer/October

Planetary Hotspots

September's Saturn/Uranus alignment remains in effect the first two weeks of the month. Mercury, and then Venus, in Virgo activate both planets. Try to resolve any issues associated with this lineup, whether they're legal matters or difficulties involving relatives. Also try to avoid travel in the same time frame.

Planetary Lightspots

Later this month the Sun and Mercury enter Scorpio, your solar fifth house. That's a plus for your social life that continues into November. Before then consider hosting a get-together at your place. The third weekend is the best for an open house or a casual dinner for close friends.

Relationships

October brings enough activity on the domestic scene to satisfy even a family-oriented Cancer. Mercury dashes through Libra, October 9–27, and the Sun is there until the 22nd, with the New Moon in Cancer occurring on the 18th. Possibly the best of all is Venus, which enters Libra on the 14th. Use it to give your home a fresh face before the holidays, or focus on a single room, adding new furniture and décor. You'll have plenty of time for large-scale domestic projects in the next three years as Saturn, which enters Libra October 29, moves through your solar fourth house. Schedule a family conference and get everyone involved. Planetary alignments have all of you on the same wavelength.

Money and Success

Your career claims a significant amount of time in early October, when the Full Moon in Aries on the 4th shines brightly in your solar tenth house. The lunar energy could bring a raise around that time; at the least you'll hear some welcome and well-deserved praise.

Rewarding Days

1, 5, 6, 8, 14, 17, 19, 24, 28, 31

Challenging Days

2, 9, 10, 11, 15, 16, 23, 30

Cancer/November

Planetary Hotspots

Saturn in Libra, your solar fourth house, and Pluto in Capricorn, your solar seventh house, clash this month to set the stage for domestic developments in December. Check your home periodically for potential problems, and take the time to update your insurance policy if you haven't done that for a few years.

Planetary Lightspots

Home life is at its best with Venus in Libra the first week of November. Finish last month's domestic projects, invite a few friends for dinner, or simply enjoy relaxing evenings with loved ones. If you feel especially ambitious, stock the freezer with holiday goodies to save yourself time later in the season.

Relationships

Keep your calendar handy to track holiday social events and your children's activities. It will be a challenge at times to keep up with it all, but organization can keep things on track and you enjoying an active social life. This busy lifestyle is sparked by the November 2 Full Moon in Taurus, your friendship sector, and the Sun, Mercury, and Venus in your solar fifth house at various times. All that energy is topped off by the November 16 New Moon in the same sign. See friends, meet people, and if you're single, ask a pal to arrange a date.

Money and Success

Mars in Leo, your solar second house, keeps money flowing your direction. But it also encourages spending, so be kind to your budget and opt for less expensive socializing. Your work life is equally positive with Mercury entering Sagittarius, your solar sixth house, on the 15th, followed by the Sun on the 21st. Some Cancers travel on business this month.

Rewarding Days

1, 4, 5, 10, 11, 13, 14, 16, 20, 21, 28, 29

Challenging Days

2, 6, 7, 8, 9, 12, 19, 27, 30

Cancer/December

Planetary Hotspots

November's Saturn/Pluto alignment is activated by three planets—Sun, Mercury, and Venus—traveling in Capricorn, your solar seventh house at various times this month. The headliner is Mercury, which turns retrograde in Capricorn on the 26th. It will only compound and delay resolution of the events that pop up. Family personalities will clash at times, and you're likely to be faced with a domestic challenge such as a major repair or a decision involving an elderly relative. Issues arise the first week of December, but the last week of the month will require action.

Planetary Lightspots

Look forward to December 31, when you can ring out 2009 and ring in 2010 in the spotlight of the Full Moon (and lunar eclipse) in your sign. Share the moment with someone you love and talk about your future and your dreams for the new year.

Relationships

Family relationships aside, December brings fun times with friends and congenial, supportive contacts with coworkers. Socialize with both groups out and about to save yourself the hassle of preparing dinner for a crowd. Plus, the more people you're around the greater the chance to connect with someone who sparks ideas and a possible a job lead. But be aware of Mercury's retrograde status and choose your words with care to avoid misunderstandings.

Money and Success

Mars turns retrograde in Leo, your second house of money, on the 20th. Keep this in mind when you're holiday shopping and cut back if necessary to prevent big bills in January. The odds favor a year-end bonus at work, which is upbeat this month with Venus and the December 16 New Moon in Sagittarius, your solar sixth house.

Rewarding Days

1, 4, 5, 6, 12, 18, 22, 23, 25, 27

Challenging Days

3, 7, 9, 10, 13, 16, 17, 20, 24, 28

Cancer Action Table

These dates reflect the best—but not the only—times for success and ease in these activities, according to your Sun sign.

	JAN	FEB	MAR	APR	MAY	JUN	JUL	AUG	SEPT	OCT	NOV	DEC
Move										16-27		
Start a class		10-11			30-31	29-30	26-27	12-13, 20-24		5-7	10-11	
Join a club				20-30		6-12				5-6		
Ask for a raise							22, 23					
Look for work		17-18						27-28		21-22	17-18, 23-30	1-4, 15-16
Get pro advice		2-3				9-10		3				17-18
Get a loan		17-18, 23, 27-28	2, 3							26-27		
See a doctor		17-18	4							21-22	17-18	15
Start a diet		17-18				8						
End relationship	23-24	21			13	9, 10						
Buy clothes	18-19							25-26			10-12, 15-16	
Get a makeover				30		23	21	17		11		
New romance							1-2	25-26			16, 19-20	
Vacation	1-2		9-19		20-21					28-30		

The Lion
July 22 to August 22

♌

Element: Fire	Anatomy: Heart, upper back
Quality: Fixed	Color: Gold, scarlet
Polarity: Yang/masculine	Animal: Lions, large cats
Planetary Ruler: The Sun	Myths/Legends: Apollo, Isis, Helios
Meditation: I trust in the strength of my soul	
	House: Fifth
Gemstone: Ruby	Opposite Sign: Aquarius
Power Stones: Topaz, sardonyx	Flower: Marigold, sunflower
Key Phrase: I will	Key Word: Magnetic
Glyph: Lion's tail	

Your Strengths and Challenges

You're an attention-getter, lovable, outgoing, and generous. People can't help but notice you wherever you go because they're drawn to your sunny smile, your warmth and upbeat attitude. A true extrovert, you're also a leader who instinctively knows how to bring out the best in people.

Your ruler, the Sun, is the planet associated with ego, so it's only natural that you're confident in your skills, talents, and abilities. Nevertheless, your pride is easily wounded and you're far more sensitive to sleights than most people imagine. The solar energy also gives you a flair for the dramatic. But some Leos let ego interfere with worldly success because they find it difficult to share the spotlight and expect the royal treatment every minute of every day.

Leo is the fixed fire sign of the zodiac, which gives you the determination to go after what you want and achieve it. When the spark ignites, nothing holds you back, and you have the follow-through to complete what you begin. Used positively, these qualities can fulfill your ambitions and set you apart from the crowd. But there's a fine line between determination and stubbornness, so learn to give in and adapt when necessary; flexibility will get you further in life. The same applies to your thinking. Generally broad-minded, you're nevertheless sometimes unwilling to compromise your strong beliefs and opinions. Be the leader you are and listen to others. They just might have a better idea that will reflect positively on you if you join the team.

Your playful spirit endears you to many, and your creative energy is exceptional. Whether you express it through the arts, ideas, your job, or hobbies, you add a distinctive zest to just about everything you do.

Your Relationships

Romance is your specialty. You know exactly how to impress a date with the dramatic flair that wins hearts, whether that's a picnic in the park or a candlelight dinner as you search for true love. Playing the field is just your style, which gives you plenty of opportunities to meet a potential mate. He or she is likely to be tough to catch, however, because you're attracted to independent souls. That's the influence of Aquarius, your partnership sign. In fact, you could make a beautiful match with someone whose Sun is in that sign.

You have much in common with the other fire signs, Aries and Sagittarius, but it could be tough to share center stage with another Leo. Gemini and Libra are intellectually in sync with you, but a Taurus or Scorpio could be too possessive.

You're an enthusiastic parent who enjoys participating in your children's activities, especially sports. You also promote learning and encourage them to expand their experiences and knowledge. But you can be a soft touch, giving in when taking a stand would be more beneficial. Go ahead and spoil them—just not all the time! You have deep feelings about family, and at least one relative probably had a profound influence on you during your childhood years. Overall, you prefer to keep family matters private and enjoy having a space within your home reserved just for you, even if it's only a comfy chair. Many Leos enjoy home remodeling and renovations and profit from real estate.

People enjoy your company and your lively, outgoing personality so it's no surprise that you have many acquaintances. An excellent networker, you're a favorite on the social scene and excel at circulating a room and charming everyone you meet. You definitely have a way with words and a talent for making people feel they're the center of your universe. Close friends, although few in number, stimulate your thinking and help keep you on track toward your goals. Long talks with them are among your fondest memories.

Your Career and Money
You're an ambitious hard worker who will stick with a career field, company, or job as long as your skills and talents are recognized. Opportunities for the future are a must, and you can excel in supervisory positions. Just remember that it takes a while to move up from entry-level to CEO. You prefer a structured, task-oriented daily work environment with measurable goals, and one where your knowledge and experience are valued. Coworker relationships, although congenial, are usually limited to business. You instead invest your energy into developing contacts that could advance your career.

You expect to be well paid for what you do and well you should—you're worth it. Most Leos are meticulous about personal financial records, but you're prone to worry, often unnecessarily, and can put too much emphasis on nickels and dimes rather than the big picture. Think long-term and aim for steady growth in savings and investments, which you should monitor. Otherwise you could find yourself poorer but wiser; the same applies to promises of sure-fire gains. If in doubt, don't. Do, however, use your sixth sense and negotiate for better terms, benefits, and compensation.

Your Lighter Side

Whatever your age, you have the fun-loving spirit of a kid who's fearless and competitive, adventuresome and spontaneous. And there's no reason not to act like one during your leisure-time hours, which many Leos fill with sports, travel, creative endeavors, and learning for the fun of it—in addition to socializing, of course.

Affirmation for the Year

People enhance and beautify my life.

The Year Ahead for Leo

The other people in your life—colleagues, friends, loved ones, your partner—are what you value most in 2009.

Expansive Jupiter enters Aquarius, your solar seventh house of relationships, January 5. That makes 2009 one of the best for love and romance, and it will bring many opportunities to invite new people into your orbit. Each will in some way be a lucky charm.

Your wish could come true this year if you're ready to take a dating relationship to the next level or you're in search of someone with whom to share your life. This will be the year of commitment for many single Leos, while couples will rekindle the fires and celebrate togetherness.

Jupiter's transit of Aquarius, which occurs only every twelve years, is also a plus for business partnerships, professional consultations, and networking. Most of all, you'll find people to be especially helpful and supportive of your endeavors. Do the same for them and develop lasting relationships that can pay off for many years to come.

There is, however, one potential wrinkle in this otherwise terrific year during which you can make the most of your people skills: Neptune. Now in its twelfth year in Aquarius, Neptune is the planet of illusion and confusion, faith and spirituality. It will encourage you to see the best in people, which is great in some circumstances. But with Jupiter also in Aquarius you'll be unusually prone to overlook what you might question in other years.

A second opinion could be well worth your time, effort, and money before making important life decisions. You should also carefully check professional credentials, read everything before you sign, and consider consulting an attorney before entering into a contract. Ask questions, avoid assumptions, push for clear-cut answers, and then back them up with your own research. If in doubt on minor matters ask someone you respect for an honest opinion.

Despite the potential downside of Neptune, you can use this planetary energy to charm almost everyone. You'll have a way with words and an extra level of charisma that will draw people to you. Of course this can work two ways. So don't be surprised when others direct their charms your way.

Saturn will begin the year in Virgo, where it will form an exact alignment with Uranus in Pisces in February and September, just as it did in November 2008. With these two planets spanning your solar second and eighth houses of money, you should try to plan ahead as much as possible for financial ups and downs. Save, spend conservatively, establish and live within a budget, and keep tabs on investments and retirement funds. Do all this and you can more easily weather the effects of restrictive Saturn and unpredictable Uranus.

This is not the year to put funds at risk no matter how much you trust someone's opinion, intentions, or honesty. Steer clear of financial agreements, loans (such as agreeing to be a cosigner), and other actions that could potentially affect your credit rating. Promises are just that and, unfortunately, not everyone is as honorable as you.

Your solar second and eighth houses are about more than money. These sectors also represent what you value personally and what you value in others. In many respects this year you'll redefine what's important to you beyond the material realm. Think about your life priority list, what you want to achieve as well as the intangibles— character and personality traits, ethics, and standards.

This planetary alignment is also about your marketable skills and talents and merging them with other people for mutual benefit. Align yourself with the right people and you have much to gain.

Saturn will move on to Libra, your solar third house, October 29. During the next three years you'll be in a learning mode, in search of information and knowledge. This would be an excellent time to return to school to begin or complete a degree or advanced certification, or to acquire practical job skills. You also could take several classes for the fun of it to learn more about a subject that interests you.

The third house is also your sector of quick trips so you'll want to keep your vehicle in good shape for weekend excursions and endless errands. You'll be on the go and at times will feel like your vehicle is your home. Part of this may be business-related.

Your work life will at some point change dramatically during the next fifteen years as Pluto transits Capricorn, your solar sixth house of daily work. You might decide to pursue an entirely new avenue of employment or establish a home-based business.

Two thousand nine isn't the best for such a major move, however, because once Saturn enters Libra it will clash with Pluto into early 2010. Power plays and frustration often accompany this align-ment and you could feel as though you're being "forced" to change your work habits or responsibilities, possibly as a result of a new boss or reorganization. This might be just the incentive you need to expand your educational horizons and return to school.

What This Year's Eclipses Mean for You
Six eclipses will occur in 2009, three of which will spotlight your solar first/seventh house axis. Each is in effect for about six months.

You'll be in the spotlight of the February 9 lunar eclipse in your sign. Use it to set an ambitious personal path for the year and to empower yourself to accomplish great things in 2009. As your confidence rises to new heights you'll be in an even better position to make the most of the year's two eclipses in Aquarius—January 7 (solar) and August 6 (lunar). Both will mirror the influences of Jupiter and Neptune in Aquarius.

But what's different about these Aquarius eclipses is that there's also one in Leo. Where Jupiter and Neptune turn your focus to other people, the Leo eclipse can help you keep things in perspec-tive. You can thus view other people with a little less idealism and more objectivity, weighing their needs and wishes and balancing them with your own.

This trio of eclipses also encourages you to strive for balance and compromise. Life is not all about you, nor is it all about other peo-ple. What the eclipses will push you to do is to take other people's desires into consideration while deciding what's best for you.

The Aquarius eclipses, plus Jupiter and Neptune, add up to what could be one of the most fabulous years for love and romance. Love the one you're with, have fun, laugh, and delight in every moment of togetherness with someone new or your partner.

If this terrific planetary lineup brings new love into your life, or deepens your feelings for someone you've been dating, you might be tempted to dash into commitment. This idea has its pros and cons. It would be great if you've known each for quite a while. With a new relationship, however, the bloom could quickly wear off once this planetary influence fades. Ask yourself and someone you trust whether you're in love or in love with love. Be wise and hold off until 2010, when you'll know the answer to the question.

The year's other three eclipses will occur in Capricorn and Cancer. Your work life will be in high focus under the July 7 lunar eclipse in Capricorn, your solar sixth house. Although you can expect an increased work load along with stressful periods, you'll also be in a position to showcase your know-how. Aim to turn in an impressive performance day after day.

The July 22 solar eclipse and the December 31 lunar eclipse in Cancer, your solar twelfth house of self-renewal, will encourage you to look inward. People may be surprised when you want to spend time alone, but make no apologies. Whether you meditate, read, or listen to music and your own thoughts, you'll feel mentally and physically re-centered and reenergized. And this will be very good for you because the sixth/twelfth house axis is also associated with health and well-being. Exercise is another good stress reliever, and you should plan to do something to release tension at the end of every busy work day.

Do yourself a favor and schedule routine medical, eye, and dental check-ups, and do the same for your family, including your pets. If a slimmer, trimmer you is your goal, the eclipses can motivate you to change your eating habits rather than just go on a diet, and to adopt an overall healthier lifestyle.

Saturn

If you were born between August 6 and 22, Saturn will contact your Sun from Virgo, your solar second house. Saturn's influence will be minor, a week or two in August or September, for Leos with birthdays from August 15 on. But **if you were born between August 6 and 14**, you'll need to be financially cautious and conservative the first seven months of the year.

Expenses are likely to be above the norm in April, May, and June, especially **if your birthday is within a few days of August 6.** Although it may not feel this way at the time, this transit will be relatively short-lived and more easily managed if you make savings a priority the first three months of the year and carefully budget your income. Saturn's influence will be prominent January through March and again in July and August **if you were born between August 9 and 14**.

Uranus

Saturn in Virgo will join forces with Uranus in Pisces, your solar eighth house of money, in February and September. Although the planetary duo is likely to bring unexpected expenses, you also could collect a past due debt or receive a settlement. Just be sure your bills are paid well ahead of time and check your credit report for any errors or long-forgotten debts. It's also possible your partner could experience a sudden gain or loss. All this will be more apparent in your life **if you were born between August 11 and 19** because Uranus will directly contact your Sun, and you should be extremely cautious about entering into any financial agreements.

Saturn-Pluto

If you were born between July 23 and 27, Saturn will contact your Sun during the last two months of the year as it begins its three-year transit of Libra. This favorable alignment will give you the opportunity to explore new ideas as well as the past. You might even have the desire to take weekend trips to nearby historical sites or research your family tree, or develop an interest in antiques and learn how to refinish furniture. The motivation to learn will be strong and bookstores or the library may become one of your favorite destinations.

Relatives, especially siblings, will have a more important role in your life this year. If you have unresolved issues with any of them you can begin to clear the air in November and December. Take the time then also to get acquainted with your neighbors; one or more of them could be helpful to you as could someone you haven't been in touch with for years.

With Pluto in Capricorn, your solar sixth house for the next fifteen years you're at the start of a long-term phase in which you'll see your work life transform itself. Some events will be initiated by others and some by you. Both will be part of an evolutionary process that will undoubtedly change your thinking about your place in the world, what you want to achieve and how best to do it, how to maximize your talents, and most importantly, how to experience the greatest satisfaction and rewards for your efforts.

This process will begin in earnest as 2009 draws to a close and Saturn clashes with Pluto. Outwardly you may find yourself in the midst of increasing conflict and controversy, with people jockeying for control. The situation will be unsettling and result in tension and frustration. Be alert earlier in the year when rumors and undercurrents could give you a hint of what to expect in the way of workplace challenges.

Inwardly you'll begin to question your future and your thinking will turn to alternatives. Education or additional training might be the best avenue to recreate your work life if you decide that's what's necessary and what you want to do. But resist the urge to establish a home-based business this year or next because the odds will be against you.

It's important to remember that as Saturn clashes with Pluto it also will favorably contact your Sun. This means you can tap into Saturn's strength and determination and make both your own.

Neptune

Neptune will be prominent in your life **if you were born between August 14 and 19**. You'll want to be especially cautious about believing everything you hear. Some people will stretch the truth and others will deliberately try to mislead you. Enjoy the romance and the charming people who come into your life, but protect your heart and your resources.

Although much of Neptune's influence will center around your interactions with other people, this mystical planet will also color your vision of yourself. You'll feel alternately inspired and centered, and confused and directionless. Knowing the difference could be a challenge at times because all these feelings will tend to blend together. That's all the more reason not to make any major life decisions this year. Once the Neptune fog clears in 2010 you'll have a better idea of where you want to go and with whom.

You, among all Leos, should take every precaution before hiring a professional such as an attorney or accountant. Check references, ask direct questions, and accept nothing less than direct answers.

Leo/January

Planetary Hotspots

There will be one quirk in an otherwise fabulous month for relationships: Mercury. It turns retrograde in Aquarius, your solar seventh house, January 11. Choose your words with care because there will be an increased chance for misunderstandings. Also double-check times and places so you don't inadvertently miss an important date.

Planetary Lightspots

The January 10 Full Moon in Cancer spotlights your solar twelfth house, so take some time for yourself. Get cozy on the couch with the latest DVDs or best-sellers and get lost in the world of fiction or fantasy. You'll appreciate the rest and relaxation during this hectic month at work.

Relationships

Jupiter makes its grand entrance into Aquarius January 5, bringing with it all the potential for romance and fortunate contacts in the year ahead. Take note of anyone you meet around the time of the January 26 New Moon (and solar eclipse) in Aquarius, whether it's a potential romantic interest or networking link. You'll reconnect at the end of February, when you'll discover just how lucky this person can be for you.

Money and Success

Get set for a hectic month at work as Mars advances in Capricorn, your solar sixth house. You have plenty of opportunities to shine and might even net a raise or bonus, thanks to favorable planetary alignments. But you'll want to be somewhat cautious because retrograde Mercury will slip back into Capricorn on the 21st. Double-check work, pay attention to details, and be careful what you put in writing. This is an excellent time to review previous work for errors.

Rewarding Days

1, 4, 5, 6, 11, 12, 17, 20, 21, 25, 26, 27, 31

Challenging Days

2, 3, 9, 10, 14, 16, 22, 29, 30

Leo/February

Planetary Hotspots

The year's first Saturn/Uranus alignment makes money matters the February hotspot. Restriction, responsibility, and change are the keywords for this planetary duo, and although all Leos will be affected to a greater or lesser degree, those born within a few days of August 13 need to be especially cautious and conservative. Extra expenses are likely and even a small financial risk could turn into a sizeable loss. It's also possible you or your mate could have a change in income or realize that could be a possibility before year's end.

Planetary Lightspots

The February 9 Full Moon (and lunar eclipse) in Leo is all about you! With it comes added confidence and charisma to charm your way into the hearts and minds of many. Go for it, ask for favors, endear yourself to others.

Relationships

The Full Moon sparks a love relationship for some Leos, but remember that the lunar energy also activates Neptune in Aquarius. That means you'll be idealistic and see what you want to see in others, which may be far different from the reality. Proceed with care. If you're part of a couple, celebrate your love with a quick getaway at month's end when Venus in Aries aligns with passionate Mars and lucky Jupiter in your solar seventh house. That's also a positive time frame for business travel and presentations.

Money and Success

Work goes more smoothly this month now that Mercury is moving forward. (It turns direct on February 1.) But you should still be alert for errors; they could surface at any time during the first half of the month. Finances gain some stability after the February 24 New Moon in Pisces, your sign of joint resources.

Rewarding Days

4, 8, 12, 13, 17, 22, 23, 24, 27, 28

Challenging Days

1, 5, 6, 7, 11, 18, 25, 26

Leo/March

Planetary Hotspots

Venus turns retrograde in Aries, your solar ninth house, on March 6, so you might want to postpone travel until late April or May. Planetary alignments make delays and cancellations possible any time this month and especially the last ten days of March when several planets clash. Legal matters proceed slowly, if at all, and a favorable outcome is unlikely if you initiate action now. In-laws and other relatives test your patience.

Planetary Lightspots

The first week of March accents fortunate contacts, at least one of which will inspire you to have faith in yourself. You also can get good advice if you first do some research and then go to the right source. Check professional credentials rather than take anyone at face value. Then ask direct questions and expect direct answers.

Relationships

Mercury in Aquarius, your solar seventh house, through the 8th, and Mars in the same sign through the 13th, have you in touch with many people. Partnership benefits from open communication and passionate moments, but workplace relationships won't be so positive. An ego clash could trigger a power play, and although you might win a few rounds, the wiser choice is to say little. Later this fall you'll be glad you kept silent.

Money and Success

February's financial stress continues with the March 10 Full Moon in Virgo which activates Saturn and Uranus in your solar second and eighth houses. Be open to change, take action to resolve issues, and turn the situation into a learning experience. If you want to make some extra money, the third week of March could bring a lead.

Rewarding Days

3, 7, 8, 12, 13, 16, 21, 22, 27, 28, 30

Challenging Days

1, 2, 4, 5, 6, 10, 11, 17, 23, 31

Leo/April

Planetary Hotspots

Finances continue to require attention this month, although without the stress level you experienced in March. Mars in Pisces, your solar eighth house, increases your earning power, but retrograde Venus, which slips back into Pisces on the 11th, somewhat diminishes the influence. Have faith. Things will begin to improve within a few days of Venus turning direct on the 17th.

Planetary Lightspots

With four planets touring your solar ninth house at various times this month you'll be ready for new adventures. Travel is a good option mid-April, for business or pleasure, if you can't wait until May. But you should also consider learning. A short-term course could benefit your career prospects and satisfy the curiosity triggered by the April 9 Full Moon in Libra, your solar third house.

Relationships

Communication with relatives is upbeat midmonth, but try to avoid talks in early and late April. The same holds true for immediate family, neighbors, and dealing with community officials. Workplace relationships are positive in the same time frame and have the potential to be this month's best connections. With only a little effort you can impress decision-makers. Be cautious, though, not to step on toes.

Money and Success

You're a shining star later in April, thanks to the Sun, Mercury, and April 24 New Moon in Mercury, your solar tenth house. And that could net you a raise or job offer. Keep your eye on the competition, however, if you're aiming for a step up. Someone who appears to be a supporter may or may not be. Share little until you know for sure who's who.

Rewarding Days

4, 5, 9, 12, 14, 17, 18, 19, 24, 30

Challenging Days

1, 2, 3, 7, 8, 13, 22, 26, 27, 28

Leo/May

Planetary Hotspots

As it does several times a year, Mercury turns retrograde on May 7. Placed in Gemini, your friendship sector, it can trigger mix-ups in your social life. But it also can affect any group activity such as job-related teamwork. Decisions made in that context are likely to be reversed or misunderstood, and will begin to come to light after Mercury slips back into Taurus, your solar tenth house of career, on the 13th. Confirm instructions and double-check all work through month's end.

Planetary Lightspots

Friends are a lightspot in your life throughout May despite the potential downside of retrograde Mercury in Gemini. The energy peaks the week of the May 24 New Moon in Gemini, when planetary alignments favor travel with friends. Take a week's vacation or a day trip to a nearby recreation area to celebrate spring's arrival.

Relationships

Jupiter and Neptune join forces in Aquarius, your solar seventh house. That's a real plus for couples and other close relationships, but be a bit skeptical about career-related promises. Some people will say what you want to hear and fail to deliver. You can, however, use this influence to sell your ideas, motivate others, and make outstanding presentations.

Money and Success

The May 9 Full Moon in Scorpio, your domestic sector, is just the incentive you need to launch a home improvement project or generally get your place in shape. You can get financing for the project if you need it, but be sure to read all the fine print and resist the urge to be a big-spender. Creativity and do-it-yourself skills can get you more for less.

Rewarding Days

6, 7, 10, 11, 14, 15, 19, 21, 24, 28

Challenging Days

1, 2, 4, 5, 12, 17, 18, 20, 25

Leo/June

Planetary Hotspots

Your solar twelfth house is the site of June's New Moon on the 22nd. This annual influence is usually a calming one in preparation for the Sun's arrival in your sign in July. But this year's New Moon in Cancer is closely aligned with Pluto in Capricorn, your solar sixth house. And that can trigger some tense moments with people and projects at work. You also could be unusually prone to colds and other viruses. If it's been a while since you've had a checkup, consider scheduling one now.

Planetary Lightspots

It's summer and the June 7 Full Moon in Sagittarius lights up your solar fifth house. Make the most of it if you want to get in shape. Join a gym, walk or bike with neighbors, or take tennis lessons. You also could get involved in your children's sports activities as a coach or fund raiser.

Relationships

The Full Moon is also a great plus for your social life, and some Leos step into a whirlwind summer romance. But watch expenses while you play. Adding even more pizzazz to summer fun is the Sun in Gemini, your solar eleventh house of friendship, through June 20, where it's joined by Mercury on the 13th. See friends, kick back, and enjoy life when you aren't wrapped up in a favorite leisure-time pursuit.

Money and Success

Mars in Taurus, your career sector, keeps you on the go at work all month. You also get the attention-getting benefit of Mercury in Taurus through the 12th and Venus in the same sign from the 6th on. Enjoy the spotlight, the praise, and possibly a raise. Make a point to turn in an impressive performance every day, which you easily can do.

Rewarding Days

2, 6, 12, 18, 19, 20, 24, 25, 29, 30

Challenging Days

1, 5, 7, 8, 11, 15, 21, 22, 27, 28

Leo/July

Planetary Hotspots

Jupiter and Neptune meet again this month in Aquarius, your solar seventh house. Think back to May. Whatever occurred then regarding a relationship comes up for review now. This double-sided influence has the potential to put you in touch with a lucky contact, but it also can encourage you to see what you want to see. Verify good news before you act, especially if money is involved. Romantic liaisons can be sensational, but don't leap into commitment.

Planetary Lightspots

Mercury in Cancer, your solar twelfth house, July 3–17, encourages you to think about the last twelve months with a focus on what you've achieved and what you've learned. This planetary influence, along with the July 21 New Moon in the same sign, boosts your sixth sense. Take note of your dreams and idle thoughts. They offer clues about new personal direction on the horizon.

Relationships

Your summer social life is all you could ask for with Venus in Gemini, your solar eleventh house, July 5–30, where it's joined by fiery Mars on the 11th. Your biggest challenge here might be keeping up with all the commitments, so try not to over-schedule yourself. Also curb your generosity. Let others pay their fair share, and choose inexpensive outings that won't stretch your budget.

Money and Success

You continue to make great career strides in early July as Venus and Mars complete their tour of Taurus, your solar tenth house. The July 7 Full Moon (and lunar eclipse) in Capricorn, your solar sixth house of daily work, steps up the pace even more. Be alert for opportunities to shine that week. Diligent efforts now could trigger a nice raise later this summer.

Rewarding Days

3, 8, 9, 14, 16, 18, 22, 23, 26, 27

Challenging Days

2, 4, 6, 12, 13, 19, 25, 28, 30

Leo/August

Planetary Hotspots

Be especially good to yourself this month, and steer clear of anyone who has a cold. You'll be particularly susceptible to viruses in early and late August when several planets connect with Pluto in Capricorn, your solar sixth house. This is a great time, however, to switch to a healthier diet or begin an exercise program because you'll have all the necessary willpower to succeed.

Planetary Lightspots

You have plenty to celebrate this month, including the August 20 New Moon in your sign. It lights up your life and gives you all the charm and charisma you need to move through each day with ultimate confidence. Set an ambitious plan for the next twelve months and invite people into your life who can boost your success quotient.

Relationships

With Mars in Gemini, your solar eleventh house, through the 24th, your summer social season continues to be filled with dates and outings. But August brings a much more important relationship factor into play: the Full Moon (and lunar eclipse) on the 5th in Aquarius, your solar seventh house. That's an ideal influence if you're in search of a soul mate. Just remember that Jupiter and Neptune in Aquarius are still active, so even if love at first sight seems like the real deal, it may or may not be. If you're part of a couple, romance your mate to the max.

Money and Success

Finances have their pluses and minuses this month. You could net a nice raise, but also be faced with unexpected expenses. That makes a conservative financial mindset a good idea. Stop and think before you shop for all but necessities and resist the urge to use credit.

Rewarding Days

3, 4, 6, 11, 12, 14, 18, 19, 23, 27, 30

Challenging Days

1, 2, 8, 13, 15, 16, 21, 22, 26, 29

Leo/September

Planetary Hotspots

Mechanical problems could pop up at any during September. Both Mercury and the Sun in Libra clash with Pluto, so it could be your car or an appliance that needs attention. But it might be tough to diagnose the problem because Mercury turns retrograde on the 7th. Keep this in mind if you need a repair and get a second opinion if in doubt. That could save you money.

Planetary Lightspots

September's best news is Venus in Leo through the 19th. You can attract just about anything you want, whether that's people, money, or an opportunity. Share your wishes with the universe and truly believe they can be yours. Romance is high on your priority list now, so set aside extra time for your partner or be alert for a new love interest who could walk into your life at any time.

Relationships

You're in touch with relatives and neighbors this month. Unfortunately, the contact is likely to be more negative than positive. The same is true to some extent with workplace relationships. Be tactful.

Money and Success

Finances continue to require a conservative approach with both the Full Moon (September 4) and the New Moon (September 18) spotlighting your solar second and eighth houses of money. Although there will be some bright spots, including another chance for a raise, you'll need to closely watch expenses and stick to your budget. Compounding the situation is Mercury, which returns to Libra on the 17th in retrograde status. That can trigger mix-ups involving money as well as delayed payments. September also brings the final Saturn/Uranus alignment in your money sectors, which will be more prominent if your birthday is near August 17.

Rewarding Days

1, 2, 7, 8, 9, 11, 16, 20, 24, 28, 29

Challenging Days

3, 4, 6, 12, 13, 17, 18, 23, 25

Leo/October

Planetary Hotspots

Mars dashes into your sign October 16 for a long stay that lasts into next year. High energy and initiative accompany this transit. Make the most of it now because Mars will turn retrograde in December, stalling personal ambitions until next spring. Remember your common sense as you zip through each day. Distractions and carelessness can trigger mishaps if you're not careful.

Planetary Lightspots

Both the Full Moon, October 4 in Aries, and the New Moon, October 18 in Libra, spark your curiosity and spirit of adventure. You could satisfy both with travel, but avoid midmonth when difficult planetary alignments increase the potential for a less than relaxing trip. Aim for month's end if you can swing it. That's also a great time for business travel.

Relationships

You might want to monitor your cell phone usage. With the Sun, Mercury and Venus in Libra, your solar third house, at various times throughout October, you'll be on the phone a lot and that can get expensive. Also be sure your computer is protected against viruses so you can safely use e-mail. Relationships are for the most part positive, although you will experience tension at work when someone tries to manipulate you. Ignore it and refuse to be drawn into in a power play.

Money and Success

Finances remain tight the first two weeks of October as Mercury and Venus contact Saturn and Uranus in Virgo/Pisces, your solar second/eighth house axis. The good news is you could collect on a long overdue debt or discover a lucky find on the sidewalk. Let major purchases wait until November if you can.

Rewarding Days

5, 6, 7, 8, 12, 17, 19, 21, 26, 31

Challenging Days

2, 9, 10, 11, 15, 23, 30

Leo/November

Planetary Hotspots

Saturn clashes with Pluto this month. This long-term influence, placed in your solar third and sixth houses, will impact your work life and trigger major changes. You'll get some inkling of the possibilities midmonth, but it will be December before you fully grasp the effects of this duo. Listen closely if a family member offers a suggestion regarding your job. It's probably on target.

Planetary Lightspots

The November 16 New Moon in Scorpio highlights your domestic sector. Host a group of friends and family for Thanksgiving or plan an open house for the last weekend of November to launch the holiday season. This is also a terrific time to tackle small household repairs and projects. Consult an expert, though, if your do-it-yourself skills aren't quite up to the task, and call a pro for anything major.

Relationships

The holiday social season gets into full swing with Mercury's arrival in Sagittarius, your solar fifth house, November 15, followed by the Sun on the 21st. You'll connect with some exciting people, and networking can result in a positive career contact. But keep an eye on your budget because all that fun can be expensive. Family ties are among the month's best, and special moments create meaningful memories. Romance zings for couples.

Money and Success

You'll have to carefully budget your time in order to meet the career demands that accompany the November 2 Full Moon in Taurus, your solar tenth house. The lunar energy has the potential to boost your status and possibly spark a promotion or job offer. Invest time and effort in reinforcing workplace relationships. You'll want these key people on your side in December.

Rewarding Days
1, 4, 5, 13, 14, 17, 18, 22, 28, 29

Challenging Days
2, 6, 8, 9, 12, 15, 19, 27, 30

Leo/December

Planetary Hotspots

Mars turns retrograde in your sign on the 20th. So be prepared for more than a few frustrations between then and early March when the action planet resumes direct motion. Rather than fight the trend, see it as an opportunity to catch up on personal tasks put on hold and to get in the habit of daily relaxation.

Planetary Lightspots

Jupiter and Neptune join forces for the last time in Aquarius, your solar seventh house. Share your love with those closest to you and embrace your spiritual connection with the important people in your life. Some Leos make a lifetime commitment, and others launch a spectacular romance full of promise for the future. If you're part of a couple, consider a quick getaway at a local luxury hotel.

Relationships

The fast social pace continues as Venus advances in Sagittarius, your solar fifth house, through the 24th. The influence peaks at the December 16 New Moon in the same sign, which also could trigger a minor windfall. Get a group together for a lottery pool, with each person contributing only one ticket. Luck could come in other forms, too—a soul mate, an addition to the family, or a promising job contact.

Money and Success

You'll be pushed to perform at work and difficult people will be more the norm than the exception as the Sun, Mercury, and later, Venus, clash with Saturn in your communication sector and Pluto in your solar sixth house. This is not the month to ask for a raise. It is the month to maintain a low profile, fulfill your responsibilities, and weather the storm with determination.

Rewarding Days

5, 6, 11, 12, 14, 15, 18, 19, 21, 25

Challenging Days

3, 7, 9, 10, 13, 16, 17, 24, 29, 31

Leo Action Table

These dates reflect the best—but not the only—times for success and ease in these activities, according to your Sun sign.

	JAN	FEB	MAR	APR	MAY	JUN	JUL	AUG	SEPT	OCT	NOV	DEC
Move										28-31	10-15	
Start a class						29-30	26-27			16-17,21-22, 26-27		
Join a club	7-9		3-4, 30-31			14-22						
Ask for a raise								20-21		14	10-11	
Look for work	1-7, 13-15, 23-25	1-3		15-16		6-12						17-18
Get pro advice	6-9	16-17, 23, 27	3, 4						1, 2	26-27		
Get a loan				21								
See a doctor				29, 30		9, 10, 23		17		28-29	6	
Start a diet	23					9, 10						
End relationship		22-23						5				
Buy clothes		17-18						1, 27		21-22		6, 10-11 14-16
Get a makeover					1-2		22					6
New romance							31	1		20-22		16
Vacation		27-28		22-30	1-3						27	

The Virgin
August 22 to September 22

♍

Element: Earth

Quality: Mutable

Polarity: Yin/feminine

Planetary Ruler: Mercury

Meditation: I can allow time for myself

Gemstone: Sapphire

Power Stones: Peridot, amazonite, rhodochrosite

Key Phrase: I analyze

Glyph: Greek symbol for containment

Anatomy: Abdomen, gall bladder, intestines

Color: Taupe, gray, navy blue

Animal: Domesticated animals

Myths/Legends: Demeter, Astraea, Hygeia

House: Sixth

Opposite Sign: Pisces

Flower: Pansy

Key Word: Discriminating

Your Strengths and Challenges

Your strength is in the details. Little escapes the attention of your keen, discriminating eye and you have knack for seeing what others miss. When compiled, all those bits and pieces of information form a complete picture in your mind that's part knowledge and part intuition. But the details can also be a challenge if you get lost in them and fail to view things from a wider perspective. Remind yourself to periodically step back and take an objective look at the specifics of a situation or project as well as your life as a whole.

Many Virgos are shy in their younger years, a trait that diminishes with life experience and expertise. But even as your overall confidence rises your mutable sign has a tendency to go with the flow, sometimes too much so. Being adaptable is one thing; reluctance to take a stand is another. Don't hesitate. Speak up.

With Mercury as your ruling planet, you excel at communication, and most Virgos are lifelong learners and avid readers. Practical, common-sense ideas are your specialty, and your sign is noted for its analytical ability. But that also encourages your brain to work overtime, worrying about what could be rather than what is, as your imagination runs wild. Rein it in and be realistic.

Ever-efficient, you have a talent for finding the quickest and best way to do just about anything. You also excel at planning and organization. That's true whether you're a neat Virgo or one who prefers an organized mess. Either way, you know where everything is and can reach into a pile of papers and pull out just the one you need.

Your Relationships

You take dating seriously and prefer a single relationship to playing the field. It's comfortable and secure—so much so that some Virgos drift along in a relationship for years without ever feeling the need for commitment. All that changes when the right person comes along to stir your passions. As one of the most sensual signs of the zodiac, you're also a sentimental romantic who treasures special events and memories, and delights in elegant, candlelight evenings. You'll know you're truly in love when you leave practical reasoning behind and embrace every magical moment of togetherness. You could make a match with Pisces, your polar opposite, or one of the other water signs, Cancer and Scorpio. Life with a Taurus or Capricorn might bring you happiness, but changeable, free-spirited Gemini and Sagittarius could unsettle you.

Virgo's home environment encourages knowledge and learning, and you probably have books and the latest technology to connect you with the world. Big rooms, big windows, and, preferably, a big home, appeal to you. Many Virgos are avid do-it-yourselfers who take on major home improvement projects that can take months to complete. Clutter can get the best of you if you're a messy Virgo, so use your organizational skills and train yourself to put things away. Virgos often get a late start as parents and usually have only one or two children. As a parent, you have high expectations and push your children to succeed in every possible way. While that can build an excellent work ethic for their adult years, they also need time and encouragement to explore their own interests. Balance constructive criticism with praise.

New people come in and out of your life regularly, usually for a purpose. A few become close friends, whom you consider to be family, especially if you live far away from your roots, as many Virgos do. You're more comfortable with these friends than you are on the meet-and-greet social scene, and enjoy people in the comfort of your own home.

Your Career and Money

Virgo has a reputation for being a workaholic. There's a good reason why: you like to be productive and you enjoy working. It's that simple. Do remember, though, that there's more to life than work, and that balance is as good for you as it is for anyone. Some Virgos push things to the max and have both a career and a side job, such as freelance work. Many choose a career in communications or another field where they can use their communication skills. Your career fluctuates as opportunities come and go, and your flexibility is an asset in adapting to changing conditions. In your daily work you need the freedom and independence to manage your own work flow without constant direction. A hands-on boss is not for you. You also do well in a teamwork environment and coworkers often become friends.

Finances benefit from your common sense and practical approach to life. At least that's usually true. Occasionally you have the urge to splurge, especially on loved ones, and can spend on impulse. That's great if you can afford it, which most Virgos can, because you have excellent earning power. Investments will be more profitable if you back decisions with research and think long-term. Be somewhat cautious with credit; it's easy to get, but tack on interest and all you have is an expensive bargain.

Your Lighter Side

No one would ever call you lazy, but you do have your moments—when no one is looking. Travel brings out this side of you, as does your favorite chair at home. Even so, your leisure time is usually productive and filled with hobbies, gardening, reading, and other practical interests.

Affirmation for the Year

My goal is a balanced lifestyle.

The Year Ahead for Virgo

Could anything make a Virgo happier than Jupiter in Aquarius? Undoubtedly there are many things, but this transit ranks right up there at the top because expansive Jupiter will spend all but the first four days of 2009 in your solar sixth house of daily work. That's sure to bring enough work to keep even a Virgo content.

The danger here is that you can take on far too much. Remember, you're only human and there are only so many hours in a day. Put them to good use, but be sure you can deliver on your promises. Otherwise, this fortunate transit could backfire.

Overall, though, you can look forward to an upbeat year on the job with excellent opportunities to showcase your skills and talents. And Jupiter's protective influence can keep you among the favored few.

If you're thinking about starting a home-based business, however, you'll want to go slow and hang onto your day job. What appears to be a great opportunity now may not be in a year or two, when it could end up being very costly. Explore the idea, and make only a minimal financial investment if you decide to go ahead.

Neptune entered Aquarius in 1998, so you've probably already experienced the influence of this planet in your work life. It represents confusion and illusion, but also faith, creativity, and inspiration. The challenge with Neptune is in knowing what's fact and what's fiction because it can mask the obvious and encourage wishful thinking. With Neptune affecting your work life, it's wise to be aware of undercurrents on the job and wary of coworkers who don't ring true. Listen to your sixth sense, keep your private life private, and be careful about whom you trust.

Jupiter will join Neptune in December, when you'll either fulfill a career goal or wonder how you could have been so off base. Take note of what happens in early February because it will give you clues about what will occur in December. Then you can plan accordingly to get the best of the Jupiter-Neptune alignment, which can motivate and inspire you to success or trigger a disappointment. Keep your options open and begin networking in earnest if your career field is prone to layoffs or you discover your company is entering a downturn or soon to undergo a reorganization. Although you may not be without a job, it is a possibility when Jupiter and Neptune join forces; dissolution is possible. A far better choice is to align yourself with the right people early in the year so you're prepared and have alternatives.

Saturn will almost complete its Virgo tour the end of October, when it enters Libra. (It returns to Virgo in April 2010 for about three months.) Thus, 2009 offers you almost the final opportunity to gain the wisdom and understanding that this planet represents.

Saturn is the planet of restriction, so you're sure to feel frustrated at times when progress seems minimal at best. This just goes with the territory when Saturn is involved. Patience is required and even if it seems like your life is at a standstill it's really not. Take a close look and compare today with where you were in September 2007, when Saturn entered Virgo. The progress you've made may not be splashy and dynamic, but it's certainly been steady with each task handled thoroughly and each achievement well-earned. So appreciate how far you've come!

The time when Saturn is in your Sun sign is often one of relative obscurity. But unlike some other planetary cycles you're mostly content with that, doing the hard work that nearly always accompanies a Saturn transit. Saturn in your Sun sign is also associated with lowered vitality so be sure to get the extra rest, relaxation and, most importantly, sleep you need now. There's an important message in this: it's the universe's way of reminding you to treat yourself well. And if a healthier lifestyle would benefit your mind and body, change your diet, emphasize positive self-talk, and begin a regular exercise program.

This is not the time to bend the rules, however, because Saturn expects everyone under its influence to tow the line. You might have a tough time getting away with even minor misdeeds such as taking a shortcut to complete a project. (Yes, some Virgos really would do this!) It's a safe bet that Saturn will deliver instant karma—an instantaneous negative repercussion—and you'll soon regret your action.

Saturn's most prominent influence this year, however, is its exact alignment with Uranus in Pisces, a contact it first made last November (2008). These two planets will form two more exact alignments this year (February and September) across your solar first/seventh house axis of self and relationships.

Uranus is the ultimate planet of change; Saturn is the ultimate planet of stability. Balancing these two diverse energies is, as you might expect, a challenge. After all, everyone prefers the status quo. Change can be positive when self-initiated, but even then it's accompanied by varying levels of stress as what's new gradually evolves into the norm.

With Uranus in your solar seventh house you can expect everything from sudden opportunities to sudden arrivals and departures—all involving other people. But Saturn/Uranus isn't all about other people. Your perspective is also shifting as you view them through the Saturn's lens. What worked in the past—people, places, and things—may no longer fit with your current life because your priorities are changing.

For some Virgos the planetary alignment will culminate with the end of a close alliance—partnership, friendship, or career ties. This can be positive or negative depending upon how you react. With Saturn in your sign it's very much up to you what happens. It's also likely that the year's events will be a mirror of your changing life direction and attitudes.

If the close relationships in your life are stable and secure, other people will still be a major theme in 2009. You'll gain a wider perspective on yourself as well as the world at large by listening to and talking with people. Some of these experiences will be quite enlightening and motivational and you'll discover that some of what you always held true was just your viewpoint. Of course you can choose to isolate yourself and your mind, but that would be a terrible waste of what could be the opportunity of a lifetime to connect with exciting people and ideas and to make the most of your practical creativity.

People are likely to depart as unexpectedly as they arrive. Each, however, will come with a purpose, and when that purpose is fulfilled, each will move on. You may or may not immediately know the reason why, but each will in some way teach you an important lesson or share a thought-provoking message.

The Saturn/Uranus alignment is also about mutual support, teamwork, and alliances that can benefit you and everyone else involved. But be a little cautious about taking on more than your fair share of the responsibility and workload. With Saturn in your sign, you'll have a tendency to do that and also to want to do everything yourself, in part so it meets your high standards. Consider this another Saturn lesson: perfection might be an ideal, but it's almost never achievable.

Saturn will move on to your solar second house of personal money October 29, when it enters Libra. Although this can restrict income and increase debt, it doesn't have to. Some people born with Saturn there amass wealth because they're thrifty, cautious, and conservative. You can do the same for the next few years as Saturn moves through Libra, where it will encourage you to save, spend wisely, and live within a budget. Because this transit is just beginning, 2009 is a great year to build up your reserves so you have money for any unexpected expenses that arise. You'll also feel more secure knowing that you have a cushion.

Pluto will spend its first full year in Capricorn, your solar fifth house of children, recreation, and romance. This sector also rules games of chance, including investments, so you'll want to be cautious about putting funds at risk. This is doubly true because Pluto will clash with Saturn from the time it enters Libra on October 29 until year's end. You also could experience added expenses involving your children and should prepare yourself to draw the line and say no if their requests are unreasonable. The same would be true if, for example, you get a sudden urge to take a 'round the world cruise or buy the most expensive car on the lot. Go for less and save the difference.

What This Year's Eclipses Mean for You

In a typical year, there are four eclipses. This year features six eclipses. Their influence will be similar to this year's planetary emphasis and alignments, focusing your attention on work, play, and personal health and well-being. Make all three a part of your life.

Your job will require much time and effort this year with two eclipses occurring in Aquarius, your solar sixth house, January 7, and August 6. Together they keep the energy flowing into that area of your life all year long since an eclipse's effect lasts six to twelve months. There's an important distinction between these two eclipses, however. The first is a solar eclipse, which is also a New Moon, signifying beginnings, new endeavors, and a fresh perspective. The second, a lunar eclipse and a Full Moon, represents conclusions and endings and is the time to complete what was begun in the New Moon, or solar eclipse, phase. What this means is that your work life will come full circle in 2009, and you have the opportunity to make your mark the first part of the year and to cash in on your efforts during the final five months. So use Jupiter in Aquarius wisely and be alert for opportunities and people that will advance your aims.

The February 2 lunar eclipse in Leo, your solar twelfth house of self-renewal, will reinforce Saturn's message about a healthy lifestyle. Get a check-up and listen to your medical professional's advice. Because this eclipse will activate Neptune in Aquarius, this is not the time to avoid reality. Tap into the strength of Saturn and Pluto and do what's necessary to improve your overall well-being, whether that's diet, exercise, ending a bad habit, or something else. Also listen to your sixth sense, which can help you tune in to your body's needs. Make leisure-time a part of every day.

The other three eclipses will span your solar fifth/eleventh house axis. All occur later in the year: July 7 lunar eclipse in Leo, July 22 solar eclipse and December 31 lunar eclipse in Capricorn.

Friends will be an important part of your life, thanks to the Leo eclipses, and the Capricorn eclipse will reinforce Pluto's influence. If you're searching for romance, these eclipses could bring someone into your life, possibly through a friend. But go slowly and keep finances and matters of the heart entirely separate. This is not the time, for example, to cosign a loan for a romantic interest (or anyone else, even a close friend or relative) or to enter into any other financial agreements. Doing so could leave you wiser but poorer.

Because the eleventh house also governs groups, you could be tapped for a top leadership position in an organization or be asked to head up a special project at work. Both are of course directly linked to this year's emphasis on teamwork and other people, and both have the potential to advance your personal and professional goals. Think about what you want to gain at the outset and then do all you can to make that happen.

Saturn

If you were born between September 6 and 22, Saturn's exact contact with your Virgo Sun can be quite empowering if you adopt its agenda and take the initiative to learn a lot about yourself from this great teacher of the zodiac. Probably the greatest personal lesson Saturn delivers is to encourage you to establish life priorities. It's that simple, although the process will require thoughtful consideration of the past as well as the future.

You may have already felt a growing dissatisfaction with your life in general. And although you link this feeling to your job, your home, your career, or certain people, it's really all about you. What worked in the past may no longer be viable because you're ready for something new. And that's where you should begin: the past. Think about where you are now and how you got there. How have your priorities changed? Your hopes? Your wishes? Your goals? A list of your current likes and dislikes is a good starting place. Then let your imagination run free and picture yourself where you want to be about seven years from now, when Saturn will contact your Sun from Sagittarius. From that you can set new goals and develop an action plan to achieve them. **If you were born between September 6 and 9**, this process will be concentrated in a short time frame—April through mid-June. But **if you were born between September 9 and 14**, initial events will occur January through March and be concluded between mid-June and the end of August. **For Virgos born between September 15 and 22**, Saturn's contact will be brief, a week or two in September or October.

Saturn and Pluto

If you were born between August 23 and 26, both Saturn in Libra and Pluto in Capricorn will contact your Sun. The Pluto influence will be active off and on throughout the year, but will intensify after Saturn enters Libra October 29. You, among all Virgos, will need to be especially cautious about financial matters, including investments. Protect your resources at every turn and don't let anyone convince you to put your security at risk. If necessary, consult a professional or a trusted, objective friend for another opinion. Listen and take the advice to heart. A positive use of this Saturn/Pluto energy would be to invest in your children's education by establishing a savings account for that purpose. You also could get involved in a new and potentially lucrative hobby such as refinishing and reselling furniture purchased at thrift stores or yard sales. This will satisfy your need for transformation, to create something usable out of something that appears to be worthless, even if you do it solely for your own home. And it's not inconceivable that you could stumble upon a valuable treasure in the process.

Uranus

Change is in the wind **if you were born between September 12 and 19**, and relationships will have a key role as Uranus contacts your Sun from Pisces. Reach out to people and widen your horizons. This is an integral part of the changes you are undergoing at this time, which can be an exciting one if you welcome new personal directions. Embrace change rather than resist it and imagine the new vistas open to you. Virgo is an adaptable sign, so you can do this more easily than most.

You'll experience the full effect of the Saturn/Uranus alignment in February **if you were born between September 12 and 14**, and in September **if you were born between September 17 and 19**. A significant relationship in your life will reach a turning point at that time, either an ending or a new beginning. This is where your personal priorities will come into play, and the decisions you make at that time will ultimately be based on what you have defined—or are in the process of defining—as what you value most in life. The alignment will also challenge you to be true to yourself while finding a workable solution to resolve any relationship difficulties. In many respects this will be a personal test of your willingness to let go of the past in order to embrace the future.

Neptune

If you were born between September 14 and 18, Neptune will inspire you to go above and beyond in your work life. Be careful. Someone, or several people, could take advantage of your work ethic and your enthusiasm. So while it's great to commit yourself to your job, heart and soul, you also need to watch out for yourself and your own interests. Do that even if it doesn't resonate with your hard-working, service-oriented attitude. In the end, you'll thank yourself and do much to limit the potential disappointment that can accompany this transit.

Virgo/January

Planetary Hotspots

Because Mercury is your ruling planet you're all too familiar with its retrograde antics. Expect the usual mix-ups, wrong numbers, and more when it switches motion on the 21st in Aquarius, your solar sixth house. Fortunately, you're great with details, and careful attention to them will be an asset at work.

Planetary Lightspots

You'll want to see your favorite friends when the January 10 Full Moon in Cancer lights up your solar eleventh house. Chances are, you'll meet some new people that week, one of whom could be your magic link to an exciting opportunity. Career networking is also featured, and you can make valuable contacts for the future.

Relationships

Love at first sight captures the hearts of some Virgos the third week of January when Venus in Pisces, your solar seventh house, aligns with Mars, Saturn, and Uranus. The planetary energy could also trigger a reunion with a former love interest who once again catches your eye. For couples, this is a marvelous time to revitalize your relationship. You'll also have plenty of opportunities to socialize, with Mars energizing your solar fifth house of recreation.

Money and Success

Retrograde Mercury aside, January has all the potential to bring significant gains in your work life. Jupiter arrives in Aquarius on the 5th, and aligns with the Sun and Mercury within a few days of the January 26 New Moon in the same sign. This will bring you to the attention of decision-makers and it could put you in the running for a promotion. Look for further developments the last week of February.

Rewarding Days

1, 5, 6, 7, 10, 13, 18, 19, 26, 28

Challenging Days

2, 4, 8, 9, 15, 22, 29

Virgo/February

Planetary Hotspots

With this month's Saturn/Uranus alignment spanning your first/ seventh house axis you can expect difficulties in close relationships. At issue is your need for security and the other person's need for independence. Resolution will be a challenge, especially if your birthday is within a few days of September 13. It's worth a try, though, if you're open to compromise. This is not the month (or year) to enter into a business or personal partnership, and be cautious if you need to consult a professional. Check credentials.

Planetary Lightspots

You could see a bigger bank balance by month's end, thanks to a lucky Venus-Mars-Jupiter lineup. A raise or bonus is possible, or you could realize a net increase from an added perk. Some Virgos will cash in on a minor windfall from a workplace lottery pool.

Relationships

Despite the relationship differences associated with the Saturn/ Uranus lineup, your social life benefits from Mercury, which turns direct on the 1st in Capricorn. Plan a few get-togethers with friends before Mercury moves on to Aquarius on the 14th. Overall, relationships will be more easygoing by month's end when the February 24 New Moon in Pisces energizes your solar seventh house.

Money and Success

February has all the potential to satisfy your strong work ethic. Mars in Aquarius, your solar sixth house, steps up the pace and your workload, and you're a key link in the information chain after Mercury enters the same sign. Even better, you'll be among the favored few the last two weeks of February when several planets activate Jupiter in Aquarius.

Rewarding Days

2, 3, 10, 15, 17, 19, 21, 22, 24, 27

Challenging Days

5, 6, 11, 12, 16, 18, 25, 26

Virgo/March

Planetary Hotspots

Finances are mixed throughout March as luck alternates with extra expenses. With careful planning and thoughtful decisions you should end the month in positive territory. Venus, the universal money planet, turns retrograde in Aries, your solar eighth house, on the 6th, which can limit resources. But it also aligns beautifully with several planets, as does the Sun in Aries from the 20th on. However, you could see a spike in expenses the week of the March 26 New Moon in Aries when the lunar energy activates Pluto in Capricorn, your solar fifth house of children, romance, and recreation. Safeguard financial information from prying eyes and be cautious with investments.

Planetary Lightspots

There's a great use for this month's Pluto influence: clean house and get rid of unneeded items. Besides giving your place fresh energy you could make a profit at a consignment shop. Do look before you toss, though. A pocket could yield cash.

Relationships

February's Saturn/Uranus alignment remains active, and related matters peak the week of the March 10 Full Moon in your sign. A relationship will thrive or end at this turning point that encourages you to think positively and move forward with confidence while blending your needs with someone else's.

Money and Success

Mercury in Aquarius, your solar sixth house, through the 7th, and Mars there through the 13th continue the fast pace at work. Focus on details as tension rises with deadline pressure. Even meticulous Virgos sometimes run the risk of overlooking important factors. Don't hesitate to ask a coworker for help if you need it.

Rewarding Days

7, 9, 13, 14, 20, 21, 22, 24, 28, 29

Challenging Days

4, 5, 10, 11, 17, 23, 25, 26, 31

Virgo/April

Planetary Hotspots

April is mostly easygoing with just a few bumps as the weeks unfold. Your goals may clash with someone else's in early April and again midmonth, and you'll need to be a little wary of a coworker who comes on too strong. This person may try to mislead you or lean on you to take on some extra work. Draw the line and put your helpful nature on hold. Do only your fair share.

Planetary Lightspots

The April 24 Taurus New Moon and Mercury in the same sign April 9-29 is all the reason you need to take off for a week's vacation or plan a long weekend getaway. If that's impossible because of work and other commitments, set aside a few weekend days to explore the cultural offerings in your city. Some Virgos travel on business this month. If you're among them, try to take an extra day or two for yourself.

Relationships

Relationships are mostly upbeat. But with Venus retrograde until the 17th in your solar seventh house, you'll want to be extra-sensitive to the needs and feelings of others, especially those closest to you. If you're undecided about a love relationship, put the decision on hold until late April. By then you'll have a better idea of how you feel and whether the union is the right one for you.

Money and Success

Money matters are this month's major emphasis. They, too, are mostly positive, but extra expenses could pop up in early and late April. You also should take precautions to protect valuables when you're out in public. The best news is you could get word of a nice raise or have the opportunity to earn some extra money the second or third week of the month.

Rewarding Days

6, 10, 11, 16, 18, 20, 24, 29, 30

Challenging Days

1, 3, 8, 13, 15, 22, 26, 27, 28

Virgo/May

Planetary Hotspots

Unlike April, this is not the month for travel unless you schedule it for the first few days of the month. Try to do that if a business trip is necessary because retrograde Mercury can trigger a delay or cancellation after it enters Taurus, your solar ninth house, on the 13th. The same holds true for important presentations and legal matters.

Planetary Lightspots

Jupiter and Neptune in Aquarius join forces in your solar sixth house. Tap into the inspiration provided by this union to dream big and aim high in your work life. Do the same for others by motivating them with praise and encouragement and you'll be rewarded by gaining yet another supporter you can rely on in the future.

Relationships

You'll be in touch with a lot of people this month, especially around the time of the May 9 Full Moon in Scorpio, your solar third house of communication. Relatives will be among them and although these relationships are generally positive, the potential exists for misunderstandings, especially with in-laws. Tune out what you don't want to hear and consider the source. Also be wary of a coworker's promises. Even if well-intentioned, the odds are they won't be fulfilled, which could leave you scrambling to catch up.

Money and Success

Your career is in high focus with this month's New Moon in Gemini on the 24th. But with Mercury turning retrograde in the same sign on the 7th and then slipping back into Taurus, you should consider May as a month to reinforce your position and lay the groundwork for great strides in June. Do, however, apply for a promotion if one is available, or send out resumes if you're job hunting.

Rewarding Days

1, 7, 8, 11, 14, 19, 21, 31

Challenging Days

5, 17, 18, 20, 25, 27, 29

Virgo/June

Planetary Hotspots

Most Virgos appreciate the sense of freedom that comes with home life. You'll enjoy the week of the June 7 Full Moon in Sagittarius, your domestic sector—somewhat. Because this Full Moon clashes with Saturn in your sign you're likely to feel hemmed in at times. Get past that and take advantage of the time to work around the house before you play. You'll be pleased with the results.

Planetary Lightspots

Mars zips through Taurus, your solar ninth house, where it's joined by Mercury through the 12th and Venus from the 6th on. That's a perfect formula for business or pleasure trips. Early June will be best for vacation travel, when you can benefit from more favorable planetary alignments, and business travel is best at month's end.

Relationships

Friends are your center of attention as the June 22 New Moon in Cancer highlights your solar eleventh house. Some of your friendships are sure to be difficult because this New Moon connects with Pluto in your solar fifth house. That also prompts some Virgos to call it quits with a dating relationship. If you're a parent, your children are likely to be a handful, and parents of teens should be especially watchful. Take it easy if you exercise; push yourself too hard and you could end up with a sprain or strain.

Money and Success

Last month's career potential comes full circle as Mercury returns to Gemini, your solar tenth house, on the 13th. It aligns beautifully with several planets, increasing the potential for praise and a possible promotion or job offer. If it doesn't come through now, you'll have other chances in July and August.

Rewarding Days
1, 8, 9, 12, 14, 18, 19, 23, 26, 30

Challenging Days
4, 5, 11, 15, 21, 22, 25, 27, 28

Virgo/July

Planetary Hotspots

This month brings the year's second union of Jupiter and Neptune in Aquarius. Think back to what happened in May concerning your job, a coworker, or travel. July may bring further developments in any of these areas or something new, such as the suggestion that additional schooling or certification would help your chances for advancement. Be prepared for weather delays if you plan to travel.

Planetary Lightspots

Your sixth sense gets a boost from Mercury, which enters Leo, your solar twelfth house, on the 17th. Calm your mind with meditation or just sit quietly and let your thoughts drift. This will help free your inner voice during waking hours or through dream images. Either or both can reveal career insights that inspire you.

Relationships

July's Full Moon in Capricorn on the 7th and the New Moon in Cancer on the 21st highlight your solar fifth and eleventh houses. That's ideal for summer fun with friends, recreational activities, romance, and quality time with children. Make all a part of your life this month as you enjoy these upbeat relationships. If you're single, ask a friend to arrange a date around the 13th, when the Sun and Mercury unite in Cancer, or join other singles or couples for a night out where you can meet people.

Money and Success

Venus travels in Gemini, your career sector, July 5–30. Take advantage of this time, when you'll be among the favored few, to impress decision-makers, apply for a job or promotion, and to develop networking contacts. The action picks up on the 11th, when Mars arrives in Gemini, setting the pace for a busy six weeks at work.

Rewarding Days

1, 8, 9, 16, 17, 20, 21, 22, 27, 29

Challenging Days

4, 6, 10, 13, 19, 25, 30, 31

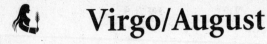 # Virgo/August

Planetary Hotspots

With this month's New Moon in Leo, your solar twelfth house, you'll want to treat yourself with maximum kindness. Adequate sleep, nutritious foods, and daily time to relax and unwind are important not only to counteract the effects of work stress but also to help prevent a cold. Try not to overdo it, and don't let yourself get run down, which can weaken your immune system.

Planetary Lightspots

August 2 marks Mercury's arrival in your sign. With your ruling planet here you'll have a way with words and added confidence for meetings, important talks, and getting acquainted with newcomers in your personal life while socializing and at work. Someone fascinating could spark a flash of insight and understanding around the time of the New Moon, partly because of your active intuition.

Relationships

Although nearly all your relationships benefit from Venus in Cancer through the 25th, the best of this planet is reserved for friendship. Placed in your solar eleventh house, it's great for social events, especially the fourth weekend of the month. You could reconnect with someone from the past around the same time, and if you're single, the reunion might spark a romantic liaison.

Money and Success

Mars in Gemini, your solar tenth house, through the 24th accents an action-packed career month—especially the week of the August 5 Full Moon (and lunar eclipse) in Aquarius. Try to plan ahead so you have plenty of time to complete projects and meet deadlines despite the many interruptions this influence promises. Do that and your star will shine with those who count.

Rewarding Days

3, 4, 6, 11, 12, 17, 20, 23, 24, 30, 31

Challenging Days

1, 2, 8, 9, 15, 21, 22, 25, 29

♍ Virgo/September ♍

Planetary Hotspots

The final Saturn/Uranus contact is activated by the September 18 New Moon in Virgo, which is closely aligned with both planets. Stress will surround a close business or personal tie (possibly both) as the issue of independence vs responsibility again arises just as it did when these planets connected earlier this year. For some, the lineup will trigger an ending, while others will redesign their relationship to better suit both people's needs. You might want to put any relationship decision on hold, however, because with retrograde Mercury returning to your sign on the 17th, there will be further developments in October.

Planetary Lightspots

Your powers of attraction are at their best from the 20th on, when Venus begins its annual transit of your sign. It's a plus for dating and socializing that extends into October, giving you all the charm and charisma you need to attract helpful people into your life.

Relationships

Although the Saturn/Uranus alignment adds stress to some relationships, others benefit from the September 4 Full Moon in Pisces, your relationship sector. The same is true of Mars, which spends the entire month in Cancer, your solar eleventh house. That's great for evenings and weekends with friends.

Money and Success

Extra expenses, possibly to fund your children's activities, may pop up this month. You also should carefully check statements and pay bills early because Mercury turns retrograde in Libra, your solar second house of money, on the 7th. Safeguard financial information and other valuables, especially when you're in a crowd.

Rewarding Days

1, 2, 7, 8, 13, 20, 21, 24, 26, 29, 30

Challenging Days

5, 6, 10, 12, 15, 17, 23, 25, 27

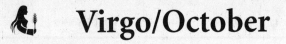 # Virgo/October

Planetary Hotspots

Mars begins its long trip through Leo, your solar twelfth house, on the 16th. The red planet will be there through early June 2010, so now is the time to get in the habit of evening relaxation. For you that might be working on a hobby project. That's great as long as you can turn off your brain at bedtime. Otherwise you could be short on sleep when you need to be at your best and brightest.

Planetary Lightspots

With Mercury as your ruling planet, most Virgos are avid readers who amass a wide variety of information. You'll be even more so in the coming weeks, starting with the Sun's arrival in Scorpio, your solar third house, on the 22nd, followed by Mercury on the 28th. That's only the beginning. Stock up on books because your curiosity will accelerate in November.

Relationships

Last month's Saturn/Uranus influence continues the first two weeks of October as Mercury and Venus contact both planets. Use the time to resolve any lingering issues, and to reach a final decision regarding a relationship, especially if your birthday is near September 18. Honest talk is a good starting place.

Money and Success

October's Full Moon, October 4 in Aries, and New Moon, October 18 in Libra, highlight your solar second/eighth house axis of money. You could realize a profit by month's end from a raise or bonus, but add to savings before you spend just in case extra expenses occur. Most important is Saturn, which enters Libra on the 29th to begin its three-year transit of that sign. Set goals to build your net worth in the next few years and eliminate debt.

Rewarding Days

1, 7, 8, 10, 11, 14, 17, 23, 24, 29

Challenging Days

2, 3, 9, 15, 16, 18, 20, 30

🦁 Virgo/November 🦁

Planetary Hotspots

Quick trips and long-distance travel are this month's hotspot. Not that every single one will be difficult, but the potential exists for delays and cancellations, especially if you plan to travel around the November 2 Taurus Full Moon or the November 26 Scorpio New Moon, your solar third/ninth house axis. Also be especially alert during your daily commute and while running errands because an accident could happen in a flash through no fault of your own.

Planetary Lightspots

Family time is at its best from the 15th on, when Mercury enters Sagittarius, your domestic sector. It's joined by the Sun on the 21st, which is great for planning a December get-together. You'll also have the incentive to get your place in great shape for the holidays. As you clean, watch for items that could bring a profit at a consignment shop.

Relationships

November's Scorpio influence is sure to have you in touch with many people, including relatives and neighbors. You'll also have added opportunities to get better acquainted with coworkers in a casual after-hours setting, which could spark a lucky networking connection or a new romance the second week of November.

Money and Success

Finances benefit from Venus in Libra, your solar second house, the first week of the month. But November also brings a Saturn/Pluto clash that urges ultimate caution with investments. Take no risks, even those that appear to be safe. Also curb your generosity and emphasize savings. You'll be glad you did when December's planetary positions activate this alignment.

Rewarding Days

5, 7, 10, 13, 14, 16, 18, 20, 21, 22, 24, 29

Challenging Days

2, 6, 8, 9, 12, 15, 19, 23, 25, 27, 30, 31

 Virgo/December

Planetary Hotspots

Mars turns retrograde in Leo, your solar twelfth house, on the 20th. Expect some frustrations with this placement when projects and decisions are delayed or shelved. Patience and stress relief are good temporary remedies that will see you through this period which lasts until early March.

Planetary Lightspots

Home is your favorite location this month, especially the week of the December 16 New Moon in Sagittarius, your solar fourth house. Even better is Venus in the same sign, December 1–24, which is as great for entertaining friends and relatives as it is for adding new décor. If you feel ambitious and creative, take a few days off to redo a bedroom or bathroom.

Relationships

A friendship or romantic relationship is likely to be difficult as the Sun, Mercury, and Venus travel in Capricorn, your solar fifth house, this month. If you have children, be prepared for the ups and downs of parenting, especially if your birthday is near August 23. Stay close to home on New Year's Eve, the date of the Full Moon (and lunar eclipse) in Cancer, your friendship sector; it directly contacts Pluto in Capricorn.

Money and Success

You might want to consider cutting back on holiday spending. Homemade gifts are great for friends and coworkers, and continue to be cautious about personal and financial information and investments. On December 2, a bright Full Moon in Gemini, your career sector, makes you an attention-getter. It also could trigger a bonus or a step up because it's beautifully aligned with the Jupiter-Neptune union in Aquarius, your solar sixth house.

Rewarding Days

4, 5, 6, 8, 11, 12, 14, 16, 17, 21, 22, 23

Challenging Days

3, 7, 9, 10, 13, 15, 20, 24, 28, 31

Virgo Action Table

These dates reflect the best—but not the only—times for success and ease in these activities, according to your Sun sign.

	JAN	FEB	MAR	APR	MAY	JUN	JUL	AUG	SEPT	OCT	NOV	DEC
Move		17, 18	14, 15			6, 7	31	1		21, 22	17, 18	2-5, 14-16
Start a class			14-15					25, 26			9-16	
Join a club				29, 30		22-24	11-12, 16, 17, 20-21	16, 17		10, 11	6, 7	
Ask for a raise				19		30	27			16		
Look for work		15-17, 22-23	1-4				10			26, 27		
Get pro advice		24-26		20, 21						28, 29		
Get a loan		27, 28		24		16, 17					27	
See a doctor		23	3		1, 29		22	6, 19				
Start a diet		22, 23		18, 19			10					
End relationship						14, 15	12	5				
Buy clothes	23, 24					9, 10		30, 31				17
Get a makeover		11				27, 28		20, 21			15	
New romance								2, 3			19-21	17, 18
Vacation	5-7	2, 3		24-26		1-12	16, 17			5-7		

The Balance
September 22 to October 22

Element: Air

Quality: Cardinal

Polarity: Yang/masculine

Planetary Ruler: Venus

Meditation: I balance
conflicting desires

Gemstone: Opal

Power Stones: Tourmaline,
kunzite, blue lace agate

Key Phrase: I balance

Glyph: Scales of justice,
setting sun

Anatomy: Kidneys, lower back,
appendix

Color: Blue, pink

Animal: Brightly plumed birds

Myths/Legends: Venus,
Cinderella, Hera

House: Seventh

Opposite Sign: Aries

Flower: Rose

Key Word: Harmony

Your Strengths and Challenges

Your comfort zone is balance and you strive for the middle ground in everything from relationships to your career to leisure-time activities. When the scales tip one way or the other you're out of sync with yourself and your world. You value cooperation and compromise as well as harmony. But when necessary, you're a master strategist who can outthink most any adversary.

Libras are known for their indecisiveness. That's true of you at times, but not always. It just appears that way to those who fail to understand your mind. Your airy sign makes you a thinker, but it can be tough for you to reach a conclusion. The reason is simple: you have the unique ability to see both sides of any question. While that might be an advantage in certain situations, it becomes a challenge if you perpetually sit on the fence.

Ever the diplomat, you have a charming, tactful way with words and can leave people wondering whether they heard praise or criticism. You're also popular on the social scene, and many born under Venus-ruled Libra are attractive. Venus also gives you an eye for beauty and possibly artistic talent, and you know instinctively how to achieve just the right look in clothing and home décor.

Your sixth sense aids your exceptional people skills, and you're a good listener who can remain emotionally uninvolved. Despite all your grace and charm you can be aloof at times. For one so personable you also maintain the distance of decorum except with those in your inner circle. And although you dislike controversy, when pushed too far, your temper is unforgettable.

Your Relationships

Life without a mate is unthinkable to most Libras because yours is the universal sign of partnership. You feel incomplete without someone to call your own. Yet for someone who is so attuned to one-on-one relationships, you enjoy group activities with a date and friends. You're drawn to those who share your need for communication and you place a high priority on mental rapport. Love can bloom during long late-night talks. But you can mistake infatuation for love and prematurely dash into commitment. So give things a chance to develop and really get to know your intended. You could feel the sizzle with Aries, your opposite sign, and the other fire signs, Leo and Sagittarius, might spark your interest. You have much in common with your fellow air signs, Gemini and Aquarius, but life could be bumpy with Cancer or Capricorn.

Tradition guides your family life, and you want quality time with loved ones on a daily basis. Dinner and conversation is your ideal, schedules permitting. You keep in touch with elderly relatives, one or more of whom could live with your family at some point. In décor you favor the traditional and colors and furnishings that create a feeling of calm and serenity. You may have grown up in a highly structured environment with your every moment planned by a parent. Out of that comes a need for private time and space in your own home, as well as encouraging independence in your children, who become more friends than children in adulthood.

You're loyal to your many friends, and take pride in having a wide circle that includes well-connected people. And no small part of your popularity on the social scene is your ability to make each person feel like the center of your universe. You entertain friends in royal style, classy and elegant, whether it's a backyard barbecue or a formal dinner. Many Libras have a large number of acquaintances from their involvement in clubs and organizations, where your leadership skills are at their best.

Your Career and Money

With your people skills you can be successful in most any career, especially those that require working with the public. You're patient and sensitive to clients' or customers' needs, and bring out the best in coworkers, encouraging them to succeed. But loyalty can keep you in a job when it would be in your best interests to move on. A congenial workplace and a pleasant atmosphere are vital to job contentment; anything less motivates you to send out resumes.

You have wealth potential and, with wise investments and savings, can ensure comfortable retirement years. Real estate could also be lucrative, so you should aim for home ownership and annual home improvements to increase the value of your property. Many Libras receive an inheritance from a family member, and some gain through collectibles and antiques. But as careful as you can be about budgeting, you also have an eye for the finer things in life; live within your means and your excellent earning power.

Your Lighter Side

It's a fact: you have a sweet tooth, and if you're like most Libras, candy and other treats are irresistible. And although most people are unaware of it, you can be lazy to the max. Enjoy it! Knowing how to relax is a gift and one that keeps you in top form when job pressure and other stressors prompt you to call for a time-out. So curl up in your favorite chair with a bag of candy and a best seller and savor the moment—guilt free.

Affirmation for the Year Ahead

A balanced lifestyle is my path to success.

The Year Ahead for Libra

Love, play, fun, and frolic are in your 2009 forecast, thanks to Jupiter in Aquarius, your solar fifth house of recreation, pleasure, creativity, and children. Whatever your age, the time is right to be a kid again and let your lighthearted inner self emerge.

Known as the planet of good fortune, Jupiter is much more than that. It's really the planet of opportunity. And just about any time Jupiter shines its benefic rays your way, you'll have a lucky streak. It's up to you, however, to seize the opportunity and run with it.

Romantic and social opportunities top the list of possibilities this year, which is one of the best for singles on the dating scene. Not that you'll necessarily find a soul mate. You might, but Jupiter in your solar fifth house is more about playing the field and filling your evenings and weekends with fun. Jupiter is just as terrific for couples in love, who can rediscover the sizzle of romance.

You'll also have an active social life and the free time to see friends and host get-togethers. All this activity on the social scene will put you in touch with many people, which is great for networking as well as widening your circle of friendship. You might also want to fill some of your leisure-time hours with sports, exercise, cultural events, and weekend trips. If you want to get in shape, consider joining a gym, learn to play golf or tennis, or walk, bike, or skate with a neighbor.

If you're a parent, you'll be a proud one this year with many reasons to cheer your children's successes. More importantly, you'll find it easy to connect with your children and delight in enjoyable hours together. Some Libras will welcome an addition to the family.

Creativity is another fifth house theme. Take advantage of this year to explore yours. Learn a new hobby, redecorate your home, delve into scrapbooking, or master a computer graphics program. Use your imagination. Now is the time to develop or perfect your innate talents, which will in some way benefit you in 2010, when Jupiter moves on to Pisces, your solar sixth house of daily work.

Jupiter has another side: expansion. And while that can be fortunate, it also can manifest as too much of a good thing. One cookie is a treat; 15 cookies can add a pound. So focus on balance, which your sign is noted for, and keep all things in perspective. This will be especially important as Jupiter draws closer to its exact May and December alignments with Neptune, also in Aquarius.

Neptune is the ultimate planet of romance and fantasy, but also illusion and delusion. So let your head rule your heart if you feel you're in love. It might or might not be the real thing because when Neptune is involved it's easy to fall in love with love. Shy away from commitment until next year, when the bloom could quickly fade. And, if you date a coworker, be sure to keep business and pleasure entirely separate.

You'll also want to be cautious with investments. Don't let anyone talk you into putting funds at risk, despite promises and guarantees, which are easily made but just as easily broken. The same applies to games of chance. Try your luck on the lottery the end of May and in mid-December with a single ticket, or get in on a group buy with friends or coworkers. If Jupiter and Neptune want to hand you a lucky win, it will take only one ticket.

Saturn spends much of the year in Virgo, your solar twelfth house of self-renewal, where it encourages you to look within. Look to the past to identify issues that hold you back and then take steps to resolve them. This is an important step because Saturn will enter your sign October 29. You might catch yourself worrying more. If so, ask yourself why you're doing that instead of using the cardinal quality of your sign to take action. The reason might surprise you and also help you put the past to rest.

But Saturn doesn't operate solo this year. It will form an exact alignment with Uranus, planet of change and the unexpected, in Pisces, your solar sixth house, in February and September, just as it did last November (2008). Think back to what was going on in your life at that time. It could give you a few clues as to what to expect this year when these planets meet again.

Job-related changes are a strong possibility because Pisces is your sign of daily work. Use your sixth sense, listen, and observe what's going on around you, especially if your career field is prone to layoffs or your company isn't doing as well as it should be. A major company reorganization is also possible. Be prepared, be proactive, and do all you can to protect your position or to network your way into a new one. You also could simply decide it's time to move on if a promotion is blocked or a supervisor pushes your limits. Keep in mind, though, that if you make a sudden exit it could be next year before you're able to land a comparable position.

Do yourself a favor and get routine medical, dental, and eye check-ups because the solar sixth/twelfth house axis also governs health. With Saturn, the planet of structure and rules, involved, be wise and follow your health professional's advice if he or she suggests, for example, exercise or a healthier diet. Uranus can help you make these and other positive changes if you tap into its energy.

Saturn will enter your sign October 29, and although it will briefly return to Virgo in mid-April next year for about three months, you'll nevertheless begin to move into this new phase. During the few years that Saturn is in your sign it will challenge you to redefine and prepare yourself for new personal directions. This will be a time when your knowledge and experience will be valuable and when you can benefit from gaining more of the same. You'll also learn to rely on yourself more than you have in the past and thus further develop your inner strength. Many people need more sleep when Saturn is in their sign, and you also should make rest and relaxation a priority so you're at your best day after day. It's all about treating yourself well.

You may have already experienced the influence of Pluto in Capricorn, which completed its transition from Sagittarius into this sign in November 2008. During the next fifteen years as it moves through your solar fourth house, changes are likely in your domestic and family lives. You could relocate, possibly multiple times, extensively renovate your home, or see relatives move in or out. It's also possible you will become involved in managing a relative's affairs and that a parent will require your assistance.

What This Year's Eclipses Mean for You

Six eclipses will occur in 2009 (most years there are four), emphasizing your career, home and family, your love life, leisure-time, and friendship.

The year begins with a January 7 solar eclipse in Aquarius, your solar fifth house, just two days after Jupiter enters the same sign. That's a terrific combination to boost your social life and it increases the odds for singles looking for a new romantic relationship. The influence continues throughout the year, maximizing Jupiter's influence, thanks to an August 6 lunar eclipse also in

Aquarius. Make the most of this year's many opportunities to play, enjoy quality and quantity time with your children, and to love the one you're with.

Complementing the Aquarius eclipses is a February 9 lunar eclipse in Leo, your solar eleventh house of friendship and group activities. Besides the obvious boost to your social life, you'll cross paths with many new people, some of whom will become good friends. Others will be excellent networking contacts. If you're involved in a club or organization, give careful consideration to a leadership position. It could increase your visibility and put you in touch with important people. Or, find a group that shares your interests and use it to widen your circle of friendship. One word of caution applies, however. This eclipse will activate Neptune in Aquarius, so be a little skeptical of anyone except those you know well. People may stretch the truth and tell you only what you want to hear.

Your career sector shines brightly as two Cancer eclipses spotlight your solar tenth house. Both have the potential to put you in the fast lane, a mover-and-shaker with high visibility. The first, a solar eclipse, will occur July 22, and the second, a lunar eclipse, will light up the sky December 31. This means you'll begin to realize your career possibilities later this year and into 2010. Use the time before then to study your options, set goals, and develop an action plan.

As your career comes into focus so will your domestic life when the July 7 lunar eclipse in Capricorn spotlights your solar fourth house. At times it will be a challenge to manage both and do it well. But you're more than up to the task and can succeed with the help of family members and colleagues. Ask for help when you need it, especially after Saturn enters Libra (October 29), when you'll want to do it all yourself. Some Libras will relocate for a new career opportunity or a promotion.

Saturn

If you were born between October 7 and 22, this will be a year of consolidation and preparation as Saturn contacts your Sun from Virgo, your solar twelfth house. You can successfully work through any lingering issues, especially those that occurred seven, fourteen, twenty-one, or twenty-eight years ago, when Saturn also contacted your Sun. Do the same with regrets, which are likely to come to the forefront now; recognize them, resolve them, and put them behind you. Then you'll be ready for new beginnings when Saturn enters your sign.

This is also the time for completion. Look around you and identify everything that's unfinished, whether it's a project, something you've always wanted to do or learn, or anything else you've perpetually put off until tomorrow. Tomorrow has finally arrived! The more you do to clear the slate now, the better prepared you will be to move forward during the next several years.

This process will be completed in a short time frame—mid-April through June—**if you were born between October 7 and 9**. For **Libras born between October 10 and 14**, the events and thoughts that occur during the first three months of the year will come full circle in July and August. **If your birthday is October 15 or later**, Saturn will contact your Sun in September or October, and again next year **if you were born between October 19 and 22**.

Saturn-Pluto

If you were born between September 23 and 27, you will be among the first of your sign to have Saturn in Libra join your Sun. Although Pluto will contact your Sun throughout 2009, its major influence will be apparent after Saturn enters Libra, October 29.

Saturn's transit to your Sun is a time of rewards, and challenges. It also will bring responsibilities and hard work, and you may feel as though your life is heavily structured, thereby limiting your freedom. This is true to some extent, but it's also your perception of your current life and lifestyle, and the influence of those around you. In reality you are very much in charge of you and your life, and the choices you make now will guide you for the next fourteen years, when Saturn will contact your Sun from Aries, your opposite sign.

Pluto is the planet of transformation, discarding the old and reworking it into something new. In essence this is what Pluto will do this year as it forms a difficult contact with your Sun from Capricorn. Pluto is all about power and control, so at times you will feel in control of yourself and your environment, and at other times completely the opposite. This is all part of Pluto's learning process that can be captured in a word: self-control. Master that and you will emerge from this Pluto-Sun transit in a much stronger position to move forward in the world.

There is no denying that life will be challenging—even difficult—at times with both Saturn and Pluto contacting your Sun. And with Pluto in your solar fourth house, events will be centered in your domestic and family life. If a relationship is unsteady, this planetary alignment could trigger a break, mostly because you are evolving and becoming a "new" person, redefining yourself with fresh goals and personal ambitions that clash with your old way of life. Another person (or other people) is merely the catalyst. You also could find it necessary to assume responsibility for an elderly parent or relative. But you should try to avoid becoming a full-time caregiver for this person, because it could be extremely disruptive to your own family life.

On a practical level, you'll want to be sure your home is fully insured and to promptly deal with any needed repairs. Make regular visual inspections of your property and educate yourself on what to look for if you live in an area prone to termite damage. One of the best uses of the Saturn/Pluto transit would be major home renovations, as well as cleaning out storage spaces, discarding unwanted items, and de-cluttering, all with the intent to allow fresh energy into your home.

Uranus

If you were born between October 12 and 19, you can expect changes in your work life to a greater or lesser extent as Uranus contacts your Sun from Pisces. Events will unfold rapidly in February **if your birthday is between October 13 and 15**, and in September **if you were born between October 17 and 19**, the times when Saturn and Uranus will form an exact alignment.

You could find yourself suddenly unemployed or suddenly promoted, or a new job opportunity could unexpectedly appear. If you have a choice in the matter, consider all the potential ramifications, positive and negative, in your decision-making process. This is vital because your work life will continue to be somewhat unstable until Uranus moves into Aries the middle of next year (2010).

It's equally possible you'll feel the increasing urge to move on, to find a job that's a better fit with your skills and talents. But the challenge will be to decide what job, what career, what direction to take next. With a myriad of possibilities, your thoughts will drift here, there, and everywhere, and it will be difficult to set your sights on a clear goal. Be patient if this is how you feel. In time you'll gain the needed focus and the future will come together.

Neptune

If you were born between October 14 and 19, mystical Neptune will favorably contact your Sun from Aquarius, your solar fifth house. Your sixth sense will get a boost from this transit, and you can easily tap into the inspiration and creativity that are Neptune at its best. Your faith in yourself will grow, and you'll feel a spiritual connection with the universe. The romance of a lifetime could bloom when someone new walks into your life and love at first sight sparkles with promise.

Even this positive contact to your Sun has its potential downside, however. Idealistic Neptune can encourage you to see life, people, and yourself as you wish them to be, not as they are. So be cautious in matters of the heart, as well as finances. There is no such thing as a safe bet. You also can choose to daydream your way through this period, filling your mind with idle hopes and wishes. But that would be a waste of this marvelous creative energy urging you to express your talents.

♎ Libra/January ♎

Planetary Hotspots

January has all the potential to be an upbeat domestic month. But there's also the chance for conflict and controversy at month's end. Keep your cool when retrograde Mercury meets Mars in Capricorn and put important family decisions on hold until mid-February. It will be tough to get everyone on the same wavelength. A mechanical problem is also possible so keep an eye on appliances. Domestic repairs are best left to experts; it will be less expensive in the long run.

Planetary Lightspots

Despite the potential domestic downside, January is also filled with busy days and lots of family activities. If you want to get your place in shape, now is the time. Favorable planetary alignments are ideal for cleaning, de-cluttering, and organizing. Then show off the results by hosting a get-together the fourth weekend of the month.

Relationships

The week of the January 26 New Moon in Aquarius, your solar fifth house, is one of the best for romance, socializing, and play, especially because it's preceded by Jupiter's January 5 arrival in the same sign. If you're a parent, or hope to be, you could have much to cheer about, and if you're single, someone exciting could walk into your life.

Money and Success

You'll be an attention-getter around the time of the January 10 Full Moon in Cancer, your career sector. And with Venus, your ruling planet, in Pisces, your solar sixth house of daily work, you could see more money in your paycheck. But you'll also want to be aware of who's saying and doing what the last week of the month, when you could catch a hint of changes on the horizon.

Rewarding Days

1, 4, 17, 20, 21, 25, 26, 27, 31

Challenging Days

2, 3, 9, 16, 29, 30

♎ Libra/February ♎

Planetary Hotspots

A friend or romantic interest could disappoint you the week of the February 9 Full Moon (and lunar eclipse) in Leo, which is closely aligned with Neptune. Take it in stride and consider it a lesson in human nature. The same could happen with a group association such as a club or organization when you discover your mission and values differ from theirs.

Planetary Lightspots

Playtime and socializing are in the forecast, thanks to Mars, which dashes into Aquarius, your solar fifth house, on the 3rd, followed by Mercury on the 14th. That's also an ideal combination for romance for couples and singles alike. If you're searching for love, a magical someone could sweep you off your feet sometime during the last two weeks of February.

Relationships

Family relationships benefit from open communication as Mercury travels in Capricorn, your domestic sector, through the 13th. Take advantage of the opportunity to clear up any misunderstandings that occurred while Mercury was retrograde last month. Overall, close relationships are at their best in mid-February when Venus in Aries, your solar seventh house, connects with Mars and Jupiter.

Money and Success

The first Saturn-Uranus alignment of 2009 activates your solar sixth/twelfth house axis February 5. You can expect workplace tension and change, possibly because of a company shake-up. There will be little you can do other than to go with the flow and protect your position. Fortunately, the stress begins to ease around the time of the February 24 New Moon in Pisces, your solar sixth house.

Rewarding Days

3, 4, 7, 13, 17, 19, 22, 23, 27, 28

Challenging Days

5, 6, 10, 11, 12, 18, 25, 26

Libra/March

Planetary Hotspots

Be prepared. At least some personal plans will stall from the 6th through mid-April as Venus, your ruling planet, travels retrograde. Placed in Aries, your solar seventh house, it's also likely to affect some close relationships. If your feelings are wavering, consider putting the decision on hold until the end of May, when all will become clear. This is not the time to make a romantic commitment or to form a business partnership.

Planetary Lightspots

Looking for a slimmer, trimmer you? Now is the time to get started. With Mars in Aquarius, your solar fifth house, through the 13th, you can more easily begin a regular exercise program. Start slowly and give your body a chance to adapt. Join a gym, walk with neighbors, or give yoga a try. Also schedule a checkup if you haven't had one in a while.

Relationships

Your social life gets interesting the first week of March, with Mercury in Aquarius, your solar fifth house. This is also a terrific influence for parents and children, and you'll both enjoy doing things together. Family relationships, however, could be rocky around the time of the March 26 New Moon in Aries, which contacts Pluto in Capricorn, your solar fourth house. Be especially tactful.

Money and Success

Tension surrounds your work life when the Virgo Full Moon on the 10th activates Saturn and Uranus. Expect more change, frustration, and added responsibilities. This might be enough to push you to seek a new position. That may or may not be the best thing to do because you could simply go from one difficult situation to another. More promising opportunities may appear this summer.

Rewarding Days

3, 7, 8, 12, 13, 20, 21, 22, 27, 30

Challenging Days

4, 5, 6, 11, 17, 18, 19, 25, 31

Libra/April

Planetary Hotspots

The pace picks up at work through the 21st thanks to Mars in Pisces, your solar sixth house. It's also likely to spark conflict, so keep your cool and use your tactful charm when difficult situations and people get to you. It will be a challenge because retrograde Venus slips back into Pisces on the 11th. Fortunately, Venus turns direct on the 17th, so month's end is a much calmer environment.

Planetary Lightspots

The bright, shiny April 9 Full Moon in Libra has you in its spotlight. It's beautifully aligned with Jupiter and Neptune in Aquarius, your solar fifth house, which is ideal for romance, creativity, and memorable moments with your children. Make all a part of your life that week, and also pamper yourself with a massage or spa day.

Relationships

Much of the month features positive personal relationships. But retrograde Venus in Aries, your solar seventh house, through the 10th can trigger misunderstandings. Take the initiative to clear up any lingering issues once this planet turns direct and returns to Aries on the 24th. A family clash is possible in both early and late April, possibly because of an extra expense for a home repair. Check credentials before you hire anyone.

Money and Success

The April 24 New Moon in Taurus spotlights your solar eighth house of joint resources. It could boost your bank account with a raise or cost-saving perk. Any financial dealings, however, require careful attention. Read all the fine print if you apply for a mortgage, refinance your home, or make an interest-free major purchase. There could be a catch.

Rewarding Days

4, 8, 9, 16, 18, 19, 20, 23, 24, 30

Challenging Days

1, 3, 7, 13, 14, 15, 22, 26, 28

Libra/May

Planetary Hotspots

May is mostly easygoing with one exception: Mercury turns retrograde in Gemini on the 7th, and retreats into Taurus on the 13th. That's sure to restrict the information flow and can also cause mix-ups in money matters. Check statements as soon as they arrive and pay bills early. Better yet, hold off on major purchases, new credit, and major financial decisions until later in June.

Planetary Lightspots

Travel appeals to you with this month's New Moon in Gemini, your solar ninth house, on the 24th. But a better choice might be to make reservations for a summer trip. With Mercury retrograde much of the month, lost luggage and delays are possible. Check out nearby locations instead. It's a good alternative to satisfy your curiosity and sense of adventure.

Relationships

Relationships benefit from Venus and Mars in Aries, your solar seventh house. The duo is a plus for everything from love to social events to passionate moments. Singles looking for a new romance could make a match the last week of May, which is also a great time for family activities. With warmer temperatures and summer on the way, why not join your kids in tennis lessons?

Money and Success

You could end the month with a bigger bank balance, thanks to the May 9 Full Moon in Scorpio, which could trigger a small windfall or a long-awaited check. Get things moving by cleaning closets and drawers, the basement and garage. Then cash in on unneeded items at a consignment shop or neighborhood yard sale, both of which could net you a tidy profit.

Rewarding Days

2, 6, 7, 10, 11, 15, 16, 21, 24, 28

Challenging Days

1, 4, 5, 12, 13, 17, 18, 20, 25, 27

Libra/June

Planetary Hotspots

A mechanical problem with your car or an appliance could pop up the week of the June 7 Full Moon in Sagittarius, your solar third house. On another level, your thoughts will turn to the past, and regrets and worries will occupy your mind. Take action to resolve what you can't change, possibly through a self-help book or support group, and do the same with current situations that hold you back.

Planetary Lightspots

Early June brings positive planetary alignments with Pluto in Capricorn, your solar fourth house. Put them to good use around the house to get your place in shape for summer, inside and out. A careful search could yield bargains in home décor, and creative solutions can save money. Use the difference for new furnishings.

Relationships

Stay tuned for good news the first week of June as Venus in Aries, your solar seventh house, connects favorably with Jupiter and Neptune. That's also a terrific time for socializing and romance, as is midmonth, when you can have positive, productive discussions with relatives and coworkers. Month's end is a different story, however. Avoid touchy subjects at home and at work.

Money and Success

Mars spends all of June in Taurus, your solar eighth house, where it's joined by Mercury through the 12th and Venus from the 6th on. That's a recipe for profit that could earn you or your partner a nice raise or gift from a family member. But think again if your thoughts drift toward a home-based business around the time of the June 22 New Moon in Cancer, your career sector. It's unlikely to develop as you wish.

Rewarding Days

6, 9, 12, 17, 19, 20, 23, 24, 29, 30

Challenging Days

1, 2, 7, 8, 11, 13, 15, 22, 25, 28

Libra/July

Planetary Hotspots

Finances require restraint if you hope to see your bank balance rise by midmonth. Venus in Taurus, your solar eighth house, through July 4, and Mars in the same sign through the 10th have all the potential to net some nice gains, including a raise. But you're also in the mood to spend, and weekend and evening fun can get expensive if you're not careful. Set a budget and stick to it.

Planetary Lightspots

The urge for fresh scenery and new adventures is triggered by three planets moving through Gemini, your solar ninth house, at various times this month. Take a long weekend at a nearby destination or plan a vacation for August. Next month might be a better choice for travel because career commitments will keep you busy now. Traveling on business? Grab an extra day or two for you.

Relationships

Jupiter and Neptune join forces in Aquarius, your solar Fifth House, making this month terrific for love and romance. Complementing that lineup is Mercury in Leo, your friendship sector from July 17 on and the Sun in the same sign after the 21st. See friends, join another family for a day of amusement, and consider hosting a casual event the week of the July 7 Full Moon in Capricorn.

Money and Success

July has the potential to be your best career month of the year, thanks to Mercury in Cancer, your solar tenth house, July 3–16. Promote yourself, offer to do presentations, talk with people. All can contribute to the potential of the July 21 Cancer New Moon which aligns beautifully with Uranus in Pisces, your solar sixth house of daily work. That equation could equal a major success, job offer, or added responsibilities you welcome.

Rewarding Days

3, 8, 9, 14, 18, 22, 23, 26, 27

Challenging Days

4, 5, 6, 13, 19, 24, 25

♎ Libra/August ♎

Planetary Hotspots

Tension rises in early and late August when several planets clash with Mars and Pluto. Accomplishing much of anything will be a challenge at best, and the better choice is to stay on the sidelines rather than get involved in conflict despite your frustration. No matter what you say, people are unlikely to change their thinking or to fulfill your needs and requests.

Planetary Lightspots

Take that vacation as Mars advances in Gemini, your solar ninth house, through the 24th. Midmonth is a good choice to get the best of August's planetary lineups. Consider a trip with friends to a resort or rent a beach cottage with another family that offers plenty of activities for kids. Even business travel is refreshing and it could link you with a networking contact or a new romantic interest.

Relationships

Between the August 5 Full Moon in Aquarius, your solar fifth house, and the New Moon in Leo, your friendship sector, on the 20th, your August calendar is made to order for summer outings and get-togethers. But don't put too much faith in a friend who makes a big promise; it's unlikely your pal will deliver. The same applies if you feel an instant attraction to someone. Take things slowly.

Money and Success

Your work life is both satisfying and stressful as easy weeks alternate with difficult ones. Work ahead as much as possible, and be sure to confirm instructions. Also listen to rumors and your sixth sense the last two weeks of August. You could pick up on emerging developments and thus be better prepared for next month's Saturn/Uranus alignment.

Rewarding Days

4, 6, 11, 14, 18, 19, 20, 23, 24, 27

Challenging Days

1, 2, 8, 9, 15, 16, 21, 22, 26, 29

♎ Libra/September ♎

Planetary Hotspots

Your solar twelfth and sixth houses are this month's hotspot as Saturn and Uranus connect for the last time in Virgo/Pisces. The alignment is activated by the September 18 New Moon in Virgo so expect that week to be stressful. These two planets last met in February; circumstances and situations will be similar this time regarding your job, including the potential for sudden changes. But with Mercury retrograde from the 7th on, first in Libra and then in Virgo, you'll want to postpone major personal decisions until later in October. You also should monitor your health. Get a check-up if it's been a while, and do your best to prevent a cold or other virus.

Planetary Lightspots

Kick back and give yourself the gift of relaxing evenings and weekends after Venus enters Virgo on the 20th. Do something nice for yourself and share your time with loved ones, who will appreciate the extra attention as much as you will.

Relationships

Friendship is at its best while Venus is in Leo, your solar eleventh house, through the 19th. But a clash with a relative or someone in the workplace can make life difficult. Choose your words with care and resist the urge to vent your true feelings, which could have repercussions this month or next.

Money and Success

Despite the potential downside and stress associated with your work life, you'll also have fulfilling days, especially around the time of the September 4 Full Moon in Pisces, your solar sixth house. Initiative and high energy can help you make your mark with Mars in Cancer, your career sector, but be careful not to step on toes.

Rewarding Days

1, 2, 7, 11, 13, 15, 20, 21, 24, 28, 29

Challenging Days

3, 5, 6, 10, 12, 18, 19, 22, 25

♎ Libra/October ♎

Planetary Hotspots

Mercury and Venus in Virgo continue to activate last month's Saturn/Uranus alignment during the first two weeks of October. Consider this an opportunity to resolve any lingering issues in preparation for Saturn's October 29 arrival in your sign. Even though Saturn will briefly return to Virgo next spring, now is the time to plan for the next exciting phase of personal growth. And with the New Moon in your sign on the 18th, you'll have the backing of the fresh start indicated by this lunar energy.

Planetary Lightspots

The New Moon is one great reason for an October celebration. Venus is another. Your ruling planet arrives in your sign on the 14th to boost your powers of attraction. You'll feel at one with yourself with this positive influence, confident, self-assured, and ready to welcome all that you wish for. Make it happen!

Relationships

The October 4 Full Moon in Aries, your solar seventh house, has the potential to connect you with many people in your career and personal life. They'll support your efforts, as you will theirs, and for many Libras this will be a bright spot in a close relationship. Your solar fifth house is also in the picture as several planets activate Jupiter and Neptune in Aquarius to boost your social life. But family relationships may be challenging midmonth.

Money and Success

Mars in Cancer continues to activate your career sector through the 15th, where it could trigger a job offer or a step up. At month's end the Sun and Mercury advance into Scorpio, your solar second house, to put a positive spin on finances.

Rewarding Days

8, 11, 12, 13, 16, 17, 20, 21, 25, 26, 31

Challenging Days

2, 3, 9, 15, 18, 22, 23, 24, 30

♎ **Libra/November** ♎

Planetary Hotspots

Saturn in Libra and Pluto in Capricorn square off in your solar first and fourth houses. Although it will be December before you experience this influence to its fullest, you can expect it to involve your domestic life, especially if your birthday is near September 22. A major home repair is a possibility or a relative may need your assistance. This is not the time, however, to begin a home improvement project or to welcome a new roommate.

Planetary Lightspots

The daily pace is sure to pick up when Mercury arrives in Sagittarius, your solar third house, on the 15th, followed by the Sun on the 21st. Both these planets also have the potential to put you in touch with interesting people, one of whom could be a valuable career connection. Socialize and network at every opportunity, and get acquainted with your neighbors.

Relationships

Mars is in Leo, your solar eleventh house, throughout November. In fact, it will be there until early June because it turns retrograde next month. Take advantage of this high-energy planet to get involved in a club, professional organization, or interest group where you can meet people and be a leader. Even if it doesn't last, you'll benefit from the connection and it will fulfill a purpose.

Money and Success

Finances get a boost from this month's Full Moon on the 2nd and New Moon on the 16th in Taurus/Scorpio, your money sectors. Even better is Venus, which arrives in Scorpio on the 7th. Build up your bank balance! But don't risk your hard-earned money on anything that sounds like a sure bet. Chances are, it will leave you poorer but wiser.

Rewarding Days

4, 5, 7, 8, 13, 14, 17, 20, 21, 22, 28

Challenging Days

2, 6, 9, 11, 12, 19, 23, 25, 27, 30

 Libra/December

Planetary Hotspots

Mercury in Capricorn, your solar fourth house, from the 6th on activates last month's Saturn/Pluto alignment, as does the Sun in the same sign after the 20th. You'll feel the stress and strain in your domestic sector throughout much of December, but events will continue to evolve into January because Mercury turns retrograde on the 26th. This is not the time to buy or sell property, especially with anyone who's not a legal partner, or to initiate major household changes. Be sure your home is adequately insured. You also might find much of your time occupied with added family responsibilities.

Planetary Lightspots

You have an extra special way with words through the 24th, thanks to Venus and the December 16th New Moon in Sagittarius, your solar third house of communication. Both can trigger unexpected good news, and your thinking is sharp and on target. If you're an avid reader you'll be more so this month, so stock up on books.

Relationships

Mars turns retrograde in Leo, your friendship sector, on the 20th. That will undoubtedly slow the social pace, but not throughout much of December because this month also features the final Jupiter-Neptune merger in Aquarius, your solar fifth house. Make the most of it and enjoy the holidays with your favorite people.

Money and Success

The year draws to a close under the December 31 Full Moon (and lunar eclipse) in Cancer, your career sector. This eclipse will prompt some Libras to retire. If you're among them, give the decision serious thought and decide first what you plan to do with those extra hours. If you're still on your way up the career ladder, be prepared for major developments in 2010. Position yourself.

Rewarding Days

5, 6, 11, 12, 14, 15, 16, 19, 21, 23, 25

Challenging Days

3, 7, 9, 10, 13, 20, 24, 28, 29, 31

Libra Action Table

These dates reflect the best—but not the only—times for success and ease in these activities, according to your Sun sign.

	JAN	FEB	MAR	APR	MAY	JUN	JUL	AUG	SEPT	OCT	NOV	DEC
Move	1-4					9-10					19-20	8-9, 17-18
Start a class		17-18				5	31	1		21-22	17-18, 22-23, 27-28	1-5
Join a club					1-2		22-31	1		17-22	8-9	6-7
Ask for a raise	19							25			16	
Look for work	28-29		15-19	20-21						28-29		
Get pro advice		4-5, 27		23-24							27	
Get a loan		2-3										
See a doctor		24-25		20-21		21		21		14	10-11	
Start a diet				20-21			11					
End relationship				24	20-21							
Buy clothes		22								26-27		
Get a makeover		12-13					26-27			16-17		10
New romance		8								25-28		19-20
Vacation							12-30					

SCORPIO

The Scorpion
October 22 to November 22

♏

Element: Water

Quality: Fixed

Polarity: Yin/feminine

Planetary Ruler: Pluto (Mars)

Meditation: I can surrender my feelings

Gemstone: Topaz

Power Stones: Obsidian, amber, citrine, garnet, pearl

Key Phrase: I create

Glyph: Scorpion's tail

Anatomy: Reproductive system

Color: Burgundy, black

Animal: Reptiles, scorpions, birds of prey

Myths/Legends: The Phoenix, Hades and Persephone, Shiva

House: Eighth

Opposite Sign: Taurus

Flower: Chrysanthemum

Key Word: Intensity

Your Strengths and Challenges

As a Scorpio you take life seriously, and at times you feel you're on a path of destiny as you pursue your life purpose. Your soul runs deep and you have an innate understanding of both the light and dark sides of life.

Your determination is relentless and you'll push yourself to the point of exhaustion to achieve a goal, which can be detrimental to your health. Obstacles are irrelevant to you and your willpower is in a class of its own. Anyone who tries to circumvent your efforts soon learns you will not be deterred, sometimes to the point of ruthlessness.

You have a magnetic, mesmerizing charisma that intrigues those around you. Yet you're cautious about expressing your views. When you do, you need only a few words to say it all. This adds to your mysterious aura, as does your classic poker face that reveals nothing—even when you're seething inside. Your steely mask is also your magic wand because you're an expert at keeping people guessing.

You're intuitive (and possibly psychic), perceptive and shrewd, all of which gives you a decided edge. Besides being a step ahead of most everyone, you watch and wait and take action only when the timing is to your advantage.

But you're also intense, and some Scorpios are controlling and manipulative, using their personal power to dominate others rather than to better themselves and their own lives.

Your Relationships

People place their trust in you because they recognize your honesty and integrity. They also share secrets because they know you respect a confidence. Your circle of friends and acquaintances is wide, but you know them far better than they know you. This gives you a distinct advantage in just about every area of life.

You're a romantic with a big heart. But you're hesitant to express your emotions until you're sure the feeling is mutual. It's a matter of self-protection; only those who know you well are aware of your sensitive soul. Your passion runs deep once you find your soul mate, but you can be possessive and even jealous, as can your mate. Trust, however, is what builds a foundation for lasting love. You could find happiness with one of the earth signs—Virgo, Capricorn, and especially Taurus, your opposite sign. Compatibility runs high with your fellow water signs, Cancer and Pisces, but you could clash with dramatic Leo or independent Aquarius.

You like to be in control of your environment. That may be achievable in some arenas, but probably not in your home life. There, anything goes and the unexpected is often the norm rather than the exception. Many Scorpios opt for contemporary home décor or an eclectic mix that makes a statement. Family communication is also important to you, and there are impromptu gatherings of friends in your home. As a parent you're protective of your children and can be a powerful motivational force in their lives. But you also tend to see the best in them when a more realistic view would be to their advantage. Find a balance between spoiling them and giving them the life skills they need.

You're choosy about your friends. You have many acquaintances, some of whom are business colleagues, but your inner circle is small and select. The social circuit isn't your scene; you much prefer casual evenings and lively conversation with people you know well. And more than a few Scorpios cherish their pets as best friends. You also might develop good friends through involvement in a charitable or service organization, which is a great way for Scorpios to network and meet new people.

Your Career and Money

Think big and think "big cheese." That's you! You have great potential to achieve a top career spot where you can grab more than a little limelight. Develop your leadership skills on the way up as you encourage others. Then you'll have the supporters you need when you need them. You prefer a fast-paced work environment where your initiative is valued. Endless meetings are not for you; neither is sitting behind a desk. If your career requires an office workplace, be sure any job comes with enough freedom to structure your work so you don't feel hemmed in.

Your earning power is among the best of the zodiac. You also go on occasional spending sprees. That's great when you can afford it, but don't go into debt to get what you want. Despite your financial savvy, income and expenses fluctuate somewhat so it's wise to plan ahead. You could do well with investments if you take the time to do thorough research, and can often find the best interest rates.

Always read the fine print before signing any contract, even those that appear to be routine.

Your Lighter Side

Scorpio is the sign of transformation, something you do almost unconsciously. You can take someone else's junk and transform it into something beautiful or useful, or resurrect what others have written off as a long-lost cause. Personally, you have the inner strength to reinvent yourself physically and mentally. What others call hurdles, you call possibilities.

Affirmation for the Year

People and knowledge enrich my life.

The Year Ahead for Scorpio

Your domestic life will benefit from lucky Jupiter in Aquarius, your solar fourth house of home and family. This happy influence will fill your year with upbeat and memorable events with friends and family, all centered in your home.

You might decide to purchase or rent a new home that, if not your ultimate dream home, will at least come close to it. If you're content with your current location, you could add on, redecorate, or remodel to suit your needs. For some Scorpios this expansion is triggered by an addition to the family.

This is a great time to get involved in your community or home-owners association as a volunteer or elected official, or to lend your expertise to a charitable organization or another project to benefit your city or neighborhood. Among the many people you'll meet could be several who become lifelong friends and possibly someone who benefits your career. This will help to satisfy your current need to establish roots and to create the feeling of security that can come through an investment of time, energy, and commitment in your immediate environment.

You'll want to splurge on your home and family this year. Go for it if you have the disposable income, but don't go into debt. Spoil those you love—and yourself—a little, but keep in mind that if you overdo it with your children now, they'll see that as the new norm and expect even more. Give them quality and quantity time instead; share your love more than your money.

Some family members will be open to your requests and willing to do all they can to help you. The more likely scenario, with compassionate Neptune also in Aquarius, is that a relative will look to you for financial assistance. Only you can decide whether to lend a hand, but keep in mind that a loan probably won't be repaid.

Be sure to check credentials and references before you hire a contractor to do home improvements. Do the same if you plan to work with a realtor for a home purchase. Whether you rent or buy, take the time to drive by the property morning and evening, week-day and weekend. Also be sure to include an inspection clause in a real estate purchase contract before you make an offer. Buy less than you can afford and carefully read all documents so you don't end up with an expensive financial surprise in the future. You might also want to consider flood insurance if your home could be at risk.

It would be a good idea to get acquainted with your children's friends this year, and to be alert for times when peer pressure could become a problem. And if you have teens, don't tempt them by leaving them home alone when you're out of town.

Saturn spends most of the year in Virgo, your solar eleventh house, moving on to Libra on October 29. (It will briefly return to Virgo next year.) Known as the karmic planet, Saturn in your friendship sector can put you in touch with soul mates and people from the past. Each person who comes into your life will have a purpose that goes beyond socializing, and some will become career contacts. You'll know you've made a karmic connection because there will be an instant attraction, although not necessarily a positive one. In fact, you may at first dislike the very person who can do you the greatest good and teach you a valuable lesson. Saturn works two ways; you're also in a position this year to do the same for others by sharing your knowledge and experience through word and deed.

Virgo is also your solar sign of groups, which reinforces the Jupiter-Neptune in Aquarius influence. That's all the more reason to invest your skills and talents in a community or neighborhood cause or to join a group of like-minded people who want to change the world—or a small part of it—to make it better for everyone. But you could easily end up doing most of the work yourself, whether by choice or chance. Saturn here is a lesson in teamwork and sharing the load, and an opportunity to hone your leadership skills.

Part of Saturn's story this year is its exact alignment with Uranus in Pisces, your solar fifth house of creativity, recreation, romance, and children. This planet of the unexpected adds another dimension to Saturn's 2009 influence. Saturn represents stability, and Uranus represents change, so the two are definitely at odds. Blending the diverse energy will be a challenge, and much of it will involve other people. Think back to November 2008. The events that occurred then may give you a clue about what to expect from these two planets this year.

The Saturn/Uranus alignment could trigger the sudden reappearance of an old friend or classmate, someone you haven't seen in years. A former romantic interest could also reappear and express interest in resuming a relationship. Only you can make that decision, but think carefully and remember all the reasons you parted ways. People rarely change, at least not their basic personalities.

If you're a parent, your children can benefit from your increased involvement in their lives. They could surprise you in some way, such as the sudden surfacing of a hidden talent, so do all you can to support and encourage them in both ongoing and new interests. You could have an emerging star on your hands. Also provide the structure children need and deliver a consistent message, day in and day out.

Explore your own creativity through a new hobby or by perfecting skills. You might discover you have a talent that could become a sideline business endeavor in time. Aim for what's practical and useful, be innovative, and create a new mousetrap!

You'll also want to be cautious with investments and other financial matters, especially in February and September, when Saturn and Uranus will form an exact alignment.

Once Saturn moves on to Libra, your solar twelfth house, you'll be content to step out of the social scene to spend more time with yourself, and your favorite solo activities. During the next few years you should evaluate your life and the overall progress you've made. Congratulate yourself on your successes and resolve any regrets, even those from the distant past. This will prepare you for Saturn's arrival in your sign in 2012, when you'll begin a new phase of personal development and explore new directions.

On a practical level, you might have to purchase a new vehicle during the last two months of 2009, when Saturn in Libra clashes with Pluto in Capricorn, your solar third house. That's definitely a time when you'll want to be extra cautious on the road.

Also be cautious about what you say and write to whom. It will be easy to hit the "send" button on an e-mail when you're upset or frustrated, both of which are possible with this Saturn/Pluto alignment. Knowing who's a supporter and who's not could be a challenge as well, so use your Scorpio sixth sense and willpower, listen, observe, and reveal little about what you know. A power struggle is possible with this configuration.

Like Saturn in Libra, Pluto will give you much to think about this year, and your thoughts will turn inward. Try not to dwell on what you can't change. Take action instead and let Pluto, your ruling planet, empower you and your determination to succeed.

What This Year's Eclipses Mean for You

There will be six eclipses this year, unlike the usual four. Three of them will span your solar third/ninth house axis, and the others your solar fourth/tenth house axis.

The July 7 lunar eclipse in Capricorn, your solar third house, and the two Capricorn eclipses in Cancer (solar eclipse, July 22, and lunar eclipse December 31) will spark your interest in travel and learning the second half of the year and into 2010. Plan a luxury trip to an exotic destination or a romantic getaway, or re-center with a series of weekend trips to nearby locations. Where you go is irrelevant. What's important is to expand your horizons. You might also want to consider a week-long gourmet cooking school in a relaxing setting, or join a group on a historical tour. But try to go before Saturn activates Pluto the end of October; otherwise you could experience delays, difficulties, and cancellations.

The Cancer/Capricorn emphasis is equally good for learning. Take a class for the fun of it or one to boost your job skills, or learn a new language. If you feel especially ambitious, consider returning to school for a degree or advanced certification to enhance your marketability. Overall, the energy generated by these eclipses (and Pluto in Capricorn) will motivate you to read and learn, to expand your knowledge of your immediate environment and the world at large, and to better understand yourself and what you want from life.

The other three eclipses, in Leo and Aquarius, will focus your attention on home, family, and career. This year-long influence can stretch you thin as you try to juggle all three. Fortunately, you'll have help from Jupiter, which enters Aquarius just two days before the January 7 solar eclipse in the same sign. An August 6 lunar eclipse, also in Aquarius, keeps the energy flowing the rest of the year. The combination is enough to trigger a local or long-distance move for some Scorpios. This could be the net result of a February 9 lunar eclipse in Leo, your career sign, which will increase your visibility and the potential for a new position or promotion.

Saturn

If you were born between November 6 and 21, Saturn will connect with your Sun from Virgo, your solar Eleventh House. This favorable contact can bring you wonderful opportunities to meet new people, get involved in a good cause, and simply enjoy lazy days and evenings with your closest friends.

People from the past are likely to reenter your life. One of them, or someone new, could become a lifetime friend—a soul mate friendship that's secure and comfortable, from the first, with an instant rapport that makes you feel as though you've known each other forever. You also could be involved with elderly people or establish a firm friendship with someone who's much older than you and have some responsibility for his or her care.

There is one potential pitfall, however. When Saturn, the teacher, is in the eleventh house, the lesson is teamwork. That might be a challenge for you because you like taking charge and being in charge. But you can have the best of both this year if you're open to other ideas and willingly share the load and the limelight. Remember, a good leader is also a good follower.

This Saturn challenge is likely to be more pronounced **if you were born between November 6 and 13.** The influence will be strongest April through June **if you were born between November 6 and 8,** and in January through March and July and August **if your birthday is between November 9 and 13.**

Saturn-Pluto

If you were born between October 23 and 27, Pluto in Capricorn, your solar Third House, will contact your Sun off and on throughout 2009. This favorable connection will encourage deep thinking as it motivates you to question everything from long-held beliefs to the mysteries of life to your identity and desires. These feelings and thoughts will become more pronounced once Saturn enters Libra October 29. With both planets contacting your Sun through year's end, you'll delve more deeply into your subconscious and strive to understand why you think and act the way you do. Seek realistic answers and take action to resolve any regrets that surface. If you and a sibling, or another relative, have had difficulties in the past, this is the time to address them. Even if the outcome changes nothing, you will feel at peace for having made the effort.

On a practical level, use your common sense when you're out and about, even in your own neighborhood. If you walk, go with a group. If you're going somewhere new, get exact directions and go with a friend or family member. It's also possible you could have a problem with a noisy or otherwise difficult neighbor, or need to adapt to neighborhood changes, such as a new street or utility work.

Uranus

If you were born between November 11 and 18, expect the unexpected in your social life and your love life as Uranus contacts your Sun from Pisces, your solar fifth house. With this quirky planet in favorable alignment with your Sun, you'll have plenty of pleasant surprises to keep your evenings and weekends lively, including the chance for love at first sight. You might even surprise yourself and actually welcome impromptu get-togethers as Uranus increases your comfort level with change—at least to a point! This Uranus-Sun contact is also a plus if you're a parent. Your children can enlighten you if you let them, and you can do the same for them.

Uranus doesn't operate solo this year, however. It will form an exact alignment with Saturn in Virgo, across your solar fifth/eleventh house axis, in February and September. You can manage this diverse energy more easily than many signs because both planets are in signs favorable to yours. Even so, a close relationship—child, friend, lover—will be stressful on some level during those months. Sometimes the best choice is the toughest one, and the more difficult path can yield the greatest rewards.

Neptune

If you were born between November 14 and 18, Neptune will contact your Sun from Aquarius, your solar fourth house. Check your home periodically for water leaks—pipes, water heater, appliances, etc. Something simple to repair is likely, but a full-fledged flood, or even a gas leak, is possible. Be sure your home is fully covered by a reputable insurance company, and be cautious about whom you hire for home improvements or repairs.

Neptune also will operate on a more intangible level this year. You'll be inspired and disappointed, creative and disillusioned. It all goes with the territory when Neptune is involved with your Sun. But the high points are likely to outweigh the low ones. Do yourself a favor and put your faith in yourself rather than other people; it will lessen the chance for Neptune's downside to emerge. Even so, a family member is likely to let you down in some way. That's human nature and also your perspective. Be realistic and try not to put anyone on a pedestal.

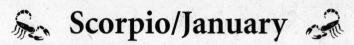# Scorpio/January

Planetary Hotspots

Your spirit of adventure comes alive under the January 10 Full Moon in Cancer. If you plan to travel, try to do it that week rather than at month's end when retrograde Mercury will join forces with Mars in Capricorn, your solar third house of quick trips and communication. The Mercury-Mars union could trigger the need for a car repair, and you also should be alert on the road. Ease up on the gas.

Planetary Lightspots

Home life appeals to you in 2009 more than it has in recent memory, thanks to Jupiter, which enters Aquarius, your solar fourth house, January 5. Outline home improvement plans for this spring and summer, but wait until mid-February to set them in motion. With Mercury retrograde this month, the best ideas will surface in February and March.

Relationships

Look forward to plenty of opportunities for socializing and romance as Venus advances in Pisces, your solar fifth house. A new love relationship is possible the third full week of January when Venus aligns with several planets. But don't be quick to shun anyone who doesn't fit your idea of perfection. He or she might be your soul mate. If you're a parent you can be your children's best motivator and example this month.

Money and Success

Life perks along in this area throughout January. Use the time to reinforce your position by speaking up. Be a leader and share your great ideas. People will eventually adopt them even if they're not initially accepted. Give some thought to your career goals for the year ahead and develop a realistic plan to implement them.

Rewarding Days

1, 5, 6, 10, 13, 18, 19, 23, 28

Challenging Days

2, 3, 9, 15, 16, 29, 30

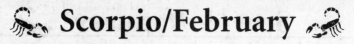 Scorpio/February

Planetary Hotspots
Your career is a hot topic with the February 9 Full Moon (and lunar eclipse) lighting up your solar tenth house. That's great for your worldly ambitions, but career responsibilities can strain family relationships. The goal here is balance. Manage that and you'll benefit from a strong support system and all the benefits that accompany transiting Jupiter in your domestic sector.

Planetary Lightspots
This month's lightspot is yours for the asking as long as you practice effective time management. Family and domestic life has all the potential to be active and rewarding with Mars in Aquarius from February 4 on and Mercury in the same sign after the 13th. Both planets join forces with Jupiter in Aquarius during the last two weeks of the month. Enjoy the company of loved ones, connect with long talks, and work together around the house.

Relationships
Tension surrounds a friendship or dating relationship in early February, when Saturn and Uranus form an exact alignment across your solar fifth/eleventh house axis. You can expect the same stress in any group involvement, where tradition will clash with progress. The best choice might be to cut ties and move on, especially if you were born within a few days of November 13. Be alert and aware of what's going on in your children's lives. Meet their friends, and steer your kids into confidence-building activities.

Money and Success
Except for a stressful few days the first week of the month, your work life is satisfying, fulfilling, and upbeat. The third week of February will be especially rewarding because you have all the potential to be a standout as Venus contacts Mercury, Mars, and Jupiter.

Rewarding Days
3, 10, 15, 17, 19, 21, 24

Challenging Days
1, 5, 6, 18, 25, 26

Scorpio/March

Planetary Hotspots

Venus turns retrograde in Aries, your solar sixth house, on the 6th. As a result you can expect slow progress and mix-ups at work through mid-April. Coworker relationships will cool with this influence and you're unlikely to get the usual support from them. And, some coworkers will be plain difficult this month, controlling and demanding. Keep a record so you can discuss the situation with a supervisor, if necessary.

Planetary Lightspots

You'll enjoy the comforts of home this month—when you have time! With Mercury and Mars in Aquarius, your solar fourth house, home life is hectic. It's also a great month to tackle home repairs and minor improvement projects. Keep an eye on appliances and pipes; one could spring a leak.

Relationships

Despite Venus retrograde, which affects most relationships more or less, March brings you many opportunities to socialize with friends. Some Scorpios feel the zing of love at first sight midmonth when the energy of the March 10 Full Moon in Virgo, your friendship sector, is also active. Take a chance on someone new and ask a friend to arrange a date. If you're a parent, your children will surprise you this month, and it's still wise to monitor their activities and get to know their friends.

Money and Success

Relationships aside, you have a busy month at work ahead of you. Deadline pressures mount as March unfolds, culminating with the March 26 New Moon in Aries, your solar sixth house. That week brings praise and possibly the promise of a raise. Go all-out to impress decision-makers and take minor setbacks in stride.

Rewarding Days

1, 7, 13, 14, 15, 18, 20, 22, 24, 28, 29

Challenging Days

2, 4, 5, 6, 11, 17, 19, 23, 26, 31

Scorpio/April

Planetary Hotspots

April is an easygoing month overall, but you'll have to contend with Venus retrograde, first in Aries and then in Pisces, which it re-enters on the 11th. The good news is Venus turns direct a week later on the 17th and returns to Aries on the 24th. So be ready to use all your charming people skills to deal with the difficult folks you'll encounter both during and after work hours.

Planetary Lightspots

The April 9 Libra Full Moon lights up your solar twelfth house, where it aligns beautifully with Jupiter and Neptune in Aquarius, your domestic sector. This makes home the best getaway to relax and unwind. Give yourself the gift of laid-back evenings—or at least an hour—to read, watch TV or DVDs, or to enjoy quality time with loved ones. Better yet, try for a few days off.

Relationships

Relationships have their bright side this month. Mercury in Taurus, your solar seventh house, has partners on the same wavelength and is ideal for entertaining friends, April 9–29. Aim for the first or second weekend if you want to host a get-together. The April 24 New Moon in Taurus prompts some Scorpios to take a relationship to the next level or to establish a home of their own. This is also a positive influence for professional consultations.

Money and Success

Your solar sixth house is active this month with several planets traveling through Aries, your sign of daily work. You can accomplish a lot, but difficult planetary alignments in early and late April advise against pushing others—or yourself—too hard. Besides, the more you try to fight the tide the less progress you'll make. Let things unfold as they will and save yourself the frustration.

Rewarding Days

4, 6, 7, 11, 16, 20, 24, 25, 29, 30

Challenging Days

1, 3, 8, 13, 14, 22, 26, 27, 28

Scorpio/May

Planetary Hotspots

You'll have to contend with the antics and frustrations of Mercury retrograde the last three weeks of May. It reverses direction on the 7th in Gemini, your solar eighth house of money, so be sure to check statements for errors and pay bills early. If you can possibly avoid it, postpone major purchases and financial decisions until later in June. Mercury then returns to Taurus on the 13th, where it can affect relationships. Clarify thoughts before you speak and choose your words with care so you don't unintentionally upset someone close to you. Also confirm dates, places, and times.

Planetary Lightspots

The May 9 Full Moon in Scorpio is all about you. Take some time that week to pamper yourself with a spa day, a massage, or dinner with someone you love at an elegant upscale restaurant.

Relationships

Other than the potential downside of Mercury retrograde, you'll enjoy seeing friends and spending time with your favorite people as the Sun advances in Taurus through the 19th. They'll inspire and confuse you, amaze and puzzle you. Listen between the lines for the strong motivational message. But be cautious if you need a home repair. Go with someone known and trusted, and if in doubt, get a second opinion. Do the same if you need to consult a professional.

Money and Success

May is a high-powered month at work with Mars in Aries, your solar sixth house, through the 30th. Budget your time to manage the increased workload, and don't rely on others to come through for you. If they do, great. But be sure you have a contingency plan. Venus also spends the month in Aries, which has you among the favored few. Make the most of it.

Rewarding Days

3, 7, 8, 10, 14, 15, 19, 21, 22, 23, 31

Challenging Days

1, 5, 12, 13, 17, 18, 25, 27, 29

Scorpio/June

Planetary Hotspots

June's New Moon in your solar ninth house is usually a positive influence for summer vacation travel. But this year it forms an exact alignment with Pluto in Capricorn. Postpone the trip and enjoy a few days with Jupiter and Neptune in Aquarius and the comforts of home. It's also possible the lunar energy could trigger conflict with an in-law or another relative.

Planetary Lightspots

Venus continues to be your lucky charm at work the first week of June before it moves on to Taurus on the 5th. Talk with people and reinforce your position with great ideas and an outstanding performance. The effort could net rewards before month's end.

Relationships

Mars spends the month in Taurus, your solar seventh house, where it's joined by Mercury through the 12th and Venus from the 6th on. That's a terrific lineup for love, romance, business talks, important appointments, and just about anything that involves other people. They'll be your prime focus this month, and you'll attract the interest and attention of many. Even minor difficulties can be resolved with well-chosen words.

Money and Success

June also has a financial emphasis with the Full Moon in Sagittarius, your solar second house, on the 7th. This is your personal financial sector, and you could feel a pinch that week when extra expenses arise. Your solar eighth house of other people's money is also in the picture with the Sun in Gemini through the 20th, and Mercury in the same sign from the 13th on. That duo could bring a raise or minor windfall just when you need it most. Set aside time to update your budget.

Rewarding Days

4, 6, 8, 9, 10, 14, 18, 23, 24, 26

Challenging Days

1, 3, 5, 11, 15, 21, 22, 25, 27

Scorpio/July

Planetary Hotspots

Relationships range from rocky to rewarding July 1–10. Although you can manage to steer clear of some difficult people, that might be impossible with certain family members. Consider the source, say little, and try not to let them upset you as Venus and Mars in Taurus, your solar seventh house, clash with several planets.

Planetary Lightspots

You have another chance this month to schedule a summer get-away. Aim for midmonth when planetary alignments favor family or romantic fun at a vacation destination. If you plan to attend a reunion you could connect with a potential romantic interest or someone who can help advance your career. The same is true if you plan to travel on business near the July 21 New Moon (and solar eclipse) in Cancer.

Relationships

Take advantage of the July 7 Full Moon (and lunar eclipse) in Capricorn, your solar third house, to meet and get together with neighbors and relatives you enjoy. This Full Moon also forms a beneficial contact with Saturn in Virgo, your solar eleventh house, making July a great month to see friends. Plan social events and also consider a weekend trip with your closest pals where you can relax and talk. If you're involved in a club or organization you might be asked to take on a leadership role, and you also could be successful in spearheading a community project.

Money and Success

Finances are generally positive throughout July, primarily because of Mercury and Venus in Gemini, your solar eighth house. You might even gain from a lucky win in the first few days of July, which are good ones for investing in a lottery pool at work.

Rewarding Days

1, 12, 14, 16, 17, 20, 21, 28, 29

Challenging Days

3, 4, 6, 15, 23, 24, 25, 30

Scorpio/August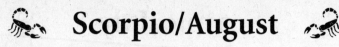

Planetary Hotspots
Try to take it easy at month's end when Mercury is in Libra, your solar twelfth house. Difficult planetary alignments could trigger a cold or mishap, so you'll also want to be extra careful on the road and if you work with tools. People are generally uncooperative in the same time frame when it's best to maintain a low profile. If travel is on your agenda, try to avoid the last week of August.

Planetary Lightspots
Domestic life is at its best the week of the August 5 Full Moon in Aquarius, your solar fourth house. You'll be in sync with your partner and other family members, making this an ideal time to discuss matters important to all of you. Tackle your household to-do list the same week and you can zip through it all in record time.

Relationships
Friendship is all you could wish for this month, thanks to Mercury in Virgo, your solar eleventh house, August 2–24, and the Sun in the same sign after the 21st. Plan a day trip with your best friends, and evenings out where you can socialize with a group. If you're single, ask a pal to introduce you to a potential match midmonth when planetary alignments could trigger a whirlwind romance.

Money and Success
Your August career potential culminates with the New Moon in Leo, your solar tenth house, on the 20th. Give it your all in the days leading up to the New Moon and be sure to talk with anyone who can further your aims. You could find yourself in an enviable position by month's end or in September, so subtly promote yourself. Apply for a promotion if you see an opening.

Rewarding Days
4, 5, 6, 7, 12, 17, 20, 21, 25, 30, 31

Challenging Days
1, 2, 3, 8, 9, 10, 16, 22, 24, 29

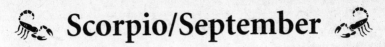 Scorpio/September

Planetary Hotspots

Saturn and Uranus form their final connection in Virgo/Pisces, your solar eleventh and fifth houses. Expect the issues to be similar to those that occurred in February—difficulties with friends, groups, a romantic interest, and possibly children. But even as the September 18 Full Moon in Virgo triggers the Saturn/Uranus lineup, both planets are in easy contact with your Sun, so you should be able to manage the conflict better than most. Think positively and be open to change.

Planetary Lightspots

Mars spends the entire month in Cancer, your solar ninth house. This makes August ideal for a change of scenery. If that's impossible, consider an alternative such as a spa day, a one-day recreational class, or a museum tour. Try to take a vacation or an extra day or two for yourself if business travel is in your plans.

Relationships

Before the Saturn-Uranus alignment takes effect, however, you can enjoy summer fun with friends and family the week of the August 4 Full Moon in Pisces, your solar fifth house. Spend a day at a nearby recreation area or be a kid again and take your children to the zoo or an amusement park. The lunar energy also sparks your creativity, which is great for hobby projects.

Money and Success

Career success meets or exceeds what you experienced in August, thanks to Venus in Leo, your solar tenth house, through the 19th. This is a terrific period to impress people and to interview if you're in the market for a new position. Snap up every opportunity to showcase your skills and talents.

Rewarding Days

2, 8, 9, 13, 14, 21, 22, 26, 28, 29

Challenging Days

3, 5, 6, 12, 17, 18, 23, 25, 27

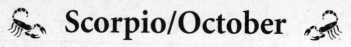 # Scorpio/October

Planetary Hotspots

Several planets travel in Libra, your solar twelfth house, the site of the October 18 New Moon. This has its upside and downside, just like every transit. On the positive side, this is the time of year when you can briefly step out of your busy life and look within while enjoying your own company. But some difficult planetary alignments increase the chance for a cold or flu, so be especially good to yourself. Stay warm, eat well, sleep, and relax in the comfort of your own home.

Planetary Lightspots

Look forward to October 22. That's the date the Sun arrives in your sign, followed by Mercury on the 28th. Begin thinking about where you want to go and what you want to do in the next twelve months so you're set to charge at November's Scorpio New Moon. Aim high and think big!

Relationships

The effects of September's Saturn/Uranus lineup are still active as Mercury and Venus complete their Virgo transit. Work through any lingering issues during the first two weeks of October, even if only in your mind, and continue to give your children your love and support. If you're weighing the pros and cons of a dating relationship, ultimately it may be best to put yourself first. People seldom change.

Money and Success

The October 4 Aries Full Moon spotlights your solar sixth house. Expect work to be hectic but satisfying as the lunar energy has you well-connected and a key player in the week's events. Teamwork is the way to go, and you can successfully convince others to support your ideas by being open to compromise.

Rewarding Days

1, 5, 6, 10, 11, 14, 19, 23, 24, 27, 29

Challenging Days

2, 3, 9, 13, 15, 16, 18, 25, 30

Scorpio/November

Planetary Hotspots

Saturn in Libra clashes with Pluto in Capricorn this month, but you're unlikely to experience much of its effect until December. Nevertheless, the first hint could emerge midmonth when someone pushes your hot button. Because these planets are in your solar twelfth and third houses, you might find yourself lost in thought at odd moments, remembering the past. Put regrets behind you and look to the future.

Planetary Lightspots

You have a lot going for you this month, thanks to the Sun, Mercury, Venus, and the November 16 New Moon in your sign. It's a terrific lineup for charm, charisma, and strong powers of attraction. Step into each day with confidence, knowing you have luck and talent going for you, and launch your new solar year with an ambitious personal agenda.

Relationships

The November 2 Full Moon in Taurus, your solar seventh house, has you in touch with many people who are drawn to you and your winning ways. Because this Full Moon is closely aligned with Mercury in your sign, you'll be at your talkative best, choosing all the right words to win supporters for your plans and projects. Capitalize on it in your personal life and your career.

Money and Success

Your career sector is action-packed with Mars in Leo, your solar tenth house. Do all you can this month to complete projects and promote your abilities because progress will stall in December when the red planet turns retrograde. Finances are positive this month with a chance for a raise, and you could net a small windfall the end of November, which is a great time to shop sales.

Rewarding Days

7, 10, 11, 16, 17, 20, 21, 24, 26

Challenging Days

2, 6, 8, 9, 12, 15, 19, 27, 30

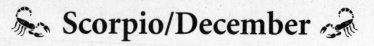 # Scorpio/December

Planetary Hotspots

Mars turns retrograde in Leo, your solar tenth house, on the 20th. Expect to be frustrated at times because decisions will be put on hold and projects stalled until early March when Mars turns direct. Find a good daily stress reliever and wait it out, knowing that nearly everyone around you is in some way experiencing a similar effect.

Planetary Lightspots

You'll want to enjoy as much time as possible at home in your space this month. It's the comfiest place to be with Jupiter and Neptune forming their last merger in Aquarius, your solar fourth house. That's also a great reason to host a get-together for friends midmonth when the Sun and Venus align with Jupiter and Neptune.

Relationships

Relationships are more challenging than not in early and late December as the Sun, Mercury, and Venus in Capricorn, your solar third house, connect with Pluto, also in Capricorn, and Saturn in Libra. In addition to potential conflict with neighbors and relatives, including in-laws, these planetary alignments and the December 31 Full Moon in Cancer, your solar ninth house, make travel inadvisable. So you might want to postpone a vacation or hometown visit until next year. The odds for a delay or cancellation increase with Mercury's switch to retrograde motion on the 26th. Drive carefully.

Money and Success

Money flows your direction with several planets, including Venus, and the December 16 New Moon in Sagittarius, your solar second house. You also benefit from December's first Full Moon, on the 2nd, in Gemini. The combination could bring you a nice year-end bonus in addition to some unexpected and much appreciated gifts.

Rewarding Days

4, 5, 6, 8, 12, 15, 18, 21, 22, 23, 27

Challenging Days

3, 7, 9, 13, 17, 20, 24, 28, 31

Scorpio Action Table

These dates reflect the best—but not the only—times for success and ease in these activities, according to your Sun sign.

	JAN	FEB	MAR	APR	MAY	JUN	JUL	AUG	SEPT	OCT	NOV	DEC
Move	1-3									26-27		
Start a class	5-7	3						29-31				17-18
Join a club								20-24		1-9	10-11	
Ask for a raise		17								21-22	17-18	14-16
Look for work		8-9, 27-28		23-24		16-17						
Get pro advice		2				18-19				7		
Get a loan		4-5					18				4-5	
See a doctor		27		23		29-30	27			16		
Start a diet				23-24								
End relationship				24		18-19		12			2	
Buy clothes	5-6	24-25		20-21			12			5-7		
Get a makeover								25-26			15-16	
New romance		25-26									25-26	
Vacation						22-24	16-17	17-18		6-11		

SAGITTARIUS

The Archer
November 21 to December 21

Element: Fire

Quality: Mutable

Polarity: Yang/masculine

Planetary Ruler: Jupiter

Meditation: I can take time to explore my soul

Gemstone: Turquoise

Power Stones: Lapis lazuli, azurite, sodalite

Key Phrase: I understand

Glyph: Archer's arrow

Anatomy: Hips, thighs, sciatic nerve

Color: Royal blue, purple

Animal: Fleet-footed animals

Myths/Legends: Athena, Chiron

House: Ninth

Opposite Sign: Gemini

Flower: Narcissus

Key Word: Optimism

Your Strengths and Challenges

Sagittarius is the adventurer of the zodiac, and each day brings new horizons to explore in your perpetual quest for truth and knowledge. Travel is a high priority for many Sagittarians, while others prefer mental journeys to expand their world view. What you seek is not just information, but understanding. The "whys" intrigue you—everything from how a civilization evolved to the inner workings of the mind. But as open-minded as you are, at times you're just the opposite and quick to judge something as pure nonsense rather than listen objectively to other opinions.

You're optimistic and outgoing, enthusiastic about life and your daily pursuits. And with expansive Jupiter as your ruling planet, more is nearly always better in your mind. If only life weren't so short! Jupiter is also the planet of luck, which most Sagittarians have in abundance. Yes, you could win the lottery, but your brand of good fortune is linked more to opportunities and your knack for spotting and seizing them. Just be sure to put your idealism on hold and look at the realistic facts before jumping in.

You're generous and sincere, friendly and confident. But you also can be blunt and speak the plain truth when a more tactful approach is needed. Learn to soften your message with kind and supportive words that will endear you to others and advance your aims.

Your Relationships

Even if you're not the "love 'em and leave 'em" type (some Sagittarians definitely are), you delight in playing the field. To you, love, like life, is an adventure to be explored to the fullest. You're passionate and spontaneous, and can fall in and out of love in a flash—at least until you meet someone who's as lively and free-spirited as you are. Mental rapport is also a must, and you bypass anyone who doesn't share your thirst for knowledge and information. You could feel the zing of true love with Gemini, your opposite sign, and Sagittarius is compatible with the other air signs, Libra and Aquarius. Fiery Aries and Leo have much in common with you, but Virgo and Pisces are likely to lack the spontaneity you desire.

You have a strong spiritual connection with family, even the people you're not particularly close to, and strive for a home life that's peaceful and serene—the place where you can escape the stresses and strains of daily life. Ocean colors can help you achieve this goal. Sagittarian parents are actively involved in their children's lives, pushing them to succeed in everything from sports to school. But consistency can be a challenge, so remind yourself to deliver the same values-based message day in and day out. Your children will benefit from it and both of you will doubly enjoy those moments when you give in and spoil them.

You're popular with friends, coworkers, and just about everyone you meet. They're attracted to your sense of humor, and you have a sixth sense about what makes people tick. As much as you enjoy your wide social circle, you treasure your best friends and would find life incomplete without them. These are the people you share your inner feelings with, the ones who are always there for you, as you are for them. You prefer going places and doing things with a friend to spending leisure-time alone. Love grows out of friendship for many Sagittarians who need and want a mate who's also a best friend.

Your Career and Money

You're likely to change careers at least once during your lifetime and probably several times. With so many interests, skills, and talents, it's only natural to expect your career life to evolve to keep pace with your ever-increasing knowledge. You're a natural teacher, whether or not that's your profession. What you need in your career is the ability to share what you know, formally or informally. But you should also take care not to lose sight of the big picture. The search for the perfect career, which doesn't exist for you or anyone else, can encourage you to leap from one to another. So try to limit major shifts in career direction to those that will contribute to lifetime success. A comfortable, stable work environment is a must. And despite your energy, you're happiest in a job where you can work at your own pace, handling each task thoroughly and completely. A high-pressure job isn't the best option for you.

You can stretch a dollar further than most people when necessary. An extravagant spender at times, and conservative at others, the sooner you learn to save and invest for the long term, the greater your wealth potential. Doing that will also minimize the impact of tight financial periods because you'll have a nest-egg to fall back on. Home-ownership could net you sizable gains, and you might also receive a family legacy. If you're handy, you could profit from owning rental properties.

Your Lighter Side

For one who's so adventuresome and action-oriented, you're a lover of peace and harmony who's far more sensitive than most people realize. All this, plus your understanding of human nature, make you a fine negotiator and consensus-builder. You want people to get along and thus emphasize cooperation and compromise, both of which can also advance your personal goals.

Affirmation for the Year

I strive for personal, financial, and career success.

The Year Ahead for Sagittarius

Jupiter will stimulate your mind this year as it travels in Aquarius, your solar third house of communication. This makes 2009 ideal for learning and growth, and you'll have a burning desire to be in the know, up on all the latest information in your own world and the world at large.

The obvious choice to satisfy this need for information would be to take a class or two for fun, to boost your job skills, or to complete your education or earn advanced certification. And online learning might be the best avenue because Aquarius is the sign of technology. It would also give you more flexibility to accommodate this year's fast-paced daily life.

Structured learning isn't the only option, however. You could gain the same satisfaction from delving into a subject that's always interested you or perfecting your hobby skills. Chances are, you'll go few places without a book in hand and also be more interested in news and educational programs. If you've always wanted to be a writer, 2009 is a great year to give it a try. Join a writer's group or take a class in creative writing.

You'll want to be sure your vehicle is in top shape all year long because you'll be on the go, both in town and probably on weekend jaunts. Satisfy your curiosity with day trips to nearby historical sites, to visit friends, and to nature preserves. You'll especially enjoy just getting out of town for a change of scenery now and then.

This year will bring lots of contact with people in your immediate environment—neighbors, siblings, and other relatives. Many will bring you luck, although you may not fully realize it until 2010 or even several years in the future.

Jupiter will align with Neptune, also in Aquarius, in May and December. This connection has its upside and, unfortunately, its downside. At their best, Jupiter and Neptune will inspire you and take your creativity to new heights—even if you've never before discovered this side of yourself. This duo will also encourage you to have faith in yourself and your abilities and to discover, or rediscover, your spiritual connection with the universe.

But Neptune also represents deception and disillusionment. So you need to be cautious about believing everything you hear and trusting just anyone. Some people will talk a good game but fail to deliver on their promises, much to your disappointment. You also can fall into the trap of self-deception, believing what you want to believe rather than seeing a situation for what it is. This makes it wise to seek an objective opinion before making important life decisions. Listen to the feedback and take it to heart.

Saturn will almost complete its Virgo transit this year, entering Libra October 29, and returning to Virgo for a few months in 2010. Since its September 2007 arrival in Virgo, your solar tenth house, you've undoubtedly experienced Saturn's influence in your career—restriction, frustration, and achievements. All of these are characteristic of Saturn, the planet that nearly always delivers rewards if you follow its rules.

Saturn is all about structure, responsibility, and accountability. It's also the karmic planet that quickly lets you know when you step out of line. But Saturn's transit of your solar tenth house is also the time when you can rise to the top because this is a career pinnacle. If you feel you have yet to achieve your goals, make that a priority this year. You won't have another opportunity like this for twenty-eight years.

But Saturn won't operate entirely on its own this year. Uranus, planet of the unexpected, will be in the mix as it forms an exact alignment with Saturn from Pisces, your solar fourth house.

On its own Uranus in your domestic sector could trigger a move or an extensive home remodeling project. Matched with Saturn, this could be the result of relocation for a new position or promotion.

Uranus in your sign of home and family can also indicate changes in family life, such as a relative or roommate moving in or out. If at all possible you'll want to avoid adding one of these people to your household now. It's unlikely to work out, despite your hope that it will. When Saturn and Uranus join forces (February and September), the living arrangement will become difficult at best and intolerable at worst. You especially don't need this hassle this year when your career life will place added demands on your time.

As you're busy making your mark in the outer world, your family could begin to feel neglected, which reflects the bigger picture of this Saturn/Uranus alignment: relationships and balance. Give your support system equal time. They'll appreciate it and you and your career will benefit from the rest and relaxation that results from quality time with loved ones.

It's also possible you'll experience major changes in your workplace or career. You might decide it's time to try a new field of endeavor or pursue a new job when it becomes apparent you've gone as far as you can go. That would be a great proactive move if it's done for the right reasons and not just because you want something new in your life. Tune in to what's happening around you at work, especially if your career field is prone to layoffs or you suspect your company isn't as stable as it once was. If either of these possibilities seems likely, be proactive: network and send out resumes.

Saturn moves on to Libra, your solar eleventh house, October 29, to begin its nearly three-year tour of this sign. You'll feel the effects of this planet in your friendships and group activities, where teamwork and mutual support will be your challenges. That's eminently doable because Libra mixes well with your sign.

You now have the opportunity to learn a lot about people, whether they're acquaintances or close friends. Some are sure to disappoint you, while others will be a stabilizing force in your life. It's all just another Saturn learning experience that encourages you to seek and share wisdom.

Some of the people who enter your life in the next few years will have a karmic connection. Be alert and watch for them, because each will have an important message or experience to share with you. Chances are, you'll recognize anyone who falls into this category because you'll have an instant, indefinable connection. And don't be surprised if these same people move out of your life once their purpose has been fulfilled.

It's also possible you'll reconnect with one or more people from the past: old friends you haven't heard from in years, former romantic interests, and possibly even a long-lost relative. Whether you resume the relationship is up to you, but you should at least try to discover the reason why these people have resurfaced in your life.

Libra is also your sign of groups, so you could feel the urge to get involved in a professional or humanitarian organization, which will also give you many opportunities to meet people and network. But draw the line early and stick to it; otherwise you could find yourself doing all the work while others sit back and accumulate accolades. The challenge here is that you could take on a heavy load of responsibility just because you feel you're the best person for the job. That may be true, but you'll be better off sharing the load. Teamwork is one of Saturn's lessons as it transits your solar eleventh house.

This will be Pluto's first full year in Capricorn, the sign it first entered in early 2008. With this planet occupying your solar second house of personal resources for the next fifteen years, there's no time like the present to get serious about your lifetime financial priorities, including budgeting and retirement. What you do now can result in wealth or just the opposite, so think and plan carefully and put your financial goals in writing where you can review them at least monthly. It's all a matter of establishing your security needs and then building the foundation to achieve them.

But your second house is about more than money. It's also about your personal values and ethics, which is a Sagittarius theme. You'll be pushed to make these decisions as well, especially after Saturn enters Libra and connects with Pluto, urging you to stand behind your beliefs.

What This Year's Eclipses Mean for You

There will be six eclipses in 2009, unlike the more usual four that occur most years. Each eclipse either reinforces or adds another dimension to the influence of the outer planets.

One solar eclipse (January 7 in Aquarius) and two lunar eclipses (February 9 in Leo, and August 6 in Aquarius) will activate your solar third/ninth house axis. This puts the learning and communication emphasis of Jupiter and Neptune even more in the forefront, making 2009 one of the best to stretch your mind and explore your creativity.

While your solar third house (Aquarius) emphasizes information-gathering, your solar ninth house (Leo) is all about knowledge, Sagittarius's lifelong quest. So consider expanding your mental horizons even further and explore the idea of not just learning but returning to school for a degree or specialized training to enhance your career prospects. Even if you already have all the necessary education there are other options. For example, you could learn another language, take several classes to update your education, or pursue a leisure-time interest as a first step toward a new or sideline career.

Relatives, including in-laws, will have a bigger role in your life this year. As with anything else, some of these relationships will be positive and others will try your patience. Such is life. Enjoy the uplifting ones and the inspiration that comes from learning little known facts about your roots. But don't let any relative talk you into something that isn't in your best interests—even if it's tough to say no.

The other three 2009 eclipses will occur in Capricorn and Cancer, your solar second and eighth houses of money. They'll amplify Pluto's financial influence, and also can trigger gains later in the year. The Capricorn lunar eclipse, July 7, is followed two weeks later by a solar eclipse in Cancer, July 22. The second lunar eclipse will be in Cancer, December 31, extending the financial emphasis into 2010.

This is the year to get your financial life in order. Pay off debt and try not to incur more, and commit to a regular savings plan. If you invest, be conservative; 2009 (and 2010) is not the year to put funds at risk. It's possible you could receive a surprise inheritance, or one much larger than expected, from a relative or friend. Take the time to organize your financial records and to review insurance policies to be sure you're adequately covered. Pay premiums and taxes when they're due. Overall, this is not the year to push your luck in money matters but to do all you can to ensure financial security for today and the future.

Saturn

If you were born between December 5–21, your career life will be a major focal point as Saturn contacts your Sun from Virgo. This year can be a real turning point in your work life. Much depends upon your job performance in recent years and your willingness to accept responsibility. Give it your all now, with clearly defined goals and a game plan to get you where you want to go. If there's one thing you can bank on when Saturn contacts your Sun, it's that you will reap exactly what you deserve—so be sure you deserve only the very best!

It's also possible you could decide your current career is no longer viable, that you need something more stimulating and challenging to make your mark in the outer world. Explore your options if you're feeling the push for change. Especially for you, this year's Leo/Aquarius influence makes the timing ideal to get the schooling you need to launch a new life path.

Make rest, relaxation, and most of all sleep, top priorities this year because Saturn can reduce stamina. A healthy diet and moderate exercise will also help maintain your energy level.

Saturn-Pluto

If you were born between November 21–26, Pluto will contact your Sun from Capricorn, your solar second house, off and on throughout 2009. This means that you, more than most Sagittarians, need to be extra cautious about money and safeguarding your financial information. Make a pact with yourself to live within a budget and to pay off any accumulated debt.

Saturn will enter Libra, your solar eleventh house, October 29, where it also will contact your Sun as it clashes with Pluto. Follow the lead of this planetary duo when they encourage you to realign not only your immediate and long-term financial goals but your personal and career priorities. You may discover that what you thought was important really isn't, or vice versa.

Having this Saturn/Pluto connection aligned with your Sun also makes it wise to avoid any financial involvement with friends or an organization. For example, don't cosign a loan or invest money in a joint venture with a friend (or anyone else). The end result will not be to your liking and could have serious financial repercussions. What you can do with this planetary energy, however, is guide a friend in need to helpful resources.

Uranus

Uranus is sure to shake up your home life **if you were born between December 10–18**. A sudden urge for change could prompt you to move across country, into a new home in a nearby location, or to begin an extensive remodeling project on your place. Proceed with some caution, however, especially **if you were born between December 13–16**, because Saturn and Uranus will form an exact alignment with your Sun. This duo could trigger a major job change in February or September, including the possibility of relocation.

Uranus's contact to your Sun is about more than home life, however. This can be an exciting time of personal change if you welcome new opportunities and new directions. The tough part will be to decide which path to take because so many will be open to you. If you want to recreate yourself, 2009 is your year to get in shape, slim down, follow your dreams, or rediscover a long-dormant talent. But be careful. Change for the sake of change isn't always the wisest choice. Keep that in mind if you feel the urge to break free from your life and a close relationship.

Neptune

Unleash your creativity **if you were born between December 13 and 17**, as Neptune contacts your Sun from Aquarius. Write, do crafts, invent something, paint, dance, sing, become a motivational speaker, or anything else that stimulates your mind, your talents, and your creativity. You'll have few opportunities in your lifetime like this one, so get inspired and make the most of it.

That's positive. The other side of Neptune is you'll attract people who will tell you what you want to hear and others with good sob stories. Keep this in mind and be skeptical of anything that sounds too good to be true. If in doubt, ask someone you trust for an objective opinion. Ultimately, though, the best choice is to put you and yours first.

♐ Sagittarius/January ♐

Planetary Hotspots

Finances require close attention and careful management this month. Between the January 10 Full Moon in Cancer and Mercury traveling retrograde in Capricorn (your money signs), the potential increases for mix-ups and unexpected expenses. Check your credit report this month and try to use cash instead of credit. The urge to splurge will be strong the last week of February.

Planetary Lightspots

Good news is headed your way. For that you can thank lucky Jupiter, which enters Aquarius January 5. Stay tuned around the 18th for exciting developments involving someone close to you. Some Sagittarians will hear news of a lucky win or settlement, and family ties benefit from Venus in Pisces, your domestic sector.

Relationships

Relationships are both stimulating and frustrating this month. Some people enlighten you, much to your surprise, especially around the time of the January 26 New Moon in Aquarius, your communication sector. Listen closely even if you disagree with their views. Upon reflection you might discover it's your perspective that's out of sync. Learn from it and adapt.

Money and Success

The odds favor career success and the chance for a bigger paycheck this month. Much depends upon your willingness to take on added responsibilities and possibly to relocate. Postpone the decision until February if you can. By then you'll have a better idea of what's involved. If you're job hunting, send out resumes the week of the New Moon and look for feedback in early February.

Rewarding Days

4, 5, 11, 12, 17, 20, 21, 26, 27, 31

Challenging Days

2, 3, 9, 10, 16, 22, 29, 30

🏹 Sagittarius/February 🏹

Planetary Hotspots

Changing conditions surround your career or domestic life in early February as Saturn and Uranus form an exact alignment spanning your solar fourth/tenth house axis. The effects will be especially prominent if you were born within a few days of December 12. Sudden career-related developments, including downsizing and restructuring, are possible, and some Sagittarians will relocate for job reasons. A family member may require more of your time and attention, and there could be changes in your living situation with someone moving in or out. Tension begins to ease by the time of the February 24 New Moon in Pisces.

Planetary Lightspots

Need a break? Plan a trip when the February 9 Full Moon (and lunar eclipse) activates your solar ninth house. Or, use the lunar energy, along with the influence of several Aquarius planets, to launch a new course of study to enhance your career options.

Relationships

Your social life benefits from Venus in Aries, your solar fifth house, which could trigger a new romance the third week of February, when the love planet connects with Mars and Jupiter in Aquarius. This lineup could also yield a networking contact and hoped-for good news that will brighten your future.

Money and Success

Although you may have a financial challenge in early February, money matters slowly return to positive territory as Mercury begins to advance in Capricorn, your solar second house. (It turns direct on the 1st.) You'll also be able to resolve any recent financial issues within the first two weeks of February, and could receive a minor windfall midmonth.

Rewarding Days

4, 8, 13, 17, 22, 23, 27, 28

Challenging Days

5, 6, 9, 11, 12, 18, 25 26

♐ Sagittarius/March ♐

Planetary Hotspots

The effects of last month's Saturn/Uranus alignment continue the first three weeks of March, primarily influencing your domestic sector. Home life is hectic at times and the potential for change remains high. You may need to repair or replace an appliance, or make arrangements for an elderly relative. With this strong emphasis on change you might get a sudden urge to begin a home improvement project. That's not the best idea right now. Window shop, plan, and compare costs instead.

Planetary Lightspots

You communicate with ease in early March as Mercury and Mars travel in Aquarius, your solar third house. Listen when people present alternative views. If you do, they'll inspire you to delve deeper into the subject under discussion. But ease up on the gas and stay off the phone when you're behind the wheel.

Relationships

The Sun and Venus in Aries, your solar fifth house, promise an active social life. If you're single you could meet a new romantic interest around the time of the March 26 New Moon in the same sign. But don't be concerned if it doesn't immediately take off. With Venus retrograde from the 6th until mid-May it might be a while before you have a chance to get to know each other. If you're a parent your children may need extra time and attention now.

Money and Success

Work is likely to be stressful the week of the March 10 Full Moon in Pisces, your career sector. You'll be stretched thin, so much so that you might consider moving on or setting up a home-based business. Neither one is a wise choice this month or even this year. Be flexible, adapt, and ask others for help.

Rewarding Days

3, 7, 8, 12, 13, 21, 22, 27, 28, 29

Challenging Days

2, 4, 5, 9, 10, 11, 17, 18, 23, 31

♐ Sagittarius/April ♐

Planetary Hotspots

After two hectic months you'll appreciate the relative calm of April. Nevertheless, the domestic scene remains somewhat of a hotspot with Mars in Pisces through the 21st and Venus retrograde in the same sign, April 11–16; it turns direct on the 17th. Put this duo to work for you spring cleaning inside and out. You'll like the results and the physical work will be a great stress reliever.

Planetary Lightspots

Mars dashes into Aries your solar fifth house, on the 22nd. That's a plus for your social life, but it can bring you far more. Use this high-energy planet to get fit before summer. Begin an exercise program, walk with a neighbor, join a gym. But go easy at first despite the temptation to push yourself.

Relationships

Leave room in your busy schedule to get together with friends around the time of the April 9 Full Moon in Libra, your solar eleventh house. Opt for a casual destination where you can catch up on the latest news, or host a small group at your place. With several planets in Aries this month, including Venus from the 23rd on, romance is also high on your priority list. Love the one you're with, and also give your children extra time; they'll fill your life with joy.

Money and Success

Work is busy, satisfying, and fulfilling as Mercury, the Sun, and the March 24 New Moon in Taurus accent your solar sixth house. To get the very best from these planetary influences, however, it's important to follow through and do every task to the best of your ability. Anything less is sure to catch up with you despite having luck on your side.

Rewarding Days

4, 5, 6, 9, 13, 16, 18, 20, 22, 23

Challenging Days

1, 3, 8, 14, 26, 27, 28

Sagittarius/May

Planetary Hotspots

Mercury is retrograde after May 7, first in Gemini and then in Taurus, and it will impact relationships and your work life. Misunderstandings are likely, so try to be especially tactful in what you say and write. Also double-check work for accuracy and clarify instructions and feedback. Ask questions rather than jump to conclusions during this month that features a Jupiter-Neptune union in Aquarius, your solar third house of communication. It's just as important not to believe everything you hear. Well-intentioned or not, some people stretch the truth and make promises they can't keep.

Planetary Lightspots

Tune in to the May 9 Full Moon in Scorpio, your solar twelfth house, and slow the pace at least a little. The lunar energy is simply a reminder that you can benefit from time alone to calm your mind and body. Give it a try. Chances are, you'll come to value a daily time-out to balance your hectic life. Read, walk, enjoy a hobby.

Relationships

Socializing continues with Venus and Mars in Aries, your solar fifth house. That's perfect timing for outdoor activities with friends and family. Romance is also in the picture for couples and singles, and the May 24 New Moon in Aries brings a new relationship for some Sagittarians. If you're a parent, or hope to be, you could have a lot to cheer about in May.

Money and Success

The Sun in Taurus, your solar sixth house, through the 19th keeps up the pace at work. Be prepared, though, for frustrating days once retrograde Mercury enters this sector on the 13th. Conditions will be ripe for mix-ups, stalled and reversed decisions, and false starts. Laughter is a great antidote.

Rewarding Days

1, 6, 7, 10, 11, 15, 16, 20, 21, 24, 25, 28

Challenging Days

2, 5, 17, 18, 23, 26, 27

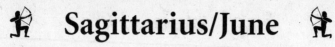 Sagittarius/June

Planetary Hotspots

The smart choice is to curb spending this month even if you should net some extra cash. Also be cautious with investments, where a conservative approach is the wise one. The June 22 New Moon in Cancer, your solar eighth house, could trigger a major expense because it aligns with Pluto in Capricorn, your solar second house. With this emphasis on your financial sectors, save all you can.

Planetary Lightspots

The June 7 Full Moon, on the other hand, is all about you. Placed in your sign, it fuels your drive and ambition and motivates you to aim for bigger and better. You can achieve a lot that week as long as you emphasize cooperation and teamwork and fulfill all your job responsibilities.

Relationships

Relationships are in focus as the Sun travels in Gemini, your solar seventh house, through the 20th, where it's joined by Mercury on the 13th. Personal ties are generally positive and upbeat, but you should keep thoughts to yourself at work in early and late June. Rely on your self-control to see through a potential clash with a demanding boss or a coworker who might try to undermine your efforts. The less said the better. Need a favor? Ask for it within the first few days of June.

Money and Success

Aside from the potential clash, June promises to be a productive and satisfying month at work. The pace is fast and your workload heavy at times. Yet you'll keep up with it by tackling one project and challenge at a time. Just be sure to clarify instructions. Apply for a promotion in early June if that's your goal; you could hear news by month's end.

Rewarding Days

2, 6, 12, 14, 17, 19, 20, 29, 30

Challenging Days

1, 3, 5, 11, 16, 21, 22, 27

Sagittarius/July

Planetary Hotspots

You'll want to see the very best in everyone this month as Jupiter and Neptune join forces in Aquarius, your solar third house. That's admirable but not very practical. Some people will puzzle you and others may deliberately try to mislead you. People will also be free with their promises but fail to deliver. So keep your wits about you and take advantage of this potentially upbeat influence to further your own aims.

Planetary Lightspots

Mercury advances into Leo, your solar ninth house, on the 17th, followed by the Sun on the 22nd. Put the planetary energy to work for you and research possible vacation destinations. Next month you'll be even more ready for fresh scenery and a summer adventure.

Relationships

You're in sync with just about everyone, thanks to Venus in Gemini, your solar seventh house, July 5–30. Supporters will appear when you need them, and others will bring you luck. The exception here could be a coworker or supervisor who demands perfection. Be gracious, tactful, and charming.

Money and Success

Money matters command your attention with July's emphasis on Capricorn and Cancer, your solar second/eighth house axis. Both the Full Moon (and lunar eclipse) in Cancer on the 7th and the New Moon (and solar eclipse) in Capricorn on the 21st have the potential to increase your bank balance. But extra expenses are also possible, so use this planetary energy to review your net worth, establish a savings and investment plan, and develop a budget that includes debt reduction, if necessary. Also take the time to comparison shop for insurance; you might find a lower premium.

Rewarding Days

3, 8, 9, 14, 18, 22, 26, 27

Challenging Days

2, 4, 6, 13, 19, 24, 25

⁂ Sagittarius/August ⁂

Planetary Hotspots

Life perks along this month with only minor ruffles to interrupt summer's flow. You'll want to be prepared for possible financial hurdles in early and late August, but you can easily resolve whatever comes up. Although a clash with a friend the last week of the month might be upsetting, you should stick to your values and hang onto your money.

Planetary Lightspots

August is your adventuresome month, with the Full Moon in Aquarius, August 5, and the New Moon in Leo, August 20, your travel and learning sectors. So pack your bags and take off for parts known or unknown. Even a weekend away can do wonders if time is limited. You might also want to check into online or local classes that could benefit your career ambitions. Then ask your employer about tuition reimbursement; with luck you'll get the funding.

Relationships

You connect with many people as Mars zips through Gemini, your solar seventh house, through the 24th. Some are lucky, some uplifting, and some frustrating. But each adds to your knowledge of human nature and the many facets of the people in your life. Take time to meet your neighbors midmonth. One of them could be the person you've been searching for.

Money and Success

There's another reason you should try to squeeze in some time off while you have the chance. Mercury paves the way for a busy September at work when it transits Virgo, your solar tenth house, August 2–24. Reinforce your position this month. Snap up opportunities to talk with decision-makers and make your mark in well-prepared presentations backed by solid ideas and maximum effort.

Rewarding Days

3, 4, 6, 11, 12, 14, 18, 19, 20, 23, 27

Challenging Days

1, 2, 8, 9, 10, 15, 16, 22, 29

Sagittarius/September 🏹

Planetary Hotspots

The final alignment of Saturn and Uranus in Virgo/Pisces, your career and domestic sectors occurs this month. You can expect more developments in matters that got your attention in February, especially if your birthday is near December 17. The planetary forces are at their strongest the week of the September 18 New Moon in Virgo, when tension rises at work and in your home and family life. Job relocation is possible, but this is not the time to purchase property or to change your living situation by, for example, acquiring a roommate. If your job situation has reached the breaking point, remain calm, keep thoughts to yourself, and try to postpone the decision until late October or November, as things may change.

Planetary Lightspots

Don't be surprised if you hear from faraway friends as Venus advances in Leo, your solar ninth house, through the 19th. A former romantic interest or school friend could be among them. However, draw the line at sharing personal information with anyone you meet online. The Internet can be deceiving. You'll also be strongly in touch with your spirituality, and a self-help book could trigger surprising insights.

Relationships

Confirm dates, times, and places so you don't miss an important event after Mercury turns retrograde in Libra, your friendship sector, on the 7th. Also keep a close eye on valuables when you're out socializing and in public.

Money and Success

Mars in Cancer, your solar eighth house, accents moneymaking opportunities, and you could end September with a bigger bank account. Hang onto it. This influence won't last forever.

Rewarding Days

1, 2, 6, 11, 15, 20, 24, 26, 28, 29

Challenging Days

3, 4, 5, 10, 12, 14, 17, 23, 25

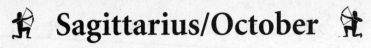 Sagittarius/October

Planetary Hotspots

Saturn enters Libra October 29 to begin its three-year transit of your solar eleventh house. You'll develop some close friendships in the next few years, and possibly find a soul mate. But this influence can also have you taking on more than your fair share of responsibility. That's partly because you'll see yourself as the best-qualified person, but also because others will rightly assume that you're willing to do much of the work. Prove them wrong. Share the load.

Planetary Lightspots

The universe offers you a gift when the Sun enters Scorpio, your solar twelfth house, on the 22nd followed by Mercury on the 28th: relaxation time. You'll value it all the more because October will be just as hectic as the past few months. Take time for yourself and your interests, and try to kick back every evening.

Relationships

Socializing is at its best much of October, which features the New Moon in Libra, your friendship sector, on the 18th, and the October 4 Full Moon in Aries, your solar fifth house of recreation. But the potential also exists for conflict with a friend or romantic interest, possibly over money. Put yourself first and don't let anyone pressure you into parting with your hard-earned paycheck.

Money and Success

Although last month's Saturn/Uranus alignment is waning, the lingering effects of this duo and its influence in your career and domestic sectors will affect you the first two weeks of October. Try to resolve these issues so you're ready to move on as Saturn enters Libra. Good news: Mars could trigger some extra cash before it completes its Cancer tour of your solar eighth house on the 15th.

Rewarding Days

3, 8, 12, 13, 17, 20, 21, 22, 26, 27, 31

Challenging Days

2, 9, 15, 16, 18, 23, 29, 30

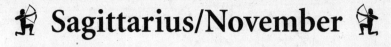 Sagittarius/November

Planetary Hotspots

Bundle up, get plenty of sleep, and fuel your body with the most nutritious foods this month. With the Sun, Mercury, and Venus in Scorpio, your solar twelfth house, at various times, you'll be unusually susceptible to a cold or the flu. If you can, take a few days off around the November 16 New Moon in Scorpio, when you'll especially enjoy cozy days and evenings at home.

Planetary Lightspots

Mercury arrives in Sagittarius on the 15th, followed by the Sun on the 21st, giving you a preview of next month's focus on you and your sign. Use these two weeks to think about new plans and personal directions so you're set to go at the December New Moon in Sagittarius. Careful thought is likely to yield goals that motivate you.

Relationships

Although Saturn in Libra, your solar eleventh house, contacts Pluto in Capricorn, your solar second house, this month, the major effects of this alignment will become apparent in December. A clash with a friend is likely this month or next and you might intentionally cut ties. The first week of November, however, is great for socializing as Venus completes its Libra transit. Do lunch with a few friends, and plan an evening out with others.

Money and Success

Your workload increases under the November 2 Full Moon in Taurus, your solar sixth house. Business travel is possible, and you might find yourself trapped in endless meetings. Find a good stress reliever such as a moderate workout or evening walk with a neighbor to clear your mind. It's also a wise idea to limit spending this month because unexpected expenses could pop up in December.

Rewarding Days

4, 5, 13, 14, 17, 18, 20, 21, 22, 28

Challenging Days

6, 8, 9, 11, 12, 19, 25, 26, 27, 30

Sagittarius/December

Planetary Hotspots

Get ready for periodic frustration in the next few months. That's the influence of Mars, which turns retrograde in Leo, your solar ninth house, on the 20th. Plans and projects will stall, and indecision will test the patience of your fire sign. Keep smiling and go with the flow. Any attempt to push and move things along will only frustrate you all the more. It will be particularly tough to get information and answers.

Planetary Lightspots

This is your month! Venus in Sagittarius through the 24th brings out your natural charm and charisma, and the December 16 New Moon, also in your sign, elevates your attention-getting status. That's perfect for holiday gatherings where you and your powers of attraction can connect with people.

Relationships

Your relationship sector shines brightly under the December 2 Full Moon in Gemini, your solar seventh house. That's as great for couples in love as it is for singles looking for a match. Seek favors if you need them and do the same for others, and spend quality time with your favorite people who will be especially pleased by your willingness to compromise.

Money and Success

Money matters are challenging this month as the Sun, Mercury, and Venus connect with Pluto in Capricorn, your solar second house, and Saturn in Libra. Adding to it is Mercury's switch to retrograde motion on the 26th, and the December 31 Full Moon in Cancer, which directly contacts Pluto. Shop sales, cut back on holiday spending, and save the difference. Also focus on your short- and long-term financial goals—or set them. Consult a financial expert if you need advice.

Rewarding Days

1, 5, 6, 11, 14, 15, 16, 19, 21, 25, 30

Challenging Days

3, 7, 9, 10, 13, 20, 24, 26, 28, 31

Sagittarius Action Table

These dates reflect the best —but not the only—times for success and ease in these activities, according to your Sun sign.

	JAN	FEB	MAR	APR	MAY	JUN	JUL	AUG	SEPT	OCT	NOV	DEC
Move	5-7	24-28		20-21		14				28-29		
Start a class		12-17				11-12				26-27		
Join a club						26-27			16-26	13		
Ask for a raise		2				9-10					20	17
Look for work				24		9-10, 18-20, 28				6-7		
Get pro advice		4-5	4								5	
Get a loan						23		17				
See a doctor						18-19		12		6		
Start a diet						19	16-17			7		
End relationship						20-21	18				5	
Buy clothes		27-28		23-24							27	
Get a makeover		21								21		14-16
New romance		27										
Vacation							22-31			12-13		

CAPRICORN

The Goat
December 21 to January 20

V3

Element: Earth

Quality: Cardinal

Polarity: Yin/feminine

Planetary Ruler: Saturn

Meditation: I know the strength of my soul

Gemstone: Garnet

Power Stones: Peridot, diamond, quartz, black obsidian, onyx

Key Phrase: I use

Glyph: Head of goat

Anatomy: Skeleton, knees, skin

Color: Black, forest green

Animal: Goats, thick-shelled animals

Myths/Legends: Chronos, Vesta, Pan

House: Tenth

Opposite Sign: Cancer

Flower: Carnation

Key Word: Ambitious

Your Strengths and Challenges

Worldly ambition defines you, although many Capricorns don't fully discover their niche in life until reaching their late twenties. But even in childhood, Capricorns feel the urge to in some way make their mark in the world. That's most likely to occur after age forty, when you and your life success potential suddenly take off. Being a late bloomer is to your advantage, however, because you get the benefit of years of knowledge and experience, which can help you dash ahead of the competition.

Capricorn is an earth sign, so you're practical, sensible, and patient. You're also responsible and conscientious, and with serious Saturn as your ruling planet, you can be overly cautious when a calculated risk could be a better choice. Start slowly with inconsequential matters; then you'll feel more at ease when faced with major life decisions.

You're efficient, organized, and thorough, and at times can be intolerant of those who fail to measure up to your high standards. Try to remember that not everyone has your drive and ambition; some people are content to simply drift through life even though that's beyond your understanding.

Yet for all the caution you exercise in certain situations, decisiveness is one of the strengths associated with your cardinal, action-oriented sign. Your vast storehouse of knowledge and excellent memory give you the ability to quickly weigh the pros and cons in almost any situation. When presented with an opportunity that feels right, nothing holds you back.

Your Relationships

Your practicality extends to dating relationships, where you're attracted to people who are as level-headed as you are. In fact, you can get so content in a relationship that you're reluctant to move on, preferring the known to the unknown. Although that might be comfortable, you'll need to break out of this pattern in order to find someone who makes your heart zing. When you do, your sensual side emerges along with your flair for romance. You could make an ideal match with Cancer, your opposite sign, which shares your need for emotional and financial security in a warm family setting. The other water signs, Scorpio and Pisces, might interest you, as could your fellow earth signs, Taurus and Virgo. But life with Aries or Libra could leave you feeling unsettled.

Home life is fast-paced for most Capricorns, with people coming and going and many family activities. But it also comes with a challenge: the need for balance. You can be so focused on your career that you dash home to sleep and dash out to work. Remind yourself that your mate needs quality time and support, and that children grow quickly. You'll also be much happier and more productive when you have a well-rounded lifestyle. As a parent you're warm and loving but also expect rules to be followed. This no-nonsense attitude is tempered by reasonable expectations, however, and you excel at encouraging your children to explore their interests and creativity within a stable, tradition-based home environment.

Your wide circle of acquaintances includes people who are financially successful and those who can benefit your career aims. You're also an excellent judge of character and quickly spot people who share your values. Some of these become your closest friends with whom you develop a deep emotional bond. Yet these friends don't necessarily know each other; in a sense you compartmentalize them because each fulfills a different need in your life.

Your Career and Money

Only those who know you well realize how truly ambitious you are. And that keeps you a step ahead of the competition because you're able to strategize, plan, and implement your next move—all without tipping your hand. You relate well with supervisors and VIPs and can successfully develop positive give-and-take relationships with those who can further your goals. Although your timing is usually on target, impatience can get the best of you, so step back and rein yourself in when necessary. In your daily work you need a lot of variety, communication, organization, and people contact. When that's in place you can be happy and successful in any work environment. You also need the freedom to multi-task and structure your own work, both of which keep you interested and involved.

You can amass considerable assets as long as your ego doesn't interfere with financial decisions. That's particularly important with investments, credit, and spending because you equate materialism with success. Rely on the same facts-and-figures practical approach you use in other areas of your life. Otherwise, and despite your cautious nature, you could become "payment poor." Although your income and expenses fluctuate somewhat, you can be thrifty and use money and credit to advantage. Capricorns often find special deals and other money-saving bargains.

Your Lighter Side

You're a hard worker, but you also know how to kick back and relax—if you let yourself! Tap into your lazy, comfort-loving side and fill some of your evenings and weekends with practical, productive hobbies such as gardening, woodworking, furniture refinishing, and artistic pastimes. Many Capricorns also enjoy photography, movies, and reading fantasy novels.

Affirmation for the Year

People enrich my life.

The Year Ahead for Capricorn

Your financial potential gets a big boost this year, thanks to Jupiter in Aquarius, your solar second house of personal money. A nice salary increase or bonus, and a windfall from an unlucky source are all possible. Although you'll attract money, you'll also be in the mood to spend freely. But this lucky influence only lasts a year, so set a goal to increase your net worth rather than just stay even. The chance to get ahead financially is a gift from the universe not to be wasted.

Your solar second house is about more than money. It represents all of your resources, including your marketable skills and talents. Give yourself credit for all you have to offer; if you feel underpaid or underemployed, begin to think about how you can change that situation, if not this year, then next.

Also take a look around your house. Too much stuff? If so, you could profit from cleaning out closets, storage spaces, the attic and basement, and then turning your discards into cash. You might even discover a hidden treasure or two that's worth considerably more than you imagine, either in your own home or at a yard sale or thrift shop. So be cautious as you toss out unwanted items, especially in May, June, and December when Jupiter will join forces with Neptune in Aquarius. What seems worthless might in actuality be valuable.

Neptune can also make a poor deal seem like a fabulous one. Remember, you always get what you pay for and some bargains are anything but. Keep that in mind if you plan to invest or purchase electronics, where an extended warranty might be worth the extra cost.

But as much as Neptune can mask the truth, it's also a terrific influence to attract just about anything you want. Try visualization, for example, if you're in search of a true bargain or aiming for a big raise, and then listen to your intuition. The combination can work wonders if you truly believe you deserve what you desire.

Saturn spends most of the year in Virgo, nearly completing its transit of your solar ninth house before moving on to Libra October 29. (It will return briefly to Virgo next spring.) This is one of the best times in your life to return to school for a degree or advanced certification to prepare for a career change or to open up new opportunities for advancement. If you began this process when Saturn entered Virgo in September 2007, you should aim to complete your education by this fall or spring 2010.

There are other choices to make the most of Saturn in Virgo. Take a class for the sheer pleasure of learning, travel where you can experience other cultures, enroll in a week-long seminar at a vacation destination to master new hobby skills, or get involved in a community historical or museum project. What you do isn't as important as doing something to expand your horizons and your knowledge.

What makes this a particularly ideal time for learning is Saturn's exact alignment with Uranus in Pisces, your solar third house, in February and September. These two planets first joined forces last November (2008), so the events that occurred then will conclude this year. Although this Saturn/Uranus lineup is itself a stressful one, both signs (Virgo and Pisces) are friendly to your sign. This means you can successfully channel the energy into positive endeavors. But don't expect everything to go exactly as planned! Uranus is the planet of the unexpected and sudden opportunities, so be ready to snap up the best of the best that come your way. Even so, it would be wise to avoid travel during the months that Saturn/Uranus is active because of the increased chance for delays, lost luggage, and cancellations.

If you've ever wanted to explore your psyche to better understand what motivates you and what holds you back, 2009 is a terrific year. Chances are, you'll be surprised by what you discover about yourself. Therapy is one option, or you could join a self-help group or read motivational, self-help books in order to maximize your potential.

Your career will be in high focus once Saturn begins its two and a half year trip through Libra, your solar tenth house. This transit is made to order for Capricorns because it's the pinnacle you've been preparing for, the time to achieve your worldly ambitions. Do all you can to firmly establish your career path while Saturn is in Libra so you can continue to capitalize on it for at least the next fourteen years.

That career path may alter course during the last two months of the year as Saturn clashes with Pluto in Capricorn. You might suddenly realize that what you thought was the ideal career direction no longer is—because you are changing. But this Saturn/Pluto alignment could also fuel your current career ambitions to the max. Be cautious if that's true. It would be easy to alienate the very supporters you need in your relentless pursuit of success.

Pluto moves slowly. It will be in Capricorn until 2024, so you may not fully experience its effects until it contacts your Sun. Nevertheless, this tiny but powerful planet will have an impact in your life this year, if only through what you experience in your immediate environment. Major changes will occur that will affect you in some way. And they will plant the seeds for the personal transformation that will occur when Pluto meets your Sun. Observe what happens around you and how the planetary energy is influencing other people and the world at large. You can benefit from this knowledge in the years to come.

What This Year's Eclipses Mean for You

Three of this year's six eclipses will reinforce the Jupiter-Neptune financial emphasis. Two will occur in Aquarius and one in Leo, your solar second/eighth house axis of personal and joint resources.

Although there are no guarantees in life, the January 7 solar eclipse and the August 6 lunar eclipse, both in Aquarius, will boost Jupiter's potential to make this a year of outstanding abundance. The February 9 lunar eclipse in Leo, your solar eighth house, adds another dimension because it brings other people into the picture. But because the Leo eclipse will also be closely aligned with Neptune, it advises the utmost caution when dealing with joint resources such as loans, insurance, legacies, investments, and partnership funds. Also take precautions to safeguard financial information and check your (and your family's) credit reports. You might even want to play it very safe and enroll in a fraud protection program. Be sure to read all the fine print before you sign any document and, if possible, avoid major financial decisions in February. Any significant money matters that occur that month are likely to resurface, or conclude, in December.

The year's remaining eclipses will spark your interest in other people. Two Cancer eclipses—July 22 (solar) and December 31 (lunar)—will light up your solar seventh house, and the final one, July 7 in Capricorn, will bring you to the attention of many. These eclipses will spotlight the close relationships in your life, both business and personal, and the value of cooperation and compromise. You'll be drawn to people and they to you, and you'll develop deep bonds with some. Others, however, are likely to disappear from your life either because they relocate or you no longer have much in common.

Some Capricorns will merge hearts in lifetime commitment as a result of these eclipses, while others will consider a business partnership. Remember Neptune? This mystical, romantic planet is terrific for Capricorns in an existing, stable relationship. But be wary if someone sweeps you off your feet or suggests you invest in a business. The same applies to home ownership with anyone other than a legal partner. Let things slide for a while, and postpone partnership decisions until at least mid-2010.

Great news: the spotlight will be on you the final six months of the year, thanks to the July eclipse in your sign. And that will trigger many opportunities to meet people and learn a lot about human nature. The eclipse energy will also boost your confidence and, in tandem with Pluto, encourage you to take an honest look at yourself and your life, where you're going, and how best to shine in the world at large. But try not to get so centered on yourself that you miss the chance to connect with someone who might be a soul mate friend or lover.

Saturn

If you were born between January 4 and 20, you'll benefit from Saturn's favorable contact with your Sun from Virgo, your solar ninth house. This is a great year to learn, grow, travel, and generally expand your horizons. Explore other cultures, see the world or a small part of it, complete or begin a degree (or study a subject just for the fun of it), or share your expertise by teaching a community or company class. What you learn now will pay off handsomely in the next few years as Saturn in Libra influences your career sector, so do all you can to set yourself up for career gains that will satisfy your ambitions.

Saturn will provide many benefits this year, but as always, Saturn will require you to put forth the effort to earn its rewards. You'll have increased stamina if you emphasize a nutritious diet and regular, moderate exercise. You'll learn what you need to learn if you have an open mind. You'll receive accolades if you take on and fulfill responsibilities. Although each requires some sort of effort, you'll find it easier than usual to make Saturn's energy work for you and thus many things will fall into place.

Pay close attention to what's happening in and around your life from mid-April through June **if your birthday is between January 4 and 7**, as Saturn will make a direct contact with your Sun during that time. **If you were born between January 8 and 12**, you'll experience Saturn's effects the first three-and-a-half months of the year and again in July and August. For **Capricorns with a birthday between January 12 and 20**, Saturn will align with your Sun in September or October.

Saturn-Pluto

If you were born between December 21 and 25, Pluto in Capricorn will join forces with your Sun throughout 2009. This can be an empowering time for you, but Pluto will also reinforce your natural tendency to take charge—possibly to the point where you'll have control issues. Try to keep your objectivity because you can easily become consumed by everything from projects to people. If you think this might be a challenge, ask someone close to you for regular feedback and then listen to the advice.

Possibly your greatest challenge during this time, however, will be the growing sense of urgency to transform yourself and your life. Used constructively, Pluto's powerful energy can reinforce your determination, willpower, and commitment to achieve just about any level of personal change from the physical to the mental. But there's another side to Pluto. This planet could prompt you to go so far as to end a serious relationship or another close alliance in order to free yourself from the past. Think carefully. Actions taken under a Pluto-Sun contact are seldom reversible.

Although Pluto will operate on its own much of the year, it will clash with Saturn in Libra, your solar tenth house, from October 29 to year's end. The intense energy of this duo could trigger everything from power plays to landing you in a top position that fulfills all your dreams. Unfortunately, a layoff is also possible, so you'll want to be alert to what's happening in your career field and your company. Most of all, don't test your luck with the boss and do try to stay out of company politics. Remember that this is the time to begin to reap the success of your efforts as you reach a career peak, and the more supporters you can gain, the better.

On a personal level, you'll want to get as much rest and sleep as possible because this Saturn/Pluto alignment can indicate diminished vitality. Schedule a health check-up if it's been a while since your last one.

Uranus

If you were born between January 8 and 16, Uranus in Pisces, your solar third house, will trigger opportunities and enlightenment. Listen to your sixth sense and to what people say. The least likely source could trigger a flash of insight that will open up new personal, financial, and professional vistas. You'll also enjoy a year of creative, clever ideas if you unleash your curiosity and let your mind wander in new directions. It's simply a matter of viewing a challenge or a project from a different perspective and then following the path to innovative solutions.

On a practical level you'll want to be cautious about what you say and write, and also when you're behind the wheel. It would be all too easy to react before you think or to take a risk on the road when you're in a hurry. February and September will require extra caution because Saturn in Virgo will form a difficult alignment with Uranus then. Legal issues may be involved with this lineup, especially **if you were born near January 10–15**, and although they could be concluded in September, it may be next year before matters are finally resolved.

Neptune

If you were born between January 11 and 16, Neptune will contact your Sun from Aquarius, your solar second house of personal resources, income, and spending. You, above all Capricorns, will need to be careful about money matters. If a deal sounds too good to be true, it probably is. If someone tries to lure you with a guarantee, steer clear of it. If you think you can quickly make a big profit, think again. Instead, let Neptune inspire you to save, invest conservatively, and thoroughly read and investigate all the details before you make any financial decisions. Be especially wary during the months when Jupiter aligns with Neptune—May, June, and December. The positive spin on Neptune is that it could trigger a sizeable bonus or raise, or lead you to a lucky, lucrative find. You also can use visualization to help bring the money you desire. Think big!

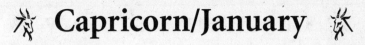 Capricorn/January

Planetary Hotspots

Handle top priorities within the first few weeks of January when the Sun and Mars in Capricorn can fuel your drive and determination. Progress slows from the 21st on, the date retrograde Mercury retreats into your sign. Daily stress relief can help manage the increasing frustration you'll feel, which will peak at month's end as Mercury meets Mars.

Planetary Lightspots

Charming words and clever ideas set you apart from the crowd this month as Venus advances in Pisces, your solar third house. You'll get the best of this planet the last weekend of January when it could trigger a quick trip for business or pleasure. Weather delays are possible, however, so plan accordingly and opt for carry-on luggage.

Relationships

People are drawn to you the week of the January 10 Full Moon in Cancer, your solar seventh house of relationships. Use it for all its worth whether you're looking for love or a career connection. Either one—or a surprise opportunity—could arrive at the least expected moment. The lunar energy also boosts your intuition, giving you new insights into someone close to you.

Money and Success

Money begins to flow your way this month with Jupiter's January 5 arrival in Aquarius, your solar second house, and the days surrounding the January 26 New Moon in the same sign bring the first indication of what this bountiful planet can do for your bank account this year. The odds favor a raise or windfall, but it could be the end of February before you actually see the cash. Try to resist the urge to splurge until then. One cautionary note: Mercury turns retrograde in Aquarius on the 11th, so pay bills early.

Rewarding Days

1, 5, 6, 13, 14, 17, 24, 25, 26, 27

Challenging Days

2, 3, 8, 9, 10, 15, 16, 22, 28, 29

☒ Capricorn/February ☒

Planetary Hotspots

If travel is a must try to postpone it until late in the month when the effects of the February 5 Saturn/Uranus alignment wane somewhat. Weather delays and schedule changes are possible with these two planets spanning your solar third/ninth houses. Mechanical problems could also pop up, either in your home or your car, and you should be wary of computer viruses. You also can expect delays in legal matters, and students will feel both motivated and challenged.

Planetary Lightspots

The time has arrived to rid yourself and your home of clutter. Get a jump start on spring cleaning by rearranging and organizing closets, drawers, and the basement as Venus in Aries, your domestic sector, motivates you to get your place in shape. It will be easy to toss out what you no longer need, and the fresh energy will clear the way for new décor later this month.

Relationships

Communication and creative thinking are assets this month, and you can easily clear up any recent misunderstandings because Mercury turns direct in your sign on the 1st. People are especially receptive to your ideas the week of the February 24 New Moon in Pisces, which is a great time to ask for favors and to enjoy the company of relatives.

Money and Success

You could be in financial luck later this month when Mercury, Venus, and Mars align with Jupiter in Aquarius, your solar second house. The same planetary lineup could trigger a spending spree, however. Do it if you can pay cash, but be cautious about using credit unless you can swing an affordable no-interest deal on a major purchase. Read the fine print.

Rewarding Days

2, 3, 4, 10, 13, 15, 17, 19, 21, 24

Challenging Days

1, 5, 6, 11, 12, 18, 25, 26

Capricorn/March

Planetary Hotspots

Your domestic sector is this month's hotspot. Planetary alignments increase the possibility for a home repair or the need for a new appliance. There also will be tense moments when personalities clash. But the main challenge is Venus, which turns retrograde on the 6th in Aries, your solar fourth house. Patience will get you further with loved ones who are apt to be indecisive at times, and this is not the time to purchase new furnishings or launch a home improvement project. Hold off until May.

Planetary Lightspots

Family life becomes a lightspot at month's end when Mercury enters Aries on the 25th. Use the last week of March to resolve any ongoing issues; encourage open, honest discussion. For the most part you'll be on the same wavelength. Listen and appreciate each other's views and then find a workable compromise to meet everyone's needs.

Relationships

February's Saturn/Uranus alignment is activated by the March 10 Full Moon in Virgo, which advises against travel. Some relatives, possibly in-laws, may require more of your time and attention. As difficult as that may be, you'll have the strength and determination to take action after Mars enters Pisces on the 14th. Continue to drive with care and don't let car maintenance and repairs go.

Money and Success

Finances benefit from Mercury in Aquarius, your solar second house, through the 7th, and Mars in the same sign through the 13th. This duo could put some extra cash in your pocket. But you'll also have the urge to splurge, especially in early March. What appears to be a great deal may or may not be because of Venus's retrograde status. Wait a day and you're likely to change your mind.

Rewarding Days

1, 3, 6, 13, 14, 15, 20, 24, 28, 29

Challenging Days

2, 4, 5, 9, 11, 17, 23, 25, 26, 31

Capricorn/April

Planetary Hotspots

After a few hectic and stressful months you'll appreciate a relatively easygoing one. Conditions still aren't great for travel, and you'll want to be especially cautious on the road the first week of April. The same holds true for major purchases because Venus is retrograde until the 17th. Also choose your words with care to prevent misunderstandings.

Planetary Lightspots

Family life continues on an upbeat path with only a few tension-filled moments in early and late April. Move forward with the planning stage on a home improvement project or give your place a spring cleaning once Venus returns to Aries, your domestic sector, on the 24th. You can easily afford to do much of what you have in mind to increase the value of your home, although creative thinking yields creative solutions that can save quite a bit of cash. Get the do-it-yourself skills you need.

Relationships

April's Taurus New Moon on the 24th spotlights your solar fifth house or recreation, romance, and children. Make all a part of your life this month as Mercury transits Taurus April 9–29, where it's joined by the Sun on the 20th. Get involved in your children's activities, socialize with friends, and take the family to a favorite weekend destination.

Money and Success

You're an attention-getter the week of the April 9 Full Moon in Libra, your career sector. All your efforts could be rewarded with a nice raise around that time, when you can also reinforce your position with decision-makers. However, be cautious about what you say to coworkers at after-hours events. Someone who appears to be supportive could be just the opposite.

Rewarding Days
6, 10, 11, 12, 16, 17, 20, 21, 25, 29

Challenging Days
1, 2, 3, 7, 8, 13, 14, 22, 26, 28

Capricorn/May

Planetary Hotspots

Mix-ups and misunderstandings plague your work and social life this month. Double-check work and confirm instructions after the 7th, when Mercury turns retrograde in Gemini. Mercury retreats into Taurus on the 13th to play havoc with your social life, increasing the chance for confusion with dates, times, and places. You'll also want to be sensitive to your children's needs during this time; a poor choice of words, although unintentional, could trigger hurt feelings.

Planetary Lightspots

The time has come for home improvements. With Venus and Mars in Aries, your solar fourth house, you can zip through domestic projects and wrap them up before month's end. Keep safety in mind. Mars could spark a mishap at the least expected moment. Then show off the results by hosting a get-together the fourth or fifth weekend of May.

Relationships

Despite the influence of retrograde Mercury, fun times with friends are on tap this month as the Sun travels in Taurus through the 19th, and the May 9 Scorpio Full Moon highlights your friendship sector. Get out and socialize, meet your neighbors, and join another family for a day at an amusement park or the zoo. Single Capricorns looking for a new relationship could be in luck midmonth.

Money and Success

Grab the chance to shine under the May 24 New Moon in Gemini, when you can impress important people. Remember Mercury's retrograde status, however. Make no assumptions and be sure you have everything covered. Leave nothing to chance. Talk of a step up could materialize in mid-June.

Rewarding Days

3, 6, 7, 8, 14, 19, 22, 24, 28, 31

Challenging Days

1, 2, 4, 5, 10, 13, 18, 20, 25, 27

Capricorn/June

Planetary Hotspots

Tread softly with those closest to you at home and at work around the time of the June 21 New Moon in Cancer. Its exact alignment with Pluto in Capricorn could trigger a power struggle or a battle of the wills when viewpoints and needs clash. Use your initiative to find a compromise that works for both of you. Remember also that your partner has the same right you do to pursue his or her own interests.

Planetary Lightspots

Let the June 7 Full Moon in Sagittarius, your solar twelfth house, inspire you to kick back a little. Not only is it good for health and well-being but even ambitious Capricorns need time off to enjoy the moment. Catch some extra sleep, and fill your evenings with quality time with loved ones and family activities.

Relationships

Mars in Taurus all month fills your social calendar, as does Mercury in the same sign through the 12th and Venus there from the 6th on. Like May, June has all the potential to be a terrific month for family outings, love, and a new romantic interest. You also can use Mars to get in shape by walking or taking a yoga class with a neighbor. If you can manage the time, plan a weekend getaway with friends at a nearby destination.

Money and Success

Aim for midmonth if you're scheduling business travel or an important presentation. People will be more receptive to your ideas. The same time frame could bring you an added perk or raise. Take the suggestion seriously if someone recommends you return to school to help advance your career. A course or two might be all you need and it's possible your employer will reimburse the tuition cost.

Rewarding Days

2, 4, 9, 10, 14, 18, 19, 23, 24, 26

Challenging Days

1, 3, 5, 7, 11, 16, 22, 27, 28

Capricorn/July

Planetary Hotspots

July perks along for the most part, with only minor glitches here and there. Be a little conservative with spending, and don't let anyone talk you into parting with big bucks as Jupiter and Neptune join forces in Aquarius, your money sector. Also try not to get frustrated when people block progress. It won't take much patience to wait things out because the flow will quickly resume.

Planetary Lightspots

July's Capricorn Full Moon on the 7th has you in its spotlight. Take advantage of this time to shine and do all you can to bring supporters into your orbit. That should be a snap if you turn on the charm, listen attentively, and give them the benefit of your knowledge.

Relationships

Relationships are also a shining star in your life this month, thanks to Mercury in Cancer, your solar seventh house, July 3–16, and the New Moon there on the 21st. The planetary influences trigger a romantic commitment for some Capricorns, and others form strong business ties with profit potential. But be wary of becoming involved in conflict or even a mildly disagreeable discussion in early July. Sometimes the best choice is to say little and let things go, and to let someone else take charge.

Money and Success

You have nearly every success factor going for you this month from the New Moon in your sign to Venus in Gemini, your solar sixth house of daily work, July 5–30. Altogether, that has you among the favored few. But don't let things go because August will be even busier and you'll want to accomplish as much as you can this month. There could be some extra cash in it for you, although that's more likely to occur in August.

Rewarding Days

1, 7, 12, 16, 17, 20, 21, 27, 28, 29

Challenging Days

2, 4, 5, 6, 10, 13, 19, 24, 25, 31

Capricorn/August

Planetary Hotspots

You'll have a high probability of conflict and frustration at work as Mercury and Mars clash with several planets this month. Do your best to keep your cool even if you're far more informed than decision-makers. There may be information about which you're unaware, and the more you push the more likely you are to alienate the very people who could help you in the near future.

Planetary Lightspots

Need an escape? Go for it if you can manage a long weekend to relax and unwind. Make it a romantic one with your partner, or join friends at a resort destination. Where you go isn't as important as the chance to get away sometime between August 2 and 25, when Mercury is in Virgo, your solar ninth house of travel.

Relationships

Even if work relationships have their challenges, you'll enjoy close ties with friends and loved ones, thanks to Venus in Cancer, your solar seventh house, through the 25th. This is one of the best influences of the year for couples, and some Capricorns will feel the zing of love at first sight with a soul mate. But it's also wise to know when to give in to a family member's wishes rather than insist upon your own agenda.

Money and Success

Cross your fingers for a nice raise this month. It could be yours around the time of the Aquarius Full Moon (and lunar eclipse) on the 5th or the Leo New Moon on the 20th, both of which are in your financial sectors. Be a little cautious though about investments and credit. Jupiter and Neptune in Aquarius can make even the worst deal seem like the best one. Also be sure you have adequate property insurance; compare coverage and costs.

Rewarding Days

3, 4, 5, 7, 11, 12, 17, 20, 21, 24, 30, 31

Challenging Days

1, 2, 8, 9, 10, 15, 16, 22, 26, 27, 29

☈ Capricorn/September ☈

Planetary Hotspots

September brings the final Saturn/Uranus contact in Virgo and Pisces, your solar ninth/third house axis. As it did in February, this alignment cautions against legal matters and travel, especially around the time of the September 18 New Moon in Virgo. You might also encounter difficulties with a relative or neighbor. However, listen closely if someone whose opinion you value again suggests a return to school. Begin now and you could achieve what you need by next summer.

Planetary Lightspots

Venus in Leo, your solar eighth house, keeps finances on track in September. You might even net a gain from this beneficial placement that also has the potential to bring a lovely gift, something you've coveted for a long time. Just continue to be cautious about credit. What you want and what you can afford might be two different things.

Relationships

Mars in Cancer, your solar seventh house, all month keeps passions alive for Capricorns in love. This also can be a favorable influence for new relationships, although you might be tempted to come on too strong. You'll also want to be alert for brewing conflict at work midmonth. Do your best to stay out of it even if that requires considerable effort.

Money and Success

Tension is more the norm than the exception in your career life this month. Although Mercury in Libra, your solar tenth house, is usually a favorable influence, it turns retrograde on the 7th, and that can trigger everything from mistakes to mix-ups to misunderstandings. Cover yourself. Get instructions in writing, and reread (and if necessary, cool off) before you hit Send on e-mail.

Rewarding Days

2, 7, 8, 9, 14, 17, 20, 21, 26, 30

Challenging Days

3, 5, 6, 12, 13, 18, 19, 23, 25

⚸ Capricorn/October ⚸

Planetary Hotspots

Last month's Saturn/Uranus lineup continues to be active the first two weeks of October as Mercury and Venus connect with both planets. This is the home stretch with this alignment so have faith and resolve any lingering issues. Travel and legal matters are still inadvisable, but you can benefit from a professional consultation, if necessary. Someone close to you has wise advice. Take it to heart.

Planetary Lightspots

Home is the comfiest place to be in early October, which features the Full Moon in Aries, your solar fourth house, on the 4th. It might be tough to find time to enjoy it as much as you'd like, but do your best because you'll benefit from time with loved ones and laid-back evenings, warm and cozy in your PJs.

Relationships

Mars wraps up its time in Cancer, your solar seventh house, on the 15th. People will support your efforts and willingly lend a hand when necessary. Just ask. At month's end, your interest turns to friendship when the Sun enters Scorpio, your solar eleventh house. Line up get-togethers for November.

Money and Success

Career matters are mostly positive, although conflict potential still exists midmonth when Mercury and Venus in Libra, your solar tenth house, clash with Pluto in Capricorn. Watch your words, and go all out to impress those who count. Do that and you could earn a promotion or significant raise around the time of the October 18 New Moon in Libra. The most important event in this sector, however, is Saturn, which enters Libra on the 29th. Although it will briefly return to Virgo next spring, this is the start of a three-year period that can be a career high point. Make it happen.

Rewarding Days

5, 6, 7, 8, 10, 14, 17, 23, 24, 28

Challenging Days

2, 4, 9, 11, 15, 16, 22, 30

⚹ Capricorn/November ⚹

Planetary Hotspots

Although Mars in Leo, your solar eighth house isn't exactly a hot-spot yet, it will be. Set a firm budget for holiday gifts and resist the urge to splurge. Money flows your way now, but that trend is likely to be reversed when Mars turns retrograde next month. And that can leave you with some hefty bills and possibly without the extra cash you were expecting to pay them.

Planetary Lightspots

Take some time for yourself after November 14, when Mercury is in Sagittarius, your solar twelfth house. Also make a point to slow the pace, even if only a little, to reduce the chance of a cold. Mostly, though, it's a great time to think about yourself, your life, and your goals, especially after the Sun arrives in the same sign on the 21st.

Relationships

You're the center of attention on the holiday social scene, thanks to the November 2 Full Moon in Taurus, your solar fifth house, and the November 16 New Moon in Scorpio, your friendship sector. Even better is Venus in Scorpio from the 7th on, which could bring a romance with a friend of a friend. If you're looking, ask a pal to introduce you to a potential match.

Money and Success

Saturn in Libra clashes with Pluto in Capricorn on the 15th. How-ever, it will be December before you experience much of the effects of this difficult lineup. The first hint might be an increasing dissat-isfaction with your career or your job. If that's true, use November to explore your options. This isn't the best time to make a sudden change, and next month may not be either. Patience and tolerance are the lessons here.

Rewarding Days

3, 4, 7, 10, 13, 14, 16, 20, 21, 22, 29

Challenging Days

2, 6, 8, 9, 12, 15, 19, 23, 27, 30

Capricorn/December

Planetary Hotspots

Your work life is satisfying and fulfilling the week of the December 2 Full Moon in Gemini, your solar sixth house. But after that, several planets kick off last month's Saturn/Pluto alignment in Libra-Capricorn, your solar tenth and first houses. And that could push you to the max and to the point of suddenly cutting ties. Don't be hasty. Mercury turns retrograde in Capricorn on the 26th, so the final outcome of this stressful period is yet to be revealed—and it could work out in your favor.

Planetary Lightspots

December's best news is the Sun's arrival in your sign on the 21st, followed by Venus on the 25th. That's a beautiful combination for making a wish come true. Visualize what you want and expect to get it as these two planets multiply your powers of attraction.

Relationships

You'll enjoy socializing with close friends far more than the party scene this month. But the December 31 Full Moon in Cancer, your solar seventh house, cautions against going anywhere on New Year's Eve because it's directly aligned with Pluto. That can also spark conflict with someone close to you in early January. Go easy on yourself and those around you.

Money and Success

Mars turns retrograde in Leo, your solar eighth house, on the 20th, and will stay that way through early March. Although this can restrict your income, its main effect will be statement errors and other money mix-ups. This is not the time to seek a loan. It is the time to safeguard valuables, and to consider fraud protection. Pay bills early; delays are possible. If someone owes you money, it might be May before you collect, so plan accordingly.

Rewarding Days

4, 5, 6, 8, 11, 12, 17, 19, 22, 23, 26, 27

Challenging Days

3, 7, 9, 10, 16, 18, 20, 24, 28, 29, 31

Capricorn Action Table

These dates reflect the best—but not the only—times for success and ease in these activities, according to your Sun sign.

	JAN	FEB	MAR	APR	MAY	JUN	JUL	AUG	SEPT	OCT	NOV	DEC
Move		27-28		23-28								
Start a class			14-15, 19 24-25	20-21						28		
Join a club			14-15					25			16-20	
Ask for a raise			4							26-27		
Look for work							18-19, 22-23, 26-27					
Get pro advice						23-24	21	17				
Get a loan							22-23, 27					
See a doctor		4, 17								21-22	5	15
Start a diet							18	15			4	
End relationship	11							17		11		
Buy clothes	6-7			25		19-20				6-7		
Get a makeover		2				9-10						
New romance		3		25								
Vacation								20-25		1-9		

AQUARIUS

The Water Bearer
January 20 to February 19

Element: Air

Quality: Fixed

Polarity: Yang/masculine

Planetary Ruler: Uranus

Meditation: I am a wellspring of creativity

Gemstone: Amethyst

Power Stones: Aquamarine, black pearl, chrysocolla

Key Phrase: I know

Glyph: Currents of energy

Anatomy: Ankles, circulatory system

Color: Iridescent blues, violet

Animal: Exotic birds

Myths/Legends: Ninhursag, John the Baptist, Deucalion

House: Eleventh

Opposite Sign: Leo

Flower: Orchid

Key Word: Unconventional

Your Strengths and Challenges

Aquarians are noted for their independence and strong will. You can be determined or stubborn, depending upon the situation, which is one example of the contradictions that characterize your fixed-sign personality.

Uranus, planet of change, is your ruler, but you welcome change only when it's your idea—and then it can't happen fast enough because you like to shake things up. Be careful, though; change for the sake of change isn't always the best choice.

You're an uncommon mix of traditional and progressive, conventional and eccentric, aloof and friendly. All of these traits are true of you, which make you a fascinating and intriguing puzzle.

Aquarius is the sign of friendship and the humanitarian, so you're generous with your time and money. You support those in your inner circle as well as organizations whose mission you value. The original networker, you get great satisfaction from connecting people with people and people with opportunities, and you nearly always know someone to contact for help or information when you need it.

Because Aquarius is an air sign, you're a communicator, albeit one who prefers to maintain at least some distance. And thus you're at times perceived as aloof when in reality you're uncomfortable with emotional expression. The intellect is your arena.

Your intuitive, insightful mind is geared to the future, and you have a knack for spotting trends, sometimes years in advance. Many Aquarians are also innovators and some are brilliant inventors. But remind yourself to also enjoy the moment while anticipating and looking forward to the next adventure, event, date, or accomplishment.

Your Relationships

You're a flirt who plays the field with ease and might even keep two dating relationships going at the same time. After all, you believe the more variety the better as you search for a partner. Long talks and walks keep you interested and you can fall in love with someone's mind. Communication is just as important once you settle into a committed relationship because you know it keeps you in touch and in sync with each other. It takes a very special person, however, to capture your independent heart. Love could sizzle with a dramatic, outgoing Leo, your opposite sign, and you might be compatible with Aries or Sagittarius. Your fellow air signs, Gemini and Libra, share your need for communication, but you could clash with Taurus and Scorpio, both of which are possessive.

Family life brings out your more traditional side and you stay in close touch with relatives. You're protective of them, and probably grew up in a loving, affectionate, and comfortable home. The same is true of your own home, although some Aquarians have difficulty letting go of anything and live with clutter—collectibles and nick-knacks on every surface and jam-packed closets and storage spaces. If this describes you, ask yourself why you find security in the things rather than the people in your life. Most Aquarians have only one or two children and some have twins. You're fond of your children, encouraging them to explore their talents and develop their curiosity. This encourages an easygoing relationship, but remember you're a parent first and a pal second, at least until they reach adulthood.

Aquarius is the universal sign of friendship so it's only natural that you surround yourself with many acquaintances and only a few close pals. Group activities appeal to most Aquarians, and you may be involved in clubs or organizations that satisfy your humanitarian goals. You can be the social butterfly working your way through a room full of people; or find a kindred soul and a corner in which to talk away the evening, exchanging knowledge and information. You accept people as they are and friends from all walks of life—as long as they fulfill one requirement: they're unique or in some way different. "Normal" people bore you.

Your Career and Money
Most Aquarians are content to remain in one career throughout their lifetimes. You might switch your emphasis or branch out into a related field, but your desire is to stick with a main area of interest. Fortunately, you have the staying power to do just that if you plan and strategize how to achieve the end result. It's wise, however, to keep your grand plan to yourself rather than risk tipping off a competitor. You have the ability to rise to a powerful position, to network your way into a spot where you can be in charge. In your everyday work life you're happiest in a family-like atmosphere and might even work in a family business. A calm working environment is a must for high productivity, as is the opportunity to initiate change and to revamp procedures, policies, and even your work

space. Your ideal would be to overhaul an entire department or company, or to take the lead in resurrecting a faltering enterprise.

In money matters you're both practical and naïve, creative and analytical. At times money slips through your fingers almost as if it disappears into thin air. You also attract what you need when you need it. Even so, it's wise to train yourself to live within a realistic budget that includes necessities, savings, investments, and fun money. Then you'll always have a nest egg to fall back on. Study facts and figures before you invest and double-check all details in loan documents before you sign. Overall, you can do well financially if you plan, think long-term, and look at the big picture. Real estate can be especially profitable, and you could receive a sizable family inheritance.

Your Lighter Side

There's a certain electrifying something about you that fascinates people. They're drawn to your magnetic charm and intrigued by your ability to say a lot but reveal almost no personal information. Only a select few, however, are privy to your full story, and that keeps most people guessing about the mysterious you and what makes you tick.

Affirmation for the Year

I'm confident and optimistic about the future.

The Year Ahead for Aquarius

Jupiter! This lucky planet will be in Aquarius for all but the first four days of 2009. The one year in twelve that Jupiter visits your sign is nearly always a memorable and fortunate one, bringing optimism and helping you attract exciting opportunities for personal growth and new directions. The toughest part might be deciding what to pursue because you'll want to do it all! That's the dilemma of this expansive planet of good fortune, so be realistic and try not to overprogram and overcommit yourself.

Devote more time in the year ahead to get to know yourself and to really zero in on your major skills and talents. You'll have the confidence to delve into new areas of interest and, whatever the outcome, you'll benefit from the experience. Try to learn all you can about yourself and your place in the world; you'll carry this knowledge with you until Jupiter again enters your sign in 2020.

Other people will be a major feature of this Jupiter transit. You'll attract those who can help you in some way, and others will bring you luck, opening doors that were previously closed. More important, this is the year to do the same for others and to make the most of your marvelous networking skills.

Jupiter joins Neptune in Aquarius as Neptune continues its long journey through your sign, which it entered in 1998. You may have already experienced the faith, spirituality, and creativity associated with this mystical planet, as well as its opposite side: disappointment and disillusionment. All sides of Neptune will be active this year as it joins forces with Jupiter in May and December.

The Jupiter-Neptune duo can inspire you to achieve great things because you'll believe in yourself and your abilities. But you should also be realistic; it will be easy to slip into wishful thinking and to see things as you wish them to be, not as they are.

The planetary energy will also touch your humanitarian heart, and you'll be more idealistic, doing what you can to improve the lives of those who are less fortunate. But rather than simply donating money or time, you'll be drawn to organizations that help others help themselves. You may do that one-on-one for elderly people in your neighborhood, for example, or for friends who can temporarily benefit from your assistance. All of these things represent the highest manifestation of Jupiter-Neptune.

But because you'll want to see the best in people this year you need to be cautious about whom you trust, especially anyone new who enters your life. Some people will tell you what you want to hear and others will deliberately try to mislead you. This is therefore not the best year for a business, financial, or serious romantic partnership.

Saturn will spend much of the year in Virgo, your solar eighth house of joint resources. By now you've probably experienced this planet's effect on money matters, since it entered Virgo in September 2007. It's not too late if you haven't yet begun to get your finances in order, especially paying off debt, which is one of the best uses of this Saturn transit. Create a budget and set payoff deadlines, beginning with those that have the highest interest rates. Try to pay cash for whatever you need.

If your finances are in great shape (and even if they're not), make savings a priority. If you invest, be conservative and think long-term. Do the same with your retirement account. Insurance is another eighth house matter, so take the time to review and update policies as necessary to be sure your home and property are adequately covered. All of these items are even more important because Uranus continues its journey through Pisces, your solar second house of personal resources.

Uranus, planet of the unexpected, can bring extra expenses as well as windfalls, and you've probably experienced this since it entered Pisces in 2003. What makes this year different is that Saturn and Uranus will form an exact alignment in February and September, just as they did last November (2008). Whatever occurred during their first contact will give you a clue as to what might happen this year. But in any case you'll want to be as conservative as possible with money so you're covered. This lineup also advises against financial partnerships and all but the safest long-term investments.

Saturn will begin its three-year Libra transit October 29, encouraging you to broaden your horizons during its trip through your solar ninth house. (Saturn will briefly return to Virgo in 2010.) This is your knowledge sector, so you should consider returning to school to complete or begin a degree program, or to get specialized job skills. This will be a real plus for your career when Saturn moves on to Scorpio, your solar tenth house, in 2012.

Even if you're set in your career and have all the education you need, you'll still have the motivation to learn, so take a class for the fun of it in person or online. Or tap into the other side of this Saturn transit and share your knowledge with others. Teach a company class or one through your community recreation department. Or get involved in a literacy project to teach adults to read. You're also likely to become an avid (or more avid) reader while Saturn is in Libra.

Pluto, now in its first full year in Capricorn since it entered this sign in January 2008, will continue to encourage you to look within yourself for answers. During its fifteen-year trip through your sign of self-renewal, you'll gain a new appreciation for what motivates you and what holds you back. Your sixth sense is also likely to become even more active, and the more you nurture it the stronger it will become.

Saturn in Libra will clash with Pluto during the final two months of the year. Although this is a difficult alignment, you can manage it better than some signs because Libra is a fellow air sign. Don't be surprised if you find yourself lost in thought more often than usual, along with a desire to spend more time alone. Give meditation a try, as well as self-help books in order to better understand yourself.

What This Year's Eclipses Mean for You

Get set to shine! Two of this year's six eclipses will occur in Aquarius—a January 7 solar eclipse and an August 6 lunar eclipse. The energy will flow all year because eclipse effects typically last about six months. Like Jupiter and Neptune, these eclipses will put you in the spotlight, an attention-getter who attracts good fortune and opportunities through other people. These eclipses also will boost your confidence and encourage you to step into each day with optimism and an eye on the future.

The February 9 lunar eclipse in Leo, your solar seventh house of relationships, will also draw other people into your life. But this eclipse will be closely aligned with Neptune, reinforcing the cautionary message about putting your faith in just anyone. This is a fabulous influence for romance. But you'd be wise to postpone a business or personal commitment until at least 2010. For couples, this eclipse can either burst your bubble or perk up your love life.

On another level, you'll want to check credentials and references before hiring a professional such as an attorney or accountant, or even a medical expert. Then be sure to ask questions rather than simply accept the advice you're given. You might have to push for answers or clarification even with a credible professional, and it would be a good idea to take notes to avoid confusion. Back up the information you receive with your own research.

Your solar sixth/twelfth house axis will be the site of the year's other three eclipses. Both a solar eclipse (July 22) and a lunar eclipse (December 31) will occur in Cancer, your sign of daily work, and there will be a lunar eclipse, July 7, in Capricorn, your solar twelfth house.

The Cancer eclipses almost guarantee that your job and work life will be a major emphasis the last half of the year and into 2010. The potential for advancement or a new job is promising, but your workload also will increase. As much as you'll want to give it your all, try to remember to treat yourself well. Relaxation and moderate exercise are great stress relievers, and even more important because the sixth and twelfth houses are associated with health. Get medical, dental, and eye check-ups, and do yourself and your body a favor by skipping fast food in favor of a nutritious diet.

This summer's Capricorn eclipse reinforces the healthy lifestyle message of Cancer and, like Pluto, urges you to take time for yourself. Get a comfy chair if you don't have one, and put a stack of books—not the computer!—next to it. That will encourage you to put your feet up and read every day, even if only for thirty minutes.

The Cancer and Capricorn eclipses also complement the Jupiter-Neptune alignment in that they can spark added incentive to get involved in a charitable organization. Hospital or hospice work might appeal to you now, and a pet-rescue group could benefit from your talents. But don't be reluctant to say no if you're asked for a large donation. Your time and talents are the best gift you can give.

Saturn
If you were born between February 2 and 19, money matters will be a major focus as Saturn contacts your Sun from Virgo, your solar

eighth house. Try not to add to your stress level by worrying even more than usual about this area of life, which you have a tendency to do. A better choice is to be proactive and take the necessary actions to ease your mind: budget, save, pay off debt, and adopt an overall conservative financial approach. **If your birthday is between February 2 and 4**, you'll need to address these issues from mid-April through June. **For Aquarians born between February 5 and 10**, decisions made and actions taken during the first three and a half months of the year will come full circle in July and August. **If you were born between February 11 and 15**, September will be a financial turning point, while **Aquarians with birthdays between February 16 and 19** will feel Saturn's effects in October and again next year.

Saturn-Pluto

If you were born between January 20 and 23, Pluto in Capricorn will contact your Sun throughout the year. The influence of this powerful planet will become most apparent, however, after Saturn enters Libra October 29, because it will clash with Pluto for the rest of the year. Placed in your solar ninth and twelfth houses, this alignment will push you to look to the past and within yourself for answers to the future, primarily in your career life. Education is a key theme, so give careful thought to how additional schooling could advance your status, either in your current field or an entirely new one. Now is the time to begin this process so you can begin to reap the benefits three years from now.

Another side of the Saturn/Pluto influence will be internal, and your thoughts will drift to the past as you examine your life. Regrets are likely to surface, but try not to dwell on them. What's past is past and by recognizing these issues and learning from them you'll be better equipped to move forward in your life. If, however, the issues are deeper ones or you simply need objective feedback, counseling might be a good option.

There is also a chance that Saturn/Pluto could also trigger legal matters. Think carefully if you want or need to initiate legal action. It will be a difficult and lengthy process that will not be resolved until next year at the earliest and possibly not for several years. And of course it would be unwise to put yourself in a position that could result in anyone taking legal action against you.

Uranus

If you were born between February 8 and 16, both Uranus and Saturn will emphasize money matters. Where Saturn will focus on joint resources, Uranus will influence your personal resources, income and spending. The nature of these two planets is quite different: Saturn represents restriction and Uranus represents change. When they clash, one or the other has to give at some point, and in the process of getting there you can expect more than a little frustration. Merging their energies is the key, and although that's easier said than done, success is possible if you change your financial thinking and approach to follow the rules: curb spending, increase assets, and eliminate debt. Ultimately this can be very positive once you adjust your habits and begin to see results. You'll thank yourself for years to come.

Unfortunately, it's also possible that your or your partner's income could decrease, or that a long-forgotten debt could resurface. Check your and your family's credit reports for errors and, if necessary, resolve them. You also should consider fraud and identity theft protection and take extra precautions to safeguard personal and financial information.

Although Uranus could bring a windfall such as an inheritance or insurance settlement, it's likely to be less than you expect or to be accompanied by special conditions or other difficulties. Be sure your home and property are adequately insured.

The Saturn/Uranus alignment will be more prominent **if you were born between February 11 and 15**, and February and September will thus be important financial months. You also should do all you can to be sure you're prepared for unexpected expenses.

Neptune

If you were born between February 11 and 16, Neptune will join forces with your Aquarius Sun throughout the year to spark your creativity, your compassion, and your sixth sense. That means you among all Aquarians will get the best of Jupiter-Neptune because both will contact your Sun in May and December. Let this influence inspire and take you in new directions of opportunity. Open your mind to different viewpoints and the knowledge you can gain by tuning in to people and the world.

But the potential is equally strong that you could experience the downside of Neptune. Be wary and wise and reserve judgment if anyone new enters your life, especially in May or June. By year's end you'll know whether the relationship is worth pursuing. Either way, someone is likely to disappoint or mislead you, and you may become disillusioned with a friendship or another close relationship. You'll also want to be cautious if you plan to consult a professional in May or December, when it will be difficult to objectively assess the information you receive. Because the Saturn/Uranus alignment will also contact your Sun, be financially ultraconservative. Don't cosign a loan, and try to avoid major purchases whether or not they involve indebtedness.

Aquarius/January

Planetary Hotspots

Patience will get your further than persistence and lessen the frustration that accompanies Mars in Capricorn, your solar twelfth house. It's there for a reason: to encourage you to take it a little easy in preparation for the fiery planet's arrival in your sign in early February. Treat yourself well, wrap up each day with a stress-relieving activity, and get plenty of sleep.

Planetary Lightspots

Wow! That's what people will say about you all year, thanks to Jupiter in Aquarius. This fortunate planet can bring out the best in you as you begin a new phase of optimism and exciting personal directions. The energy this month peaks at the January 26 New Moon, also in your sign, and gives you an extra dash of charisma. Embrace life and share your good cheer.

Relationships

Overall, relationships go smoothly this month. You're in sync with just about everyone, at your most charming with the Sun and several planets in your sign. There is, however, one minor glitch that could pop up. Mercury turns retrograde in your sign on the 11th, increasing the chance for mix-ups and misunderstandings. Choose your words with care and confirm dates, places, and times.

Money and Success

Work is hectic around the time of the January 10 Full Moon in Cancer, your solar sixth house. But it might be worth the extra effort because Venus in Pisces, your money sector, could reward you with a surprise raise or bonus. Splurge a little, save a lot. Unexpected expenses could pop up in February. You could also gain through a lucky find on the street or at a thrift store.

Rewarding Days

4, 11, 12, 16, 17, 20, 21, 25, 26, 27, 31

Challenging Days

2, 3, 6, 9, 22, 23, 24, 29

Aquarius/February

Planetary Hotspots

Money matters require careful attention this month as the year's first Saturn/Uranus alignment activates your solar second/eighth house axis. Spend as little as possible, save as much as possible, and avoid anything with even a hint of financial risk. Also take extra precautions to safeguard important information, and check your credit report for errors. Put major purchases on hold if you can.

Planetary Lightspots

A stellar lineup of planets in your sign the last week of February has all the potential to brighten your life with luck, exciting news, and the promise of good things to come. Share your enthusiasm with others, and make the most of the high energy that comes with Mars in your sign.

Relationships

You're at your most fascinating and intriguing this month, thanks to four planets traveling in your sign. And with Mercury in Aquarius and Venus in Aries, your solar third house of communication, you have a way with words that can charm just about everyone. People are drawn to you the week of the February 9 Full Moon (and lunar eclipse) in Leo, your relationship sign, which could bring a special someone into your life. Some Aquarians celebrate love with an engagement.

Money and Success

Although money matters are a challenge this month, there's also a bright spot. The February 24 New Moon in Pisces, your solar second house, can help you keep finances in positive territory if you focus on your financial goals and conserve resources. It might also give you an opportunity for a bigger paycheck or the chance to earn some extra income.

Rewarding Days

4, 8, 13, 15, 17, 22, 23, 24, 27, 28

Challenging Days

1, 5, 6, 7, 11, 12, 18, 20, 25, 26

Aquarius/March

Planetary Hotspots

People are less forthcoming with information from the 6th through mid-April as Venus travels retrograde. So expect to be frustrated at times when what you need is nowhere to be found or someone fails to come through for you. This influence also prompts you to think deeply about what you value and to ponder your life priority list. And that can be a very positive self-motivational tool.

Planetary Lightspots

You're on the go this month, especially around the time of the March 26 New Moon in Aries. The lunar energy could trigger a desire for a weekend away but, with the New Moon contacting Pluto, that's not the wisest idea; mechanical problems are possible as the Sun and Mercury clash with Pluto and join forces with retrograde Venus. Stay around home and make your plans for another time.

Relationships

Retrograde Venus can spark misunderstandings, so be sure to clarify your thoughts and ask questions rather than make assumptions. Even so, difficulties could surround a relationship with a relative or neighbor; unfortunately it's unlikely to be resolved this month. Keep that in mind and say nothing you might later regret. It will be April or May before you can clear the air.

Money and Success

Finances continue in high focus as the March 10 Full Moon in Virgo, your solar eighth house. Careful spending is still the path to follow, and remember to check your (and your family's) credit reports if you didn't do that last month. Also check statements for errors as soon as they arrive and be sure your property is adequately covered by insurance. Keep the faith. Much of this should be resolved during the first three weeks of March.

Rewarding Days

3, 7, 8, 13, 20, 21, 22, 27, 30

Challenging Days

1, 2, 4, 5, 11, 17, 25, 31

Aquarius/April

Planetary Hotspots

Look forward to a month that's far easier than the past few. Most everything is life as usual, although with Venus retrograde through the 16th you should steer clear of major purchases, contracts, and romantic commitment. Also take precautions to guard valuables when in public because it would be easy to lose a treasured item.

Planetary Lightspots

Try to schedule a week's vacation or a long weekend away when the April 9 Full Moon in Libra nudges your spirit of adventure. Fun is the main ingredient, but if you choose the right location you'll benefit from renewed inspiration to pursue exciting personal directions. Aim for a calm environment, possibly near water, that can re-center you, body and soul.

Relationships

Home life is at its best with Mercury in Taurus, your domestic sector, April 9–29, where it's joined by the Sun on the 20th. The energy culminates at the April 24 Taurus New Moon, when you'll feel especially close to family. That's also an ideal time frame to host a get-together for friends, and to get the family involved in spring cleaning and other household projects. Begin planning summer home improvements.

Money and Success

Mars in Pisces, your solar second house, gives you the initiative to boost earnings. Although an unexpected expense is possible in early April, the main reason to conserve funds and pay bills early is Venus, which is retrograde in Pisces, your money sector, through the 16th. Once it turns direct, recent financial issues begin to ease and you'll again attract exactly what you need when you need it.

Rewarding Days
4, 5, 9, 16, 17, 18, 19, 24, 30

Challenging Days
1, 2, 3, 7, 8, 13, 22, 26, 28

Aquarius/May

Planetary Hotspots

Wrong numbers, misdirected mail, dead batteries, miscommunication, and mix-ups are the norm when Mercury is retrograde. Get ready. Mercury does that on the 6th, traveling first in Gemini, your solar fifth house, and then retreating into Taurus, on the 13th. So expect this planet to affect social events and domestic activities. Confirm dates and times, and try to postpone major household decisions and purchases until later next month.

Planetary Lightspots

If it seems like you need to be everywhere at once this month, you're not far off. Mars steps up the pace of daily life as it advances in Aries, your solar third house. But with Venus there you'll enjoy almost every moment, being in touch with people and at the center of the action. Do take care on the road, however. Planetary alignments could trigger an accident if you're distracted.

Relationships

Summer socializing gets a jump-start from Mercury's brief time in Gemini. But the best is the May 24 New Moon in Gemini, which sparks a romantic liaison for some Aquarians, and brings smiles to proud parents who see their children succeed. This influence is also terrific for creative endeavors, so plan to spend some of your leisure time with a favorite hobby.

Money and Success

You have a great opportunity to make your mark and be noticed the week of the May 9 Full Moon in Scorpio, your career sector. Enthusiasm and optimism soar, which is great as long as you don't take on more than you can deliver. Be realistic about what you can accomplish in a day, a week, and a month.

Rewarding Days

2, 6, 7, 8, 10, 11, 15, 16, 21, 24, 28

Challenging Days

4, 5, 12, 17, 18, 20, 23, 25

Aquarius/June

Planetary Hotspots

It's life as usual at work until the week of the June 22 New Moon in Cancer. Then, conflict, a power play, or a clash with a coworker or supervisor are all possible because this New Moon is exactly aligned with Pluto in Capricorn, your solar twelfth house. You may not immediately be aware of or realize what's happening, so keep comments to yourself rather than risk ramifications.

Planetary Lightspots

Mars in Taurus, your domestic sector, provides all the incentive and initiative you need to work on projects, repairs, the garden, the patio, closets, and more this month. Mercury in Taurus through the 12th sparks ideas, and Venus in the same sign from the 6th on gives your artistic eye a boost. Redo a room exactly to your liking.

Relationships

Your social life is in high gear this month, thanks to the Sun in Gemini, your solar fifth house, through the 20th, and Mercury there from the 13th on. Plus, the June 7 Sagittarius Full Moon lights up your solar eleventh house of friendship. Bring it all together during evenings out with friends, and consider hosting a casual party sometime this month.

Money and Success

Finances settle down now that fewer planets are activating Uranus in Pisces and Saturn in Virgo. This month you may experience the unexpected in an entirely different way as several planets form beneficial contacts with Uranus and Saturn. A minor windfall is on the list of possibilities, or you might receive an inheritance or gift from a friend or relative. Even so, it's best to spend conservatively.

Rewarding Days

2, 6, 12, 14, 16, 17, 20, 24, 29, 30

Challenging Days

3, 5, 8, 11, 19, 21, 22, 25, 27, 28

Aquarius/July

Planetary Hotspots

You'll enjoy a mostly easygoing month with only minor challenges here and there. Among them could be a misunderstanding with a family member in early July as Venus and Mars in Taurus, your solar fourth house, contact several planets. It could be the result of your unrealistic expectations. So don't expect more from loved ones than you expect from yourself.

Planetary Lightspots

It's summer and July's Full Moon (and solar eclipse) is in Capricorn, your solar twelfth house. That's all the reason you need to designate the week of the 7th as the perfect time to slow the pace a little, at least evenings and the weekend. You'll especially appreciate the relaxation during this busy month at work. Your intuition is also active that week. Listen to your inner voice.

Relationships

Plan ahead so you can take advantage of Mercury's arrival in Leo, your solar seventh house, on the 17th, followed by the Sun on the 22nd. This is as great for your love life and your social life as is Venus in Gemini, your solar fifth house, July 5–30. A sparkling new romance catches some singles by surprise at month's end.

Money and Success

It's your time to shine on the job. For that you can thank Mercury, which transits Cancer, your solar sixth house, July 3–16, and the New Moon (and solar eclipse) in the same sign on the 21st. Extra effort could net you a perk, and a raise is also possible. If you're job-hunting or just want to check out the possibilities, send out your resume that week. It could net results by the end of August or early September.

Rewarding Days

1, 3, 8, 9, 10, 14, 18, 22, 23, 26, 27

Challenging Days

2, 4, 5, 6, 12, 13, 19, 24, 25, 30

Aquarius/August

Planetary Hotspots

If travel is in your plans, try to avoid the last week of August when Mercury in Libra, your solar ninth house, clashes with Mars and Pluto. That can trigger anything from a delay to a cancellation to a mishap, and it's unlikely you'll have a relaxing vacation experience. Skip talk with relatives, especially in-laws, during the same time frame.

Planetary Lightspots

You have an extra level of charisma to charm just about anyone in your midst the week of the August 5 Full Moon in Aquarius. The lunar energy is also a great reason (if you need one) to pamper yourself with a massage, facial, or a day off to do exactly as you please.

Relationships

The Full Moon activates Mars in Gemini, your solar fifth house of recreation and romance, which is all the more reason to plan social events and outings with friends. If you're single and looking, Mars could spark an exciting romance, especially because August also features the New Moon in Leo, your relationship sector, on the 20th. That's ideal for couples in love, and some Aquarians decide to make commitment a part of their future. If you're among them, be sure it's true love and not an illusion because the New Moon also contacts Neptune in your sign.

Money and Success

Get set for another great month at work, albeit a more laid back one than July. You're among the favored few with Venus in Cancer, your solar sixth house, through the 25th, the date Mars arrives in the same sign. So don't let things go because September will be another busy one on the job. Finances are in positive territory again this month, with the chance for a minor windfall.

Rewarding Days

4, 5, 6, 11, 14, 18, 19, 23, 27

Challenging Days

2, 8, 9, 15, 16, 21, 22, 28, 29

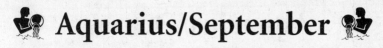 Aquarius/September

Planetary Hotspots

Saturn and Uranus align in Virgo/Pisces, your financial sector, the week of the September 18 New Moon in Virgo. Consult a financial expert, if necessary, but try to hold off on any major decisions until later in October because Mercury, which turns retrograde in Libra on the 7th, returns to Virgo on the 17th. This means the matters associated with this lineup won't fully conclude until next month. Be cautious with spending and also carefully check statements and your credit report (even if you did that earlier in the year).

Planetary Lightspots

Take the breather you deserve after the Sun enters Libra, your solar ninth house, on the 22nd. Travel isn't the best choice because of Mercury's retrograde status, but you can benefit from a little time out with an alternative—learn about whatever captures your current interest or simply devote some evening and weekend hours to reading the latest best sellers. This is also a great time to explore the self-help section at your local bookstore or library.

Relationships

Relationships benefit from Venus in Leo, your solar seventh house, through the 19th. Couples are on the same wavelength, and you'll find people genuinely helpful. But because Venus aligns with Jupiter and Neptune in Aquarius midmonth, the wise choice continues to be skepticism regarding personal or professional contacts. What you hear may not be the exact truth.

Money and Success

Your work life varies from busy to hectic with Mars in Cancer, your solar sixth house, throughout September. Keep up the pace, but retrograde Mercury makes it wise to slow down enough to double-check for errors.

Rewarding Days

1, 2, 8, 11, 12, 15, 19, 20,, 24, 28, 29

Challenging Days

4, 6, 7 13, 14, 17, 18, 22, 23, 25

Aquarius/October

Planetary Hotspots

October's major event is Saturn, which enters Libra, your solar ninth house, on the 29th. As it begins its three-year transit of this sign, your interest may turn to the wider world. But its main emphasis here is knowledge, just as it was in September, which you'll again realize around the time of the October 18 New Moon, also in Libra. Ask yourself whether your job prospects could benefit from additional education. If you've ever considered switching careers, now is the time to investigate the possibilities.

Planetary Lightspots

The October 4 Full Moon in Aries lights up your solar third house, putting you at the center of the information chain. Use it to promote yourself and your ideas, and also try for a long weekend away. The change of scenery will refresh, re-center, and inspire you to move forward into the future.

Relationships

Relationships are generally positive this month, although there is potential for conflict once Mars enters Leo, your solar seventh house, on the 16th. As much as some people will support your efforts, others will stubbornly resist. The less said the better at month's end when a clash with a coworker or supervisor is possible.

Money and Success

Last month's Saturn/Uranus alignment continues to be active the first two weeks of October as Mercury and Venus wrap up their time in Virgo. Take a close look at personal and family finances, refine short- and long-term goals, and commit to a path toward financial freedom. Unexpected expenses are still possible, but you could also net just the gain you need to cover them.

Rewarding Days

8, 10, 12, 13, 17, 21, 22, 26, 27, 31

Challenging Days

2, 7, 9, 11, 15, 16, 18, 20, 30

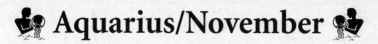 Aquarius/November

Planetary Hotspots

November brings an exact alignment of Saturn in Libra and Pluto in Capricorn in your solar ninth and twelfth houses. Although you're unlikely to experience this influence until December, you can plan ahead. If you're considering holiday travel or legal action, both could be negatively impacted next month. However, this duo can also give you all the incentive and determination you need to follow through on returning to school.

Planetary Lightspots

Home life is featured the week of the November 2 Taurus Full Moon in your solar fourth house. Get busy and tackle all those unfinished projects or initiate new ones to get your place ready for the holidays. Just be sure to include your partner in the planning stage. You might think you know exactly what you want, but brainstorming could yield the most creative ideas.

Relationships

The potential for conflict with someone close to you still exists with Mars in Leo all month. So choose your words with care and be tactful even when you'd rather be blunt. Good news: Mercury in Sagittarius, your solar eleventh house, from the 15th on, where it's joined by the Sun on the 21st, signals the start of holiday socializing, which will be at its best in December. Line up dates and outings now so you have time to see your closest friends.

Money and Success

This is one of your best career months of the year, thanks to the November 16 New Moon in Scorpio, your solar tenth house. The lunar energy, and the Sun, Mercury, and Venus in the same sign part of the month also fuel your ambitions. Think big and go for what you want!

Rewarding Days

4, 5, 7, 13, 14, 17, 18, 22, 27, 28

Challenging Days

2, 6, 8, 9, 11, 12, 19, 23, 30

Aquarius/December

Planetary Hotspots

Mars turns retrograde in Leo, your solar seventh house, on the 20th. This can disrupt relationships at times, a trend that continues through early March when the red planet will resume direct motion. More importantly, this is not the time to establish a new business or personal partnership, and you should carefully check credentials before consulting a professional such as a physician, accountant, or attorney.

Planetary Lightspots

Treat yourself especially well this month. You deserve a little pampering as the Sun, Mercury, and Venus visit Capricorn, your solar twelfth house of self-renewal, activating Saturn and Pluto. Get a massage or go all-out with a spa day. Also sleep, rest, stay warm, and eat well to avoid a cold or flu. It's possible your immune system could be lowered at this time.

Relationships

The week of the December 16 New Moon in Sagittarius is ideal for holiday social events. You're sure to be a popular guest who has just the right words and pizzazz to liven up any get-together. But consider carefully before you commit to visiting relatives, especially in-laws, over the holidays. Conflict is likely to be more the norm than the exception. And, the best New Year's Eve choice is to stay home because the December 31 Cancer Full Moon (and lunar eclipse) activates both Pluto and Saturn.

Money and Success

The lunar eclipse increases the possibility for tension in the workplace, not just the week of December 31, but into 2010. Plan ahead. Organize your time, (especially if you intend to return to school) as a precaution against stretching yourself too thin.

Rewarding Days

5, 6, 11, 12, 14, 15, 16, 19, 21, 25, 30

Challenging Days

3, 7, 10, 13, 17, 20, 24, 28, 29, 31

Aquarius Action Table

These dates reflect the best—but not the only—times for success and ease in these activities, according to your Sun sign.

	JAN	FEB	MAR	APR	MAY	JUN	JUL	AUG	SEPT	OCT	NOV	DEC
Move		2-3				6-12				6-7		
Start a class		27-28									27-28	
Join a club		17						1		21-22		14-15
Ask for a raise		25		20-21								
Look for work						22-24		17		11	6	
Get pro advice					1		22-23					
Get a loan								21			11	
See a doctor				30		10, 23	21	17				
Start a diet								17			7	
End relationship		9										
Buy clothes		5	4			16-17	13, 18				5	6
Get a makeover		22								26-27		
New romance					24		18					
Vacation								27-28		10-22		

PISCES

The Fish
February 19 to March 20

♓

Element: Water

Quality: Mutable

Polarity: Yin/feminine

Planetary Ruler: Neptune

Meditation: I successfully navigate my emotions

Gemstone: Aquamarine

Power Stones: Amethyst, bloodstone, tourmaline

Key Phrase: I believe

Glyph: Two fish swimming in opposite directions

Anatomy: Feet, lymphatic system

Color: Sea green, violet

Animal: Fish, sea mammals

Myths/Legends: Aphrodite, Buddha, Jesus of Nazareth

House: Twelfth

Opposite Sign: Virgo

Flower: Water lily

Key Word: Transcendence

Your Strengths and Challenges

Pisces, the mutable water sign of the zodiac, is known for its flexibility. You can adapt in most any situation, like the chameleon that changes its colors to reflect its surroundings. This gives you the ability to blend in or stand out and to quickly get in sync with other people and your environment. That's both a plus and a minus, depending upon the situation. There are times when the best choice is to take a stand, something you're reluctant to do if it might spark controversy. Accept that it's a necessary part of life and be true to your beliefs.

You're sensitive and compassionate, interested in the welfare of others, and some Pisces people are actively involved in charitable organizations that help the less fortunate. If you find yourself consistently putting the needs of others first, however, remember that in reality you need to look out for yourself; no one else will.

Creativity is another of your strengths. Whether it takes the form of artistic endeavors, ideas, or something else, you envision possibilities that others miss. Neptune, your ruling planet, also encourages you to inspire others and to follow your own spiritual path. Your strong faith sees you through hurdles, although you have a tendency to turn inward when worries dominate your thoughts. Meditation can recenter you, body and soul, during these times.

Idealistic and trusting, you strive to see the best in everyone. Although that's admirable, you'll benefit from asking questions and taking less for granted. Your sixth sense can steer you in the right direction here and in other life situations. Listen to your inner voice. It's an asset, and the more you listen the stronger it will become. Some people with a Pisces Sun are psychic. But keep in mind that you're also impressionable and can pick up vibrations, both positive and negative, from other people and your environment. Get in the habit of surrounding yourself with a positive energy field.

Your Relationships

You're a romantic with a heart of gold, kind and sentimental. Most people with a Pisces Sun dislike being alone and need the security that a lasting relationship provides. This motivates you to seek a mate, but dating can be challenging at times because you want things to work out and have a tendency to hang on even when you should move on. Have faith in the universe. Your ideal match may be only a date away. Love at first sight could be yours with a practical Virgo, your opposite sign, or one of the other earth signs, Taurus and Capricorn. You're in sync with Cancer and Scorpio, your fellow water signs. But life with a Gemini or Sagittarius could upset the stability you need and desire.

Your wish is to always be surrounded by peace and harmony. Although you might achieve that in many areas, home life is unlikely to be among them. There you can expect a lot of activity, including neighbors and relatives dropping in on the spur of the moment. Your home is a place for communication, and you probably have bookcases, the latest technology, and more than a little clutter. Pisces parents are fond of their children and involved in their activities, but you may tend to be overprotective of them. You want to shield them from life's ups and downs, which is a natural instinct. But in the process you may actually do them a disservice. Learning by experience and testing their independence in a safe environment is often the best way for children to prepare for the imperfect life they'll experience as adults.

Acquaintances and the social scene aren't your style. You prefer to have a handful of best friends, some of whom are for a lifetime, and to enjoy their company in small groups in comfortable, familiar surroundings. Even if you and someone close drift apart, you quickly pick up where you left off as though no time had passed. Among your friends is probably a soul mate or two. These are the people you lean on during difficult times and the ones who cheer your victories. You also learn a great deal about life from them.

Your Career and Money

Although you can do it if you have to, a career behind a desk isn't your best choice. It becomes tolerable, and even desirable, if you have the opportunity to learn, share your knowledge and possibly travel. Once dissatisfaction sets in, however, you're quick to move on in search of the perfect career opportunity. That of course doesn't exist, which is something you learn with time and experience. In your day-to-day work life you can have a significant and very positive impact on many people. You're the resident cheerleader, encouraging others, and exercising your leadership ability to bring out the best in yourself and coworkers. You also can do well as a manager.

You have excellent earning power, but also a tendency to splurge on impulse, especially for loved ones. Do yourself a favor: learn to live within a budget and make joint financial decisions with your partner. Both will go a long way toward creating the financial security you desire, as will regular savings and conservative, long-term investments. You could benefit from an inheritance or major gift from someone close to you, either a relative or friend.

Your Lighter Side

Chances are, you have a semi-secret hobby. You might be a gourmet cook, or an outstanding musician, singer, or artist. Plunge in if you haven't yet discovered this side of yourself and explore your creative energy. It's exceptional and creative endeavors are great for re-centering your soul at the end of the work day.

Affirmation for the Year

People enrich my life and my knowledge.

The Year Ahead for Pisces

People, friendship, work, play, finances, and close relationships will be in the forefront this year as the outer planets and six eclipses highlight your solar chart sectors.

Leading the way is Saturn, which will nearly complete its trip through Virgo, your solar seventh house, when it enters Libra October 29. (Saturn will return briefly to Virgo next spring.) Relationships have been a key focus since Saturn entered Virgo in September 2007. Some of these were undoubtedly difficult and others ultimately positive. The trend continues this year, and you'll have the opportunity to strengthen some ties, while others will fade into the past.

But Saturn here is not necessarily negative, despite what you may have heard or read. Many relationships actually thrive under this influence, with couples becoming closer than ever before, and others have the motivation to commit to lifetime togetherness. What you're likely to do is to consciously distance yourself from some people, possibly friends who no longer fit in your life as they once did.

Some people will enter your life for a specific reason—to teach you something or to learn from you. These may be karmic connections, and you'll feel an instantaneous bond with them. Oddly enough, you may dislike these people yet be drawn to them. That should be your first clue that the universe has brought you together for some purpose.

People from the past may resurface this year, especially old friends. But think carefully if a former romantic interest expresses a desire to resume the relationship. It may work out the second time around. The chances are greater, however, that it won't, so do yourself a favor and remember why you decided to move on.

All of these things are true of Saturn, but this serious, stable planet will be challenged by Uranus in Pisces this year. And that adds an entirely different scope to the potential events of 2009.

Uranus has been in your sign since 2003, so you've probably already experienced its ability to trigger the unexpected as well as sudden insights about yourself and your world. All these internal changes will manifest outwardly in some way. You might decide to pursue an entirely different career direction, for example, as a way to express your new-found independence, which Uranus encourages.

As Saturn and Uranus form an exact alignment in February and September across your solar first-seventh house axis you may suddenly decide to end a close relationship. Or at least that's how it will appear to other people. In reality this is something you've been thinking about for some time, at least since last November (2008) when these two planets first contacted each other. Be cautious. Changes initiated under a Uranus transit are usually irreversible, and with Saturn involved you could ultimately regret the decision.

If a relationship truly isn't working out, however, your best choice might be to part ways. Only you can decide the right thing to do, but be aware that there are alternatives if you're both open to compromise. Much of this centers on you and your changing needs and desires and whether you can find a way to fulfill them and maintain the status quo. Explore the options, first on your own and then together.

Jupiter, planet of good fortune will enter Aquarius January 5 to begin its year-long tour of your solar twelfth house. Placed here, it functions as a sort of Guardian Angel, watching over you and protecting you. Not that you'll be able to get away with anything and everything! But Jupiter here has the reputation for coming to the rescue at the eleventh hour to save the day and often at the least expected moment. Just don't rely on it to bail you out all the time.

You'll be more than usually content with your own company this year, and meditation or even listening to music can help you access your inner voice. Listen to your intuition especially in career matters, where you may benefit from hidden support. Unfortunately, the opposite could also be true because Jupiter will join forces with illusive Neptune in May and December. So be cautious about what you say to whom. Someone who appears to be a supporter may actually try to undermine your position. The toughest part will be in knowing who's on your side and who's only pretending to be.

Yet this Jupiter-Neptune union will also boost your sixth sense and encourage you to explore your spirituality. It will certainly touch your compassionate soul and inspire you to help others.

Again, caution will be necessary because some people will try to take advantage of your good intentions. Be selective and help people help themselves rather than give them a handout.

Pluto will continue its journey through Capricorn, which it entered last year. Placed in your solar eleventh house, this tiny but powerful planet will impact your friendships during the next fifteen years. You'll connect with important people as well as those who have the ability to transform your life in some way, and you'll do the same for others either one-on-one or as a driving force in a charitable organization or professional group. With Pluto involved, power plays and politics are likely to be part of the scenario, and you'll need to step back periodically and look at things objectively. Otherwise your passion for your mission could become all-consuming.

It will be later in the year, however, when Pluto will be at its strongest. Saturn, which will enter Libra October 29, will clash with Pluto through year's end. Because this is your solar eighth house of joint resources you should avoid any financial dealings with friends, groups, or organizations no matter how much people lean on you. This also would be a poor time to get involved in a fund-raising effort, for example, or to accept a leadership position that requires you to take responsibility for a group's finances.

The Saturn-Pluto alignment also advises caution with personal and family money matters. Try to avoid major financial decisions the last two months of the year, and take precautions to safeguard financial information—even with friends. This is not the time to place your faith in other people or to blindly trust anyone where money is involved.

Finances will benefit from a conservative approach the next three years as Saturn travels in Libra. Make it a priority to pay off any consumer debt and try not to incur more. Also put yourself on a budget that includes a savings plan, and try to use cash instead of credit. You'll be amazed at how little you buy and you'll be rewarded by seeing credit card balances drop and assets rise.

What This Year's Eclipses Mean for You

There will be six eclipses this year, three of which will activate your solar sixth/twelfth house axis of daily work, service, health, and well-being.

Like Jupiter and Neptune in Aquarius, the January 7 solar eclipse in Aquarius will encourage you to focus on your innermost needs and desires. This self-renewal process is a valuable one because it will prepare you for Jupiter's arrival in your sign in 2010. Think about what you'd like to achieve, both personally and in the outer world, as you touch your inner spirit through meditation or creative activities. Out of it will come a greater sense of confidence in your abilities while strengthening your faith in yourself.

The Aquarius solar eclipse will be followed by a February 9 lunar eclipse in Leo, your solar sixth house. Your work life will take on an added dimension as a result and you'll find yourself questioning and evaluating this area. But this year isn't the best to switch jobs because this eclipse will be closely aligned with Neptune. And that would make it easy for you to jump into what appears to be an ideal situation that in reality isn't at all. By next year your vision will be clearer and you'll have a better idea of exactly where you want to go.

The third (lunar) eclipse, August 6 in Aquarius, reinforces the February eclipse in the same sign. Where the first prompted you to think, this one will encourage you to act on those thoughts and ideas. Explore possibilities, talk with people, and generally outline the potential job opportunities that might be open to you. Begin networking through a volunteer, community, or professional activity. The people you contact now will bring you luck next year.

You'll have an active social life the second half of 2009, thanks to three eclipses that will highlight your solar fifth-eleventh house axis.

The July 7 lunar eclipse in Capricorn will to some extent mirror the influence of Pluto in the same sign, putting you in touch with new people and long-time friends. Some of these people will have a major impact on your life. The lunar influence will also emphasize teamwork and encourage you to become active in group activities.

Complimenting these eclipses will be two others—July 22 (solar) and December 31 (lunar)—in Leo, your solar fifth house of recreation, romance, creativity, and children. Besides boosting your opportunities for love, these eclipses will motivate you to express your creativity. Find (or further develop) a hobby that can fill your leisure-time hours with pleasure.

If you want to get in shape, these eclipses will provide the incentive. All you need do is tap into it; join a gym, walk or bike with a neighbor, or learn to play tennis or golf. You might also enjoy getting involved in your children's sports or other after-school activities. An addition to the family is in the forecast for some hopeful parents.

Saturn

If you were born between March 4 and 20, relationships will be a key theme as Saturn contacts your Sun from Virgo, your solar seventh house. At least one important relationship will reach a turning point. You may become much closer to someone in your life or decide to step away when the distance between you widens.

Overall, this year will bring relationship lessons and the opportunity to learn from others. Your people skills will be tested and compromise and cooperation will be emphasized. It's likely you'll be the one who has to give in to others, and you may feel as though someone (or several people) is trying to structure and control your life. If this happens, try to view the situation objectively and identify why you react the way you do. It may be a valuable lesson in assertiveness and learning how to manage confrontation rather than just backing away.

Uranus

Change is in the forecast when Uranus in Pisces joins forces with your Sun, as it will this year **if you were born between March 9 and 16**. The urge for new personal directions has been building for some time and now that Uranus has arrived you'll be ready to take action. This may surprise those around you who never realized this internal process was underway and, because Uranus will align with Saturn in February and November, it's likely to manifest through a relationship.

You may suddenly realize that a close relationship is holding you back, restricting your self-expression. This may or may not be true. But your perception is your reality. Before you suddenly cut ties, however, you should try to glimpse the future and also consider the possible karmic implications. Actions taken under a Uranus transit are rarely reversible.

This also can be one of the most exciting years of your life because you're open to change. You'll have the power to recreate yourself and your place in the world however you wish, and you'll also attract opportunities and fascinating people who can help you make the most of 2009.

Saturn-Pluto

If you were born between February 19 and 22, Saturn will contact your Sun after it enters Libra October 29. Pluto will do the same all year from Capricorn, where it will clash with Saturn in Libra.

With Saturn in your solar eighth house of joint resources and Pluto in your solar eleventh house of friendship and goals, finances will require attention. Although the Saturn/Pluto alignment could trigger a financial downturn, what this planetary energy will focus on is urging you to redefine and realign your financial goals. Use the first ten months of the year to do just that, as well as to build up savings so you have reserves, if necessary.

Above all you'll want to avoid any risky financial actions such as investments and entering into any contracts or agreements that could jeopardize your resources—even if you believe the loss potential is small. Do the same with major purchases and loans; try to put them off until later in 2010.

You, above all those with the Sun in Pisces, should be extremely cautious about financial and other personal financial information. Fraud protection would be a good idea. Used positively, Saturn and Pluto can give you the willpower to pay off debt and to change your financial philosophy to help ensure a comfortable retirement.

Neptune

If you were born between March 12 and 16, Neptune will contact your Sun from Aquarius, your solar twelfth house. This spiritual influence will also nudge your sixth sense, which you can take to a new level this year. Calm your mind and let your inner voice emerge. The more you do this the more trust you'll have in your intuition. You might also want to keep a journal next to your bed to record dream images. They're likely to be quite vivid this year and also insightful.

But it will also be easy to give in to the tendency to wish away any difficulties that arise this year. Try to avoid this, especially in relationship and financial matters where a direct approach will be more successful and in your best interests.

Neptune will also encourage you to let your creativity flow, and this can be an excellent outlet for daily frustrations, especially later in the year when the eclipses activate your solar fifth house.

Pisces/January

Planetary Hotspots

You may hear some confidential information around the time of the January 26 New Moon in Aquarius. Keep it to yourself, and also be cautious about sharing personal information. With several planets in Aquarius, your solar twelfth house, you also should take precautions to avoid a cold or flu, which could linger into February. Eat healthy, sleep well, and stay warm.

Planetary Lightspots

Circle January 3 on your calendar. That's the date Venus arrives in your sign to boost your charisma and powers of attraction. What you wish for can be yours the third week of the month when Venus aligns with several planets.

Relationships

People are a key theme this month. Turn on the charm if you're looking for love, which could catch you by surprise the last weekend in January. A soul mate could walk into your life. Earlier in the month, the Full Moon in Cancer on January 10 activates your solar fifth house of recreation and romance, which complements Mars and the Sun in Capricorn, your friendship sign. See friends, socialize, meet people. Couples also benefit from this month's planetary alignments and a great opportunity to strengthen ties through open communication and togetherness.

Money and Success

Someone close, possibly a friend, could lean on you for a loan or donation at month's end. Say no if that's how you feel rather than let anyone get the best of your compassionate nature. You (and your mate, if you're committed) should spend some time early this month outlining your 2009 financial goals. Establish a budget and savings goal, and plan for the inevitable unexpected expenses.

Rewarding Days

1, 5, 6, 10, 13, 14, 16, 19, 28

Challenging Days

2, 3, 8, 9, 22, 29, 30

Pisces/February

Planetary Hotspots

This month's hotspot is the year's first exact Saturn/Uranus alignment. With these two planets spanning your solar first/seventh house axis, you can expect relationship difficulties to impact your personal or professional life, or both. The planetary energy is at its peak the first week of February and active again at month's end, especially if your birthday is within a few days of February 9.

Planetary Lightspots

The February 24 New Moon in your sign energizes your life and puts you in the spotlight. Use it to launch your solar year with new directions and fresh goals designed for personal empowerment, confidence, and success. Then plan to update your progress every three months to keep yourself on track toward achieving maximum success. Take note of your dreams this month. They offer insightful images about your career, family life, and close relationships.

Relationships

Although Saturn/Uranus dominates this month's relationship forecast, you'll have plenty of opportunities to socialize and see friends through the 13th as Mercury transits Capricorn, your solar eleventh house. With this planet turning direct on the 1st, you can easily connect with pals you missed seeing in January.

Money and Success

Cross your fingers for a little extra cash the third week of February when Venus in Aries, your solar second house, aligns with Mars and Jupiter. The first week of the month, however, could bring an unexpected expense. Work will be hectic once the February 9 Full Moon in Leo activates your solar sixth house. The lunar energy also increases the chance for errors, so slow down and check the details. And, like last month, be cautious about what you say to whom.

Rewarding Days

3, 10, 13, 15, 17, 17, 19, 21, 22, 24

Challenging Days

1, 5, 6, 7, 11, 12, 18, 25, 26

Pisces/March

Planetary Hotspots

Saturn and Uranus go one more round as the March 10 Full Moon in Virgo, your solar seventh house, activates these two planets. Fortunately, once this is past you'll be able to put most of the influence behind you until these two planets align for the last time this fall. Personal relationships are the focus, and it will be tough to view situations objectively. Try, anyway. There's a valuable lesson here that both you and the other person can benefit from as responsibilities clash with the need for independence.

Planetary Lightspots

Mars zips into Pisces on the 14th, boosting your energy and initiative. Take advantage of this six-week transit to handle everything on your personal to-do list. One caution: be alert in the kitchen, on ladders, and when working with tools because this is an accident-prone influence.

Relationships

Although relationships have their challenges this month, planetary alignments also accent friendship and generally positive workplace communication. Even so, you'll be unusually sensitive to other people's comments. Try to view constructive criticism as just that rather than as negative feedback. Upon reflection you might actually find it to be enlightening.

Money and Success

Finances are mixed. On the upside is the New Moon, March 26, in Aries, your solar second house, which could bring you a well-deserved raise or a minor windfall. But an unexpected expense could arise after Venus, also in Aries, turns retrograde on the 6th. Be conservative. Save. This isn't the month to buy luxury items.

Rewarding Days

1, 6, 14, 15, 20, 24, 25, 27, 28, 29

Challenging Days

2, 4, 5, 9, 11, 17, 19, 23, 31

Pisces/April

Planetary Hotspots

Retrograde Venus slips back into Pisces on the 11th. It's sure to frustrate personal plans at times and also trigger mix-ups. The good news is the influence won't last long because Venus turns direct on the 17th and four days later merges with Mars, also in your sign. Like magic, life will get back on track and you'll be off and running.

Planetary Lightspots

The past surfaces in some way this month, and you'll find fond memories drifting through your thoughts and dreams. Turn them into reality by creating photo albums for the family and your children. You might even discover you have a talent for scrapbooking or another artistic venue that can enhance your home décor.

Relationships

Mercury travels in Taurus, your solar third house, April 9-29, where it's joined by the Sun on the 20th. The energy peaks around the time of the April 24 New Moon in Taurus, which has the potential to deliver the great news you've been waiting for. You'll also enjoy relaxing yet lively outings with friends, but keep an eye on expenses. Close ties become even stronger as the month unfolds.

Money and Success

Although there's a lingering possibility of extra expenses this month, the financial picture is mostly favorable. The week of the April 9 Full Moon in Libra is promising for lucky finds, whether in your attic, basement, at a yard sale or thrift shop. And a flash of insight could trigger a bright moneymaking idea. Follow through if it doesn't require a major investment or partnership, especially with a friend. Use your imagination instead of your money.

Rewarding Days

4, 5, 6, 10, 11, 16, 20, 21, 24, 25, 29, 30

Challenging Days

1, 2, 3, 7, 8, 13, 14, 22, 26, 27, 28

Pisces/May

Planetary Hotspots

Jupiter and Neptune join forces in Aquarius, your solar twelfth house, for the second of three times this year. This union can inspire but also confuse you. Dreams can be particularly insightful, and your sixth sense will be active. But you'll also want to see the best in people, giving them the benefit of the doubt when you should instead question their motives. Someone who appears to be supportive may be exactly the opposite, so keep confidences to yourself.

Planetary Lightspots

There's not much you'd like more the week of the May 9 Full Moon in Scorpio than to pack your bags and head for parts known or unknown. Do it if you can, even for a long weekend. But be prepared to be flexible because Mercury, which turns retrograde on the 7th, could produce a few bumps in the road.

Relationships

Retrograde Mercury will have its greatest impact in the relationship arena. Because it switches direction in Gemini, your solar fourth house, family communication could be rocky at times. It then retreats into Taurus, your solar third house, on the 13th, with the potential for mix-ups and misunderstandings in just about any area of life. If you lose something during this period, which is not uncommon during Mercury's retrograde cycle, it might magically reappear next month.

Money and Success

With both Mars and Venus in Aries, your solar second house, May brings added incentive and opportunity to build your bank balance. Just be sure that happens, because this duo also encourages spending sprees. Skip credit and pay cash to keep your budget in the black.

Rewarding Days

3, 7, 8, 14, 15, 19, 21, 22, 28, 31

Challenging Days

1, 5, 13, 18, 20, 25, 27, 29

Pisces/June

Planetary Hotspots

Your solar fourth house of home and family is June's hotspot. Although you'll delight in upbeat times with friends and loved ones, challenges also arise as the Sun and Mercury in Gemini clash with several planets. Expect everything from domestic chaos to miscommunication and short tempers to a possible mechanical problem. Call a pro if you need a repair; it will ultimately be less expensive.

Planetary Lightspots

Life perks along as Mars zips through Taurus, your solar third house, where it's joined by Venus on the 6th and Mercury through the 12th. The combination keeps you on the go and on the phone, busy with activities and in touch with many people. Be smart. Stay off the phone when you're behind the wheel because a distraction could spark a mishap.

Relationships

The bright summer Sun enters Cancer on the 21st. That's as great for your social life as it is for quality time with your children. But there's one catch to this otherwise upbeat trend: the June 22 Full Moon in Cancer aligns with Pluto in Capricorn, your solar eleventh house. A friendship could be rocky under this influence, or a dating relationship could end amidst conflict.

Money and Success

You have all the attention-getting power you need to do great things at work the week of the June 7 Full Moon in Sagittarius, your solar tenth house. There is one caveat, however. Decision-makers are watching so give it your all and meet every deadline and responsibility to the best of your ability. Be prepared, though, and plan ahead in order to balance career and family demands.

Rewarding Days

6, 8, 9, 10, 14, 18, 19, 23, 26

Challenging Days

1, 3, 5, 11, 15, 21, 22, 25, 28

Pisces/July

Planetary Hotspots

Your thoughts run the gamut from clarity to confusion as Venus and Mars in Taurus, your solar third house contact several planets. There's a simple solution when worries occupy your mind: take action. Or, if you're not quite ready for that, talk with someone close to you whose opinion you value. If a decision involves money, however, trust your instincts and choose to protect your resources.

Planetary Lightspots

Venus arrives in Gemini, your solar fourth house, on the 5th, quickly followed by Mars on the 11th. Get busy when both planets spark a desire for domestic change. Rearrange furniture, paint a room or two, and create a corner with a comfy chair you can call your own. Then show off the results by hosting a get-together.

Relationships

July is a terrific month for socializing, thanks to the July 7 Full Moon (and lunar eclipse) in Capricorn, your friendship sector, and the July 21 New Moon (and solar eclipse) in Cancer, your solar fifth house. It's also one of the best of 2009 for romance and the chance to meet a soul mate. A reunion with someone from the past could be all you hope for and more—a true soul mate. But along the way it's possible you could end a friendship with someone whose values are far different from yours.

Money and Success

The work pace begins to pick up when Mercury enters Leo, your solar sixth house, on the 17th, and the Sun does the same on the 22nd. Do as much as you can now to catch up and work ahead because August will be especially hectic. A meeting or talk near the 20th could trigger a terrific opportunity.

Rewarding Days

1, 7, 8, 9, 12, 16, 20, 21, 28, 29

Challenging Days

2, 4, 6, 13, 19, 24, 25, 31

Pisces/August

Planetary Hotspots

Be especially kind to yourself the week of the August 5 Full Moon (and lunar eclipse) in Aquarius, your solar twelfth house, and again midmonth. Either time frame could bring on a summer cold, just when your job demands your full attention. Eat healthy and get plenty of sleep to boost your immune system.

Planetary Lightspots

Now is the time to get busy around the house—to get rid of clutter and get organized. Then move on to a domestic project (or projects) that have been on hold seemingly forever. Mars provides all the incentive and high energy you need as it transits Gemini, your solar fourth house, through the 24th. Then turn your discards into profits at a neighborhood yard sale.

Relationships

Your solar seventh house comes alive this month with both Mercury and the Sun in Virgo. It's unrealistic to think all relationships will be easygoing, but most are positive and beneficial. Even those that aren't present an opportunity to learn from others and to increase your knowledge of human nature. A friendship or romantic relationship could be stressful in early or late August, possibly because of finances. Put you and yours first and have no regrets.

Money and Success

Your work life is at its best this month as the Sun moves through Leo, your solar sixth house. August 20, the date of the New Moon in Leo, fills you with fresh energy to tackle new projects and wrap up ongoing ones. But don't be discouraged if you feel your efforts are under-appreciated. They will pay off, both financially and personally, before year's end.

Rewarding Days

3, 4, 6, 11, 12, 17, 20, 25, 27, 30, 31

Challenging Days

1, 8, 9, 15, 16, 21, 22, 26, 29

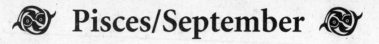 Pisces/September

Planetary Hotspots

Stress surrounds relationships the week of the September 18 New Moon in Virgo. Ongoing issues can be resolved now, in one way or another, by putting the past to rest. This is especially true if your birthday is within a few days of March 16. For some, a close relationship will end, while others will feel a renewed commitment. The outcome of this turning point mostly depends upon whether you can adapt, blend, and fulfill your changing needs within the context of the relationship. Hold off if you're unsure what to do because retrograde Mercury returns to Virgo the day before the New Moon. You could change your mind.

Planetary Lightspots

High energy accompanies the September 7 Full Moon in Pisces, which also has you in the mood to play as summer turns to fall. Get involved in your children's activities, see friends, and most of all, use your creativity in a hobby or artistic project that expresses the essence of you.

Relationships

September promises an active social life, thanks to Mars in Cancer your solar fifth house. It's also great for romance and evenings designed for couples in love. But this month also brings the potential for misunderstandings at work and in your personal life because of retrograde Mercury. Think before you speak and write.

Money and Success

Retrograde Mercury can also trigger money mix-ups as it travels in Libra, your solar eighth house, September 7–16. Check statements for errors as soon as they arrive, pay bills early, and rein in your generosity if a friend looks to you for cash. You may never see it again.

Rewarding Days

7, 8, 11, 13, 20, 21, 24, 26, 28

Challenging Days

5, 6, 10, 12, 17, 18, 22, 25

Pisces/October

Planetary Hotspots

Money matters are something of a hotspot this month, although not totally so. In fact, you can turn much of the potential negative effect into a positive one. Both the Full Moon, October 4 in Aries, and the New Moon, October 18 in Libra, occur in your financial sectors. This influence can increase your bank balance but also spark added expense as the Sun and Mercury in Libra clash with several planets. The big event, however, is Saturn, which enters Libra October 29 for a three-year transit. So take advantage of the difficult planetary alignments midmonth to assess your financial status and to set financial goals for the next several years, including savings, retirement funds, and debt reduction.

Planetary Lightspots

The Sun moves on to Scorpio on the 22nd, followed by Mercury on the 28th. This is a terrific duo for information-gathering, learning, and travel. Although the main emphasis in this area will come next month, it's time to begin thinking about how you can best utilize this influence as 2009 winds to a close.

Relationships

Last month's Saturn-Uranus alignment remains active the first two weeks of October as first Mercury and then Venus complete their Virgo transits. Consider it the final chapter in this saga, the time to reflect upon recent changes and learn from them.

Money and Success

Mark October 16 on your calendar. That's the date Mars arrives in Leo, your solar sixth house, to launch a high energy period at work that extends into next year. Interested in a new job? Plan ahead. Research the latest resume and interview techniques so you're set to launch your search the end of November.

Rewarding Days
1, 5, 8, 10, 14, 19, 23, 28, 29

Challenging Days
2, 9, 15, 16, 18, 25, 30

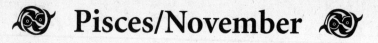 Pisces/November

Planetary Hotspots

Although it will be December before you realize the full effects of this month's Saturn/Pluto alignment, the last week of November offers hints about what to expect, especially if your birthday is near February 19. Reminder: get started now if you haven't yet assessed your overall financial picture and set concrete goals.

Planetary Lightspots

November activity centers in your solar ninth house, which features the Sun, Mercury, and Venus in Scorpio at various times along with the November 16 New Moon in the same sign. Make travel plans when the combined influence triggers your curiosity and a desire for fresh scenery. Just be prepared for delays which could be triggered by winter weather. Better yet, schedule a trip for the new year and take a mental journey now—a short-term class or a visit to your favorite museum.

Relationships

The November 2 Full Moon in Taurus accents communication and complements this month's ninth house emphasis on learning. Relationships are generally positive, although job-related stress could impact interaction with coworkers, and a relative or friend is likely to make your life difficult midmonth. Take it all in stride and consider the source. Also keep confidential matters to yourself, as tempting as it might be to pass along the information.

Money and Success

Mars continues its transit of Leo, your solar sixth house, which keeps you busy at work. That trend increases from the 15th on when Mercury arrives in Sagittarius, your career sector, followed by the Sun on the 21st. Take advantage of favorable planetary alignments to strengthen your position as you head into December.

Rewarding Days

1, 7, 10, 11, 14, 16, 20, 21, 24, 26, 29

Challenging Days

2, 6, 9, 12, 15, 19, 23, 25, 27, 30

 # Pisces/December

Planetary Hotspots

There's a simple way to at least partially control expenses, which can spike this month as the Sun, Mercury, and Venus activate Saturn and Pluto: cut back on gift-giving, especially for friends. This is not the time to spend on credit because you'll end up paying steep interest. At least as important is a cautious approach with investments, even those that sound like sure winners, and any financial dealings with friends or relatives. Don't, for example, cosign for a loan; the debt could become yours.

Planetary Lightspots

The December 2 Full Moon in Gemini, your domestic sector, is all the incentive you need to decorate your home for the holidays. While you're at it, clean out drawers and closets, and get rid of all the clutter that's accumulated in recent weeks. Then you'll be set to host a get-together for friends either the first or second weekend, this month's best choices for socializing.

Relationships

Although Pluto in Capricorn, your solar eleventh house, minimizes social opportunities, you'll enjoy seeing friends midmonth as well as after-hours outings with coworkers. Play it safe on New Year's Eve, however. That's the date of the Full Moon (and lunar eclipse) in Cancer, your solar fifth house, which clashes with Pluto. Ring in 2010 at home.

Money and Success

Expect some frustrating times at work as Mars in Leo, your solar sixth house, travels retrograde from the 20th until early March. This month, however, still brings plenty of opportunities to shine under the December 16 New Moon in Sagittarius, your career sector, with Venus in the same sign through the 24th.

Rewarding Days

4, 5, 8, 12, 15, 17, 18, 21, 22, 23, 27

Challenging Days

1, 3, 7, 9, 10, 13, 20, 24, 28, 31

Pisces Action Table

These dates reflect the best—but not the only—times for success and ease in these activities, according to your Sun sign.

	JAN	FEB	MAR	APR	MAY	JUN	JUL	AUG	SEPT	OCT	NOV	DEC
Move		4-5	3-4				18-19	15			4-5	
Start a class		3		25-26				12		6-7		17-18
Join a club		2-3				9-10						
Ask for a raise		27										
Look for work					1		20-31	1		12-13, 17-22		6-7
Get pro advice		11								14	10-11	
Get a loan							27			12-13,16 26-27		10
See a doctor		23			1		22-23		2			
Start a diet		9										6
End relationship			11							15	10-11	
Buy clothes						23		17		11		
Get a makeover		25		20-21								
New romance												
Vacation										28-31	6-21	

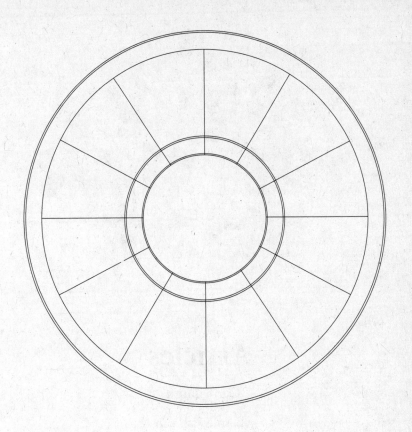

Articles

Contributors

Bernie Ashman

Donna Cunningham

Alice DeVille

Lesley Francis

Eileen Grimes

Elizabeth Hazel

Robin Ivy

Gretchen Lawlor

Aquarian Chic for Your Home

by Elizabeth Hazel

There's no real agreement about when the Age of Aquarius begins, but Aquarian trends have been gaining strength since the 1960s. As the first decade of the twenty-first century ends, the ever-moving pendulum of fashion, architecture, and decor is swinging to reflect changes in society. The technology boom and a consumer-driven economy have had a noticeable impact on houses, lifestyles, and relationships.

The Aquarius glyph—two wavy, parallel lines—implies balance, equity, harmonious placement, and flowing communications between individuals. Airy, thinking Aquarius wants the good of the group as well as accommodation for individuals within the group. This futuristic sign is ruled by both Saturn and Uranus. Traditions (Saturn) sometimes must give way to the demands of a society's changing needs (Uranus) so that all are served.

From a decorating standpoint, the planetary pair of Saturn and Uranus suggest finding innovative ways to use traditional design elements. For example, the structure and purpose of rooms and furnishings will have to be framed with fresh criteria.

Cosmopolitan Aquarius is fascinated with aesthetics drawn from other cultures. Asian ideas about design, color, and placement, including feng shui and Vashtu, are making an impact on contemporary western architecture and decor. African and South American art and textiles are becoming popular, too. Only fragmentary concepts from Asian decorating ethics fit comfortably into the architectural limitations of older American homes. Nevertheless, feng shui stresses that the primary consideration of decor is the movement and comfort of human bodies, including hospitality and the comfort of guests. Aquarius is the humanitarian sign, reinforcing the appeal of this people-centered decorating philosophy.

In Asian cities, living space is often crowded, which makes multipurpose furniture and sleek kitchen designs a necessity. In the U.S. the use of Asian fabrics and print patterns—cotton gauze, linen, Madras stripes, floral and paisley patterns, embroidered panels, and brocade—have begun to saturate decorating tastes. The focus is on textures and intricate patterns that convey an airy, relaxed elegance that has translated with ease into American decor.

Seeing a Crowded House through Aquarian Senses

When living spaces are crowded, the minimal and restrained Aquarian style seeks serenity and privacy within the urban jungle. Homes and apartments that must accommodate large or extended families must be as clutter-free as possible.

Consumerism has driven people to accumulate clothing, books, papers, CDs and DVDs, gadgets, and purposeless items that gather dust, like antiques, collectibles, and film memorabilia. Collections require space, and are difficult to display properly. An excess of anything, even if it is intrinsically valuable, becomes clutter. Most people benefit from a "can't clean it, don't buy it" attitude toward decorating.

Computer and telecommunications equipment has become part of household litter. The necessary wires and power strips can look like an explosion in a spaghetti factory. Although these items are utilitarian, few homes are designed to accommodate the sheer mass of electronic equipment that has become *de rigueur* in the past few decades.

Clutter has a psychological tie to insecurity and anxiety, so it isn't surprising that one of the first precepts of feng shui is to eliminate it. Long-term clutter accumulates unattractive and unhygienic dirt. Clutter is controllable through organization and efficient storage.

Between the collection and electronics fads, stuff is squeezing the life out of living space. Areas formerly dedicated to interpersonal communication and intimacy are now clogged with shelving units and wire jungles. Aquarian Age decor is beginning to address this issue.

People Friendly Space

Appliances have dominated living spaces design since the 1950s. Newer houses have more electrical outlets, more room for appliances, and more and larger closets for clothing. In spite of this, many American homes are not designed to accommodate computer equipment, a plethora of kitchen devices, or personal wardrobes.

In the sheer thrill of the early days of consumer electronics, people often made a point of placing televisions, massive stereo systems, or computers in highly visible locations. The mind-boggling, almost esoteric secrets of the early personal computers excused the labyrinth of wires. Thankfully, technological advances have significantly reduced equipment size, because the honeymoon is over.

Computers and televisions do not and should not replace human relationships and direct, interpersonal communication. The trend is to make electronics accessible but invisible. Televisions and computers can be housed in cabinets or armoires that close when not in use. Stereos and stereo speakers have shrunk to almost miniature proportions and can be hidden anywhere. Wall-mounted flat-screen televisions free up surface space, thus eliminating the need for television furniture altogether.

The same accessible-but-invisible trend is influencing kitchens. Kitchen appliance fronts can be adapted to match cabinetry. Storage space is increasingly efficient and space saving; some appliances are mounted under cupboards. Lost cupboard corners are now homes for lazy Susans or pull-out shelves that make every inch of cabinet space functional.

In this way, the people-centered, accessible-but-invisible aesthetic reduces technology to a subservient and understated element of the decorating dynamic.

Energy and Environment

While Americans have always had an extraordinary amount of housing space compared to the rest of the world's populations, they are now facing some of the same housing issues because of rising heating and energy costs. More people are sharing homes to defray expenses. Energy costs and long-term environmental impact are both significant forces in the Aquarian Age housing market. It's a priority to make houses and appliances more energy efficient.

Environmental friendliness has saturated decorating styles, too. Color is more nature-reflective, and room themes bring nature indoors. Colors from gardens, forests, meadows, beach, sea, and sky dominate contemporary wall paint palettes. Materials for furniture construction include renewable, biodegradable materials like rattan and wicker. Floor coverings made of natural fibers like sisal and hemp are both attractive and practical. Designers are turning to cork, stone, and other low-impact products for flooring. Natural fiber fabrics, like cotton, linen and wool, are replacing non-degradable petroleum by-products like polyester and Naugahyde.

Lighting takes advantage of natural and energy efficient sources. Lighting fixtures are made with long lasting, low voltage halogen or fluorescent bulbs. Window treatments are minimized to welcome sun light during the day time. New UV treatments for windows eliminate the dangers of ultraviolet rays on skin and fabric.

Another environment-friendly trend is recycling older items. Rather than sending furniture to the landfill, people are adding slip covers or reupholstering furniture. Wood furniture can be painted or refinished. Older furniture is also being repurposed. For instance, with a few interior shelving adjustments, old Victrola or sewing machine cabinets make very attractive storage units.

Some decorators spotlight the versatility and fun of mismatched, rehabilitated old furniture. A good example of this would be a kitchen table with mismatched chairs, all painted in the same or coordinating colors.

Functional Furniture

Americans struggle with the "form versus function" furniture equation. While an old desk may be beautiful (form), it may be too small for a computer and peripheral items (function). Furniture must be evaluated for its ability to perform the function for which it was designed. Some older pieces, particularly clothing storage and office furniture, simply don't translate well to modern demands. Nonfunctional or fragile furniture is impractical to own when space is at a premium.

Because living space competes with stuff, double-duty furniture design is becoming a necessity. Ottomans, chairs, and benches with hidden storage compartments are a popular solution. Storage tubs utilize the empty space under beds. Innovative closet designs utilize every inch of space. Futons perform as both couch and bed.

In small apartments, some older techniques are getting a facelift. Murphy beds that fold up into a recessed storage space are making a comeback. Concealed ironing boards, drying racks, kitchen work surfaces, and other equipment are being installed in new construction and rehabbed buildings. Folding step stools make overhead areas more accessible. Things that can be hidden or collapsed into walls or under shelves when not in use are another way to make space more versatile.

Rooms may have to accommodate multiple uses. A small breakfast nook in an apartment may have to serve as a food prep area, dining area, study room, and storage area. Casters make furniture easier to roll out of the way. Concealed or coordinated storage helps spaces perform in more ways for the inhabitants, and this is particularly true when the household includes children and pets.

House Style

In general, decor should complement a home's architectural style. Victorian homes have lots of small, interconnected rooms; modern homes have open floor plans, larger kitchens, and more bathrooms. Homes built before the 1960s often require smaller furniture and storage concessions. Open floor plans accommodate larger furniture, but need items like carpets and screens to define space and anchor furniture groupings. Open floor plans also require more unified color choices. Decorating is easier (and less expensive) if the chosen dwelling suits the furniture one has.

Once the house style has been determined, each room should be studied for strong and weak points. Are there big or small windows? High or low ceilings? What is or isn't in proportion? There are decorating tricks to turn liability features into assets, to minimize excesses, and to mask or distract from deficiencies. Identifying a room's liabilities is the starting point of good decorating, because it helps determine what a room needs to look polished.

Practical by nature, Aquarius's influence requires a tape measure. Pieces must fit into a room's proportions. Furniture, light fixtures, and televisions are the biggest culprits in the too big/too small battle. Furniture shouldn't block windows or doors by either size or placement, or hinder the traffic pattern.

Focal Points

Decorating wisdom dictates that each room should have a focal point. Without one, the eyes seek a place to rest without success, which in turn gives a feeling of insecurity. In the simplest terms, a room's focal point is an item that commands immediate visual attention when a person enters the room. This may be a piece of artwork, furniture, or an architectural feature, like a fireplace, that dominates the space. A room's theme and color scheme may be derived or inspired by the focal point.

Electronics are unsuitable and undeserving focal points. The reasoning behind this is quite clear: if a television, for instance, is the focal point of a room, it makes a statement that passive viewing is more important than human interactions. Mirrors aren't usually good focal points, because they should reflect a beautiful view, not people entering and exiting a room. Furniture is arranged in a semi-circle or u-shape around the focal point, and away from the walls. Televisions are side-lined in this arrangement; an accessible accessory, perhaps hidden, but not central.

This is a big step away from the days when televisions were placed in each and every room of a house. Aquarian Age decorating sensibilities emphasize the socializing and hospitality function of the living room, in contrast to the retreat-from-socializing purpose of an entertainment room.

Alternative Living Spaces

Decorating trends are opening up to new and revived types of living space. A small but clamorous minority are choosing to reside in rehabilitated warehouses and office buildings, house boats, mobile homes, and log cabins. Condominium ownership is a growing trend as people decide that exterior property maintenance is not the way they want to spend their time.

All of these new and re-imagined dwellings revolve around one key concept: downsizing. Again, less space necessitates many of the new decorating trends previously mentioned: double-duty furniture, concealed-but-accessible appliances, severe reduction of personal possessions, multi-purpose rooms, energy-efficiency and environmental friendliness.

Innovative room usage is a new trend, too. In feng shui, unused rooms (or rooms used for junk) attract bad chi, bad energy. The purpose of rooms in traditional houses is rather forcefully linked to their names: the living room, the dining room, etc. Few people have the luxury of space dedicated to expensive decor, like a dining room suite that is used once or twice a year. Residents should discuss their ideas, decide on the purpose or multipurpose of a room, and deliberately decorate to serve those needs.

Grama's China

Downsizing will become an increasing national trend in the 2010s, as aging Baby Boomers opt for smaller homes. A move from a 4,000 square-foot house into a condo with 1,500 square feet can cause a bad case of "space shock." Purchased and inherited items will face a ruthless keep-or-toss evaluation process.

A protocol for sentimental items is slowly evolving. Only the most special and/or valuable items are kept, and those items occupy special, spotlighted locations in the new, smaller home. Choices become a matter of basic household needs and size constraints. Grama's china may have to be sold or passed on to a relative.

As Baby Boomers wrestle with downsizing, American society as a whole will be affected. The less-is-better aesthetic will permeate all other age groups within the country. This is an Aquarian independence trend, combined with a dash of Aquarian emotional detachment from material items. The reduction of possessions represents freedom to travel and enjoy life, and to spend time on relationships instead of maintaining and paying for a house full of stuff.

Riding the Rainbow

Moods are influenced by colors. Aquarian Chic is expressed by using colors found in nature. Electric and primary colors are rarely used on walls and large furniture pieces, and instead are limited to accent colors. Black, red, and white are treated with great caution in feng shui, as an excess of any of these colors can have unfortunate effects on the residents of the house.

Home decor is a personality statement, and colors express personality. Time spent on developing unique personal tastes and preferences is almost always more successful than mimicking some fly-by-night decorating trend proffered by an overpaid Martha wannabe in a catalog or on a TV show. Fad colors rarely stay viable for more than a few months unless they're associated with retro chic, like the recent pink-and-black French stripes-and-dots look. Choose colors, furniture, and art that you can live with comfortably for years. Popular retro styles are always a safe decorating refuge.

For example, a friendly, sociable person might choose warm, welcoming colors (soft yellow, spring-green, rosy-pink) and French country furnishings. A conservative person may prefer colors that are rich and restrained (burgundy, deep golds, browns, forest-green) and traditional hunt club furniture. Original, quirky people may select unique color tones (teal, lavender, metallics, pale orange) to accent ultramodern furnishings and art. A person who needs a retreat from the world should choose soothing colors, perhaps a seashore-inspired color palette (stone and sand colors, muted blue-greens) with a mix of natural wood and overstuffed furniture.

A personal statement is not the same as choosing a "favorite" color for a room. Determining a room's sunlight orientation is critical to making a proper color choice. Contemporary paints are light sensitive, and the type of paint also impacts how the color looks (flat paint looks darker, semi-gloss lighter). If the focal point is artwork, take it to the paint store and don't be afraid to ask for help. Take fabric samples, too. Identify colors that echo or harmonize with the focal point. Consider both tints (lighter) and shades (darker). Select several paint sample chips, take them home, and tape these chips to the wall. Observe how the paint colors look at different times of day with the ambient light in the room. Compare the paint chips to flooring and any natural woodwork moldings or furniture. A well-chosen color will enhance the beauty of natural woodwork. It may take several weeks to narrow down paint selections to a few best-possible choices. Some stores sell paint samples so you can test a small area before purchasing gallons.

Ragging and sponging paint techniques are an easy, inexpensive way to have exciting walls, and can mask imperfections on old walls. Colors should flow between connecting rooms. Stairway decor unifies color palettes on different floors. Long-term color planning should encompass whole-house themes and transitional colors between separate areas.

The Magic Carpet Trick

It is easier to match paint, art, furniture, and window treatments to an area rug than it is to find an area rug to match everything else. Carpets are floor art, and pure wool rugs are a superb, long-lasting investment. Wool rugs have dozens of thread colors in the woven design. Carpet designs encompass all decorating styles, so a favored carpet can suggest appropriate art, furniture, accessories, and accent colors, too. As area rugs are used to define furniture groupings, it is completely acceptable to use a carpet's colors to define and inspire a room's decor. Decorating a room from the floor up can be a surprisingly successful strategy for creating a pleasing, visually coordinated room design.

Rendezvous with Retirement

by Alice DeVille

People live so much longer today and have two or more decades ahead of them to enjoy life once they leave the primary career and embark on a new venture. Buoyed by an opportunity to visualize a different lifestyle, savvy retiree wannabees allow plenty of time to invent the future. That vision varies with the individual and ranges from going full steam ahead in the same career with a different employer, a complete career shift with lots of hours, a nifty little part time job with no pain, self-employment or no work at all. If they have been living a balanced life and value time away from work, those contemplating retirement will look for opportunities to spend more time exploring social and recreational outlets that meet their goals. That may or may not include embracing a new career.

Individuals who like their work often say they don't want to leave one demanding career to take on another that is challenging and time consuming and leaves little time for fun. Yet these same individuals strongly desire a routine that involves a job. It is not unusual for someone who has been a hard core scientist or a driven financial analyst to trade in the long hours for a lower paying position with a minimum of responsibility and greatly reduced hours. Clients have told me they just want to pick up enough extra money for travel, games and investment in hobbies. Around the same time I began this article a newly-retired client told me she's looking for a side income to support her desire to gamble at blackjack. She wants to visit Las Vegas and Atlantic City several times a year.

Have you noticed firms where citizens over sixty are strongly visible? Mall stores, fast food eateries and convenience stores employ seniors for most shifts. I know of medical providers, insurance offices and real estate firms that swear by the reliability of their part-time hires. A visit to your local movie theater, bookseller or deli could also find you face-to-face with a reliable retiree working under twenty hours a week who is enjoying the people-to-people contact and little pressure. And those who don't want the income volunteer at hospitals, national forests and parks or civic organizations. Perhaps like them, you look at retirement as a stepping stone from one career to another. If you decide that working is a viable option for you, at least give yourself a few months before you commit to another routine. Have some fun—just veg out and don't make any commitments.

The Age of Enlightenment

Have you ever thought about the appropriate age in life to start planning for retirement? Do you think of retirement as a funding commitment that you make to finance the years beyond your present career? Experts say that it is never too early to begin the process. My opinion is that new hires in their first permanent position should be given orientation into retirement planning by the HR staff within a few weeks of coming on board. Companies traditionally offer pre-retirement checkups for employees in their forties so they can come up with a successful game plan. The thinking behind this target age is that by the time you enter your forties you probably have a lot going for you: a stable job, a growing family and some solid assets. Even if you have a little catching up to do, you've got time to plan for big goals like retirement. When it gets closer to leaving the fold, these companies offer retirement workshops to help the departing employees assess the Big Picture and figure out how far their money will go. Do you think it is enough to develop a savings plan and contribute to a pension plan that will take you through your idle years? Or do you believe, as many do, that there is no such thing as retirement?

The Wheel of Life: Preparing for New Horizons

In my twenties, I went to work for an individual who had a blackboard in his office on three walls. I noticed that he was marking time for some unknown reason in increments of five. When I arrived on the scene there were quite a few notations on the almost full first board and the number of checks was growing. After I got my feet wet I had the courage to ask what the notations meant. He said "days to retirement." I asked if he were close and he said he had 3-1/2 years to go. Sadly, this man was marking time to leave but not looking ahead at goals to occupy his time after he left. Within two weeks of retirement he was dead. Although he had the money and the pension, he lacked the vision to see beyond the target date to enjoy a fulfilling life.

The most important thing you can do is set goals for the future at any stage of your life. If you only have goals in a few departments of life you become bored and miss out on a number of meaningful experiences. Workaholics have this tendency. Experts suggest you develop at least two goals for these suggested areas: personal, professional, money or resources, communication, neighborhood or community, family, recreation, health, work, travel, relationships, debt reduction, spirituality, friendships, associations, and charity. It makes all the difference in the world and keeps you healthy, motivated and a joy to others.

Attitude Is Everything

We're in the midst of a population explosion in terms of the number of people in the fifty-and-over population. This baby boomer and beyond generation is healthier, better educated and more active than ever before. Boomers have more money and often two homes. For that reason they don't want to give up the lucrative salaries and the wish-fulfilling lifestyles they're used to enjoying. I have observed more and more people working past seventy years of age whether or not they are collecting Social Security benefits. Some contacts have more than one job and don't miss a beat! A common trait of the most centered among them is a sense of humor.

Often the decision to retire is based on attitude and beliefs. Here are opinions others expressed when they made the decision to retire.

- I knew it was time to retire when I had more things to do outside of work than while I'm working.

- After thirty-six years in government I was ready to retire, but I wanted to keep on using my brain. I found a job tutoring grade school students in reading and spelling and found a grateful audience and inner fulfillment.

- Burnout got to me—I knew it was time to go. Once the light bulb went off I just sat right down and started to calculate the financial plan I needed to pull away.

Several retirees said that ill health forced them out of stressful jobs that were contributing to their overall lack of wellbeing. Others said they saw the writing on the wall when management began to look for ways to thin the troops among employees in the upper-fifties age group or older. When transfers to locations that had no appeal were pushed, others with retirement eligibility knew it was time to pull the plug or be stuck somewhere far from family and connectivity.

As a Realtor® with SRES credentials (Seniors Real Estate Specialist), I work with clients over fifty who are undergoing lifestyle changes. Part of my work is to help them with financial planning. Many older people have no interest in giving up their homes and familiar spaces unless it becomes necessary due to illness or inadequate funding. Family members (usually children), fearing they will be blamed for the decision, will contact me to talk to a parent about putting their home up for sale and moving to a retirement community. Sometimes it is not in their best interest to sell the home and move on, so we look at other options.

Relocating or Staying Put

Over the years I have worked with many clients who moved from one part of the country to another after retirement. The reasons have been diverse: always planned to move to Community X, cost of living was cheaper where we moved, could afford more house somewhere else after selling our paid off residence for a huge profit, wanted a warm weather climate like Florida or Arizona, wanted to move near family or move away from family, wanted the wide open spaces vs crowded cities, sought a self-contained retirement village with an array of recreational, social, and medical amenities, decided to buy a beach house where family could gather and enjoy vacations together, and moved to a specific location based on a recommendation from a friend.

There are pros and cons to moving away from familiar places. For starters, don't do it randomly and do visit the proposed relocation spot enough times to know what living there would be like. Far too many individuals have regrets about giving up the conveniences and ease of life they left behind, and it is very expensive to correct. Unless you have your dream home picked out and have been planning a move to a cherished location, wait at least a year after retirement before considering a move.

One client told me she moved to a certain town and was miserable and could not seem to get her life together. She was bored, even though she worked and had little down time. She had very creative ideas yet felt there was no audience for her innovative ideas. When I asked why she moved there she told me an acquaintance suggested it as a carefree place to live. Just like that, she moved. Since she was well-versed in astrology I asked her why she had not considered astrocartography (relocation astrology) to determine feasible places to live. Subsequently we looked at other cities that interested her and she moved within a year to a much more compatible environment. Other "movers" with regrets indicated they missed family and wanted to move back to home base, had to travel too far for shopping or medical facilities, found product selection poor, and could not find friends with compatible interests.

Care Free Travel

Everyone dreams of the "trip of a lifetime." Start your wish list early. When you retire, you can make that adventure a reality because you have the freedom to travel when you want. Couples may share a fondness for Caribbean cruises, island hopping in Hawaii, touring the countries of Europe, Asia, or Africa, comparing the cultures of

North, Central and South America, going on a month-long trip to Australia or taking an RV tour of the USA. If you're a single retiree, group tours may have greater appeal because they're cost-effective, you meet new people and you don't have to do the driving. It is seldom a good idea to travel alone, so find a willing friend to share your adventure.

Don't have a huge travel budget? Look into home swapping with residents of countries of interest. Each of you benefits from the cultural exchange and can take advantage of the free tourist attractions in the respective locales. You could also stay at an elder hostel, although you may have to settle for some very basic cuisine if your trip includes a meal plan. Link up with AAA or AARP travel to take advantage of bargain trips.

New Routines for Domestic Bliss

All of a sudden that life you were living of getting up at 5 am and spending the next 8–10 hours at work meeting deadlines and juggling meetings comes to a halt. You'll be spending more time with your significant other and will soon discover what a retirement routine is like. Being together 24/7 after years of being gone all day or traveling for business creates a huge challenge. To say the least, you'll undergo an adjustment period. Be sure you line up enough interests to keep you busy or you'll spend your golden years tripping over your spouse.

Women who stayed at home taking care of the family undergo the greatest level of adjustment when their husbands retire. Many of them report that spouses follow them around trying to organize their chores. Spouses that were used to giving orders all the time, often asked their partner what they were going to do next if the partner sat down in the middle of the day to watch TV or read a book. Some of their answers are unprintable. Regardless of your situation, find a way to give each other space and enjoy a renewed spark in your relationship.

Money Tips

- Go over your finances to make sure you have enough income to live the lifestyle you want.

- Consult a financial planner to get a new perspective and a reality check.

- Develop a budget to make sure your retirement income covers fixed expenses as well as discretionary spending including the hobbies and recreation you want to enjoy.

- Don't tie up all your cash for your new home purchase if that is in your plans.

- Pay off as much debt as possible, even the mortgage if it doesn't take all your cash. Mortgages are still a big tax deduction so save that for last. Refinance if the rates are right to reduce the monthly payment.

- Take your social security distribution at the age that pays the highest monthly annuity to you. That will soon be age seventy for a number of individuals in the workforce. Very few retirees can live on social security alone so look at your pension, savings and investments or plan for a part-time job to supplement the allotment.

- Register for Medicare three months before you turn sixty-five. If you wait, you will pay a penalty.

- Be sure you have a will. If you own property a revocable living trust will protect your assets for your heirs. They won't have to go to probate court to collect their inheritance.

After you determine that you have enough money for retirement, schedule a consultation with me so we can work on your departure date and take a look at the time line for implementing your plans.

The Astrological Influence on Retirement

In most cases, clients who come to me to select a transition date for retirement from one main career to another phase of life have significant activity in key houses in their astrological chart. In a nutshell, they have been thinking about retirement for some time and seek validation that it's time to let go. Most notably the second house of income, the sixth house of daily work, the tenth house of career, the eleventh house of goals, and the eighth house of retirement and raises (money from other sources such as pension or social security funds) play a role in the exit strategy. Two or more houses are usually involved when the worker decides to rendezvous with retirement. Current transits form aspects between planets in the involved houses in an individual's chart. The outer planets I watch closely are Jupiter, Saturn, Uranus, and sometimes Pluto.

Jupiter relates to expansion and looking beyond the status quo for insight into redistributing assets. This planet's many themes include contentedness, good fortune, prosperity, and material and spiritual riches. After enjoying a rewarding career, the prospective retiree anticipates that life has more to offer and leaving is a step toward new adventure. A transit of Saturn signifies a change in responsibility either sought by the employee or as a result of new conditions in the workplace. Time on the job and quality perfor-mance help build a reputation of success that comes with age and experience. When Saturn drives a retirement, the prestige of a rewarding profession and achievement of goals makes it easier to finance the retirement with the promise of material security. The Uranus influence can mean conditions come up out of the blue that give the employee new options for exiting the job. They may include a sudden windfall like a buyout offer to trigger early retire-ment because the organization has new employee retention goals; the company is reorganizing and the job is changing; or manage-ment is downsizing and has to make hard decisions to reduce the numbers of employees. Pluto is slow and insidious but very deeply imbeds the psyche with life-changing ideas. When Pluto influ-ences retirement, clues have been coming for a while that suggest transforming life by uprooting or disconnecting from the workplace security blanket. Anyone with a hard Pluto aspect will have inves-tigated the pension benefits and looked at the bottom line to make sure retirement is affordable.

The planning phase of retirement means you will be assessing your net worth, so the eighth house gets a real workout. This sector relates to your budget, charge accounts, community property, credit worthiness, debt, escrow accounts, estates, funeral arrangements, insurance, interest rates, mortgages, profits from partnerships, taxes, and trusts. Examine all aspects of compensation and obligation and then invent your future.

The Final Indulgence

Pleasure is around every corner. Understand yourself and what drives you. Balance your wheel with activities that add meaning to your life. Stay in shape in body, mind and spirit. Stay connected: make plans with friends. Use the Internet to broaden your perspective. Enjoy people of all ages and appreciate nature. All dreams are possible—pursue yours with passion and you'll live a meaningful life.

In the Spirit of Your Sun Sign

by Lesley Francis

You've read them all. Every description, every adjective, every catch phrase about your Sun sign. By now, you could probably recite them *ad nauseum*, followed by whatever disclaimer you've developed to counter the less attractive aspects you perceive in those observations.

"Oh, yes, I am an Aries but I am not (a) aggressive (b) bossy (c) caustic . . ."

Anyway, you get the point. (And I am not picking on Aries. It's just that somebody's got to go first and you like to be first.)

Behind all these words, one thing stands out. Each Sun sign has its own unique path to follow, a calling, something it intends to express at its basic core. This calling is simple, yet it cannot be simplified.

On one level, it reflects a part of human development—something we choose to assimilate in order to process life here on earth, in order to experience the full potential of what it is to be human.

On another level, it points to a spiritual purpose for that particular Sun sign, something that is essential to how you live life in all ways whether you are an Aries, a Taurus, a Gemini, a Cancer, a Leo, a Virgo, a Libra, a Scorpio, a Sagittarius, a Capricorn, an Aquarius, or a Pisces.

This spiritual purpose is like a compass set for true north. It's at the heart of you. It's neither ethereal nor inconsequential. It requires deep expression. It says something about the way you take on life, how you process it. It reveals true essence.

Being aware of this purpose can help you do a number of things. You can strip away anything that doesn't further you being the best you can be, or expand your awareness of who you are and why you are here. You can shine a light on things that seemed inexplicably yet profoundly important. And, finally, your awareness of this purpose can guide you to a life more clearly, more authentically lived.

Just remember this: Not every day or every experience is created equal. So, sometimes you will feel incredibly aligned with your spiritual purpose and at other times you will wonder if it has completely disappeared. The truth is that you can block it, lose sight of it, disconnect from it; but what is intrinsically there can never really vanish. The spiritual purpose of your Sun sign is what keeps you connected to life, to how you've chosen to live it.

And, with that purpose comes a spiritual gift and a spiritual challenge. Both are meant to illuminate your journey and point you back in the direction of your spiritual purpose. Which means they can be double-edged swords. The spiritual gift can sometimes feel like a burden and the spiritual challenge a place of refuge and comfort. This is the paradox that is life.

So, consider the following observations as a door opening to the promise and the possibility, the power and the potential of who you came here to be, using the template of your Sun sign as a point of initiation. You can refine and define and rework and reassess your spiritual purpose.

Life, after all, is always a work in progress. And the choice is at all times yours.

Aries

The Aries spiritual purpose is to take a risk.

Life isn't life if you are not ready to rush headlong in one direction or another. Of course, there are many different ways to take a risk but, at the very centre of your being is the push to put yourself out there. Otherwise, life feels flat to you and somewhat out of focus.

The Aries spiritual gift is courage.

You've got more than just adrenalin at your beck and call—although the amount you possess physically and psychically scares most people. It's courage pure and simple. A resource you often take for granted *and* the fuel you truly run on.

The Aries spiritual challenge is releasing the need to be right.

Let it go already! You don't always know the answer and you don't have to.

Taurus

The Taurus spiritual purpose is to determine what is valuable.

What you do, what you say all leads to one thing—finding the rock upon which to build your world. That means looking around the world and deciding what to embrace, what to stand for. Without that, life isn't stable.

The Taurus spiritual gift is perseverance.

Ain't nobody got the will to stick with things the way you do. Once your word is given, you're in it for the long haul. That's just the way things are done.

The Taurus spiritual challenge is letting go.

You're stuck with the eternal question: How can something that was once the center of your world not be important anymore?

Gemini

The Gemini spiritual purpose is to experiment.

Life is a series of possibilities for you. Your motto? Everything is worth doing at least once. You can't possibly be satisfied with supposition. So, you sample, sample, sample.

The Gemini spiritual gift is curiosity.

It might drive everyone else crazy but you just can't fathom a life where you don't want to know *something*. Or is that *everything*? You're not sure because you never know when you're going to reach information overload (otherwise known as bored).

The Gemini spiritual challenge is to do something with what you've learned.

Life isn't always a game of Trivial Pursuit. Take time, expand your awareness and turn all that information and experience into something more substantial.

Cancer

The Cancer spiritual purpose is feeling.

Life is a constant series of feelings. You respond immediately to everything. It is your way. Knowing what you are feeling keeps you deeply connected to your life. Stop hiding this truth and embrace it. Then you will teach the planet a valuable lesson. The heart is a great place to be.

The Cancer spiritual gift is sensitivity.

There isn't a single emotional color that escapes you. You have this innate weather vane that lets you know which way the emotional wind is blowing.

The Cancer spiritual challenge is defensiveness.

Step away from the pincers. Get over the need to lash out in order to protect your soft underbelly.

Leo

The Leo spiritual purpose is to create.

Your life approach is simple. Love what you do and wait to see what happens. After all, every moment holds the promise of something new and wonderful. You really do believe you can make something from nothing with only yourself as the raw material.

The Leo spiritual gift is playfulness.

Life is supposed to be fun, right? Isn't that what it says in the Leo operator's manual? The secret you hold is you can play at anything, make anything fun. All aboard!

The Leo spiritual challenge is pride.

You just can't accept that everything you do isn't always great, that sometimes people take exception to some of those grand Leonine gestures.

Virgo

The Virgo spiritual purpose is to process.

For you, life boils down to one thing: How do things work? You have to know that, otherwise life is meaningless, without a sense of order. Life really is in the process of getting from one place to another.

The Virgo spiritual gift is discernment.

You can't imagine navigating life without examining things. It would be silly to assume that every solution suits everybody. So, you check everything out at least once to make sure it aligns with your purpose and your intent.

The Virgo spiritual challenge is criticism.

You seek perfection. If it isn't forthcoming, you turn your famous analytical scalpel, most often on yourself, in an attempt to oust the fatal flaw. Maybe there isn't one.

Libra

The Libra spiritual purpose is to bridge.

To you, the world is full of people who have just never had a chance to meet each other and, if they did, they would certainly like and accept each other. And it's your mission to bring them together and magically dissolve any negativity that might arise.

The Libra spiritual gift is being open.

Truly charitable, you can accept almost anything and anyone with finesse and *noblesse oblige*. Inclusive is the only option on your menu.

The Libra spiritual challenge is not dealing with things directly.

If your sense of fair play is violated in any way, you avoid saying so. Instead you set about righting the perceived injustice passively and surreptitiously. After all, you can't have people thinking you aren't nice.

Scorpio

The Scorpio spiritual purpose is to dig deep.

The obvious is definitely not of interest to you. Life better provide you with all the opportunities you require to plumb the depths. You want to immerse yourself totally, with no holds barred, and then emerge, shiny and new.

The Scorpio spiritual gift is passion.

Your intent is always clear. Give everything because passion is everything. What's the point of parceling yourself out, you argue. If something really is worth it, the only response is total, unreserved commitment.

The Scorpio spiritual challenge is vulnerability.

The truly ironic thing is that you cannot live the life at the level of intensity that inspires you without laying your soul bare to at least one person—yourself.

Sagittarius

The Sagittarius spiritual purpose is to seek meaning.

You are on a perpetual search for the elusive butterfly (aka the meaning of life). There just has to be something else going on beyond than all that day-to-day stuff. And it's always just beyond your consciousness.

The Sagittarius spiritual gift is enthusiasm.

You have this in limitless supply. And it's infectious. It's hard to resist all that gusto, all that Pied Piper energy. Especially since you thrive on it so well.

The Sagittarius spiritual challenge is maturing.

You just don't like the definition of being grown-up. Granted, it looks pretty uninteresting since it was invented by a Capricorn. Here's a twist. Create your own. Embrace responsibility. It actually creates more meaning.

Capricorn

The Capricorn spiritual purpose is to manifest.

What if I do this and this? This is your constant question. What will come of my efforts? This is your unending focus. You are endlessly fascinated by what the results of your efforts will be. Results certainly interest you more than the steps it takes to get there because they are the real measure of your capabilities.

The Capricorn spiritual gift is integrity.

After all, how can a structure survive if it is not built properly? And that goes for the principles of life as much as it does for buildings, roads, etc.

The Capricorn spiritual challenge is control.

Just in case it's escaped your notice, you aren't the only one seeking this out-of-reach goal. The reason it's out of reach? It's based on fear and fear is a task master that no one can ever satisfy.

Aquarius

The Aquarius spiritual purpose is to catalyze.

You believe change and growth are the only things that count. So you spend all your time getting out your electric cattle prod just to see what happens if you poke and push and electrify. What's the harm in that you wonder? It might lead to something better.

The Aquarius spiritual gift is tolerance.

Trying to decide what everybody else should be doing is just too much trouble, probably because it leads to nagging. Instead, you'd prefer to trust others to make their own choices.

The Aquarius spiritual challenge is routine.

Some things just have to be done on a regular basis. At regular times. It really isn't such a bad thing. Not everything needs to be outside the box.

Pisces

The Pisces spiritual purpose is to envision.

Your dreams run the gamut from the mundane to the truly spectacular. In each is a gem of possibility that you can make into reality. Then what you dream will truly be a vision.

The Pisces spiritual gift is compassion.

There isn't a single person on the planet that you will refuse to envelop in that unconditional acceptance that you give so easily. You take pleasure in reminding others of the beauty within.

The Pisces spiritual challenge is boundaries.

It really is just so easy for you to float off into space. Or get so caught up in someone else's life that you forget who you are. It's okay to be separate. That way you get to find out how terrific you are.

Take Action! Volunteer

by Robin Ivy

Every time an individual or small group recognizes a problem that could be addressed in the community, country, or around the globe, and decides to do something about it, the spirit of volunteering ignites. America has a history of volunteering, and many unpaid positions serve vital needs in our cities and towns.

Groups often start by raising awareness around a cause or issue, attracting other individuals who share the vision and are willing to do the work involved. Sometimes these grass roots efforts evolve into large organizations with extensive reach. For example, the American Red Cross began in 1881, when founder Clara Barton rallied a small group of friends with a common interest in protecting those injured in war. Over one hundred years later, the American Red Cross still relies on volunteer service in times of crisis and dire need. For example, the September 11, 2001, terrorist attacks on the United States, the devastating hurricane Katrina in the Gulf Coast area in 2005, and international disasters such as the Indonesian earthquake in 2006 have called for American Red Cross intervention and help.

The Sierra Club, another grass roots effort, started in 1892, and has now become the oldest and largest organization of its kind. Created to protect marine and public lands, the Sierra Club today supports pro-environmental candidates, promotes clean air and energy efficiency, and is involved in the battle against global climate change. Local and national chapters rely on volunteers for fund raising, office work, and even educational services such as designing curriculum teachers can use in their classrooms.

Why should you get involved now? As 2009 begins, the planet Saturn is deep in Virgo, a sign of dedication and service. Saturn's tour of Virgo began on September 3, 2007, and continues through most of October 2009. If you've been feeling the urge to get more involved in your community, thinking more and more about the condition of the earth and our atmosphere, or just have an interest in using your time and talents well, the timing is ideal. Saturn is the planet of organizations and structures, and Saturn in Virgo is about service to others. You recognize the work that needs to be done, and now the heavens put forth the challenge to improve, organize, and commit to the cause that attracts you. In fact the motto of Saturn in Virgo could be: "Be productive, lend a hand."

Match Your Volunteer Style

Once you decide to volunteer, determining where, when, and how to serve is the next step. Is it your nature to join a larger, more established organization like the ones discussed here? Or are you more likely to find a small group that is addressing a local issue or need? Could a hospital, hospice, or school inspire you to donate your time and talent? Perhaps you have the pioneering spirit and passion to start an organization of your own with a specific mission in mind. Volunteering takes so many forms and has so many faces! Your sign of the zodiac may have a bearing on the kind of work you're most suited to and the type of cause you're motivated by.

By exploring your Sun sign, you may see how your personality is best matched to volunteer opportunities. Are you an air sign suited to people oriented work or an earth sign preferring a hands on position? An independent sign like Sagittarius might engage in activities varying in time and purpose, while a Taurus, for example, may thrive more on regularly scheduled hours and work. According to each sign's traits, there are some suggestions ahead followed by your volunteer horoscope for 2009, during Saturn's Virgo stay.

Aries

Aries, as the first sign of the zodiac, you're a born initiator. Being involved at the launch of a volunteer group will be most exciting for some of you. Other Aries may be good at getting new projects started within existing organizations. With Mars as Aries ruler, you can draw on your energy and courage for rescue work, crisis intervention, or volunteer fire fighting. As the sign of the child, you may dedicate your talents to coaching, assisting in schools, or organizing sports and games in after-school programs. In the political world, you assume the role of presenter if your group has a voice in city council, school board, or other government meetings.

While Saturn is in Virgo, you are one of the signs most likely to be called into service. Volunteering to improve the health and well being of other individuals would be natural for you now, so you may consider hospital or hospice work. You could also help people improve their health by organizing a sports team or leading exercise classes if you are so inclined.

Taurus

As an earth sign, you're matched for hands-on, active volunteer roles, Taurus. Ruled by Venus, many of you have talent in the arts and can lend your skills in music, dance, crafts, and design in a variety of ways. Your patience makes you a great candidate for work with young people, the physically challenged or the elderly. You might entertain them with your songs, stories, or other performance art, donate your time for painting and beautifying, or use your green thumb to plant in parks or community gardens for all to enjoy. Strong and able, you also find building and constructing appealing. You could be a great asset to Habitat for Humanity, an organization dedicated to building affordable housing for those in need.

While Saturn is in Virgo, work with children and in recreational type programs should be especially appealing. You may become the Little League coach or lead children in learning expeditions in schools or outdoors. Any kind of creative work you can share with others will be highly valued by those you serve.

Gemini

Gemini, your versatility makes you a great volunteer! Finding the cause to commit yourself to may be your greatest challenge since you have so many interests. People-oriented work that keeps you on the move is likely to suit your personality well. Meals on Wheels or another service involving visits with older people or shut ins keeps you interested and makes good use of your conversational skills. Job coaching, resume writing and tutoring for people who need a boost academically or professionally would also be a way to share your expertise with others. Ruled by planet Mercury, you could also consider becoming a literacy volunteer.

Saturn in Virgo may keep your attention close to home, so letter writing, phone calls, and other work you can do on your own time are appealing this year. If you are a seasoned businessperson, you could consider helping others start small businesses. Many cities and towns have groups that help others write business plans, find space, and learn to manage finances. Many of you have the sales, communications, and problem solving skills to mentor newbie entrepreneurs.

Cancer

Your nurturing nature opens you to many volunteer roles that require caring and compassion, Cancer. How can you best express that urge to help? If you're the typical kitchen-loving Cancer, cooking, donating, and serving food are major ways to serve your community. Cancer is the sign of family and home, so you may find reward and meaning in working with the homeless at shelters or soup kitchens. Another way to tap into your caring side is to help in a local hospital where volunteers are needed in so many departments. You could rock babies in a birthing center, deliver messages and mail to patients, or even work in the gift shop, for example.

With Saturn in Virgo, community projects that affect your own town and neighborhood will hold special appeal. Is the use of green space or an energy ordinance up for debate in your town? Does the park or beach require regular cleanups? Is there an issue involving animals that you feel strongly about? Issues that directly impact life in your neighborhood draw your attention and benefit from your skills in speaking, writing, finance or fund raising this year.

Leo

Leo, you're naturally generous and people oriented, so many volunteer positions will appeal to you. Generally, you like being on the front line, and may even accept leadership roles in either new or established foundations. Since you understand children and young people, coaching or directing youth in music, art, or performances could be your calling. Community organizations devoted to kids need volunteers in most every city and town. Athletic Leos might be inspired to work with charity marathons or triathlons for worthy causes.

This year, as Saturn tours Virgo, you may be asked to help raise funds. Your extroverted personality and generous spirit are contagious and help you attract donors. You might be surprised to find yourself in the role of treasurer or business manager, helping organize accounts and allocate funds. Organizing a gala event, particularly in the name of an educational institution or children's charity, is also a great way to put your interests and talents to work.

Virgo

As the most service-oriented sign of all, you take community involvement and volunteer work seriously, Virgo. Hands on positions that show tangible results are particularly rewarding for you. Your skills might be well suited to organizing or working with a food co-op, helping plant a community flower or vegetable garden, or tutoring adults working for GEDs, or children who need extra attention. As an earth sign, environmental causes attract you, too. Many Virgos are great with animals, and shelters and rescue organizations need reliable volunteers for a variety of positions.

If you've never volunteered before, Saturn challenges you to service this year. Regularly scheduled hours, for example, committing to one day a week or one meeting a month, will match your desire for routine and efficient use of time. With Saturn in your sign, work with the elderly could be very rewarding and you may foster some interesting relationships that give back to you in terms of learning and wisdom. On the other hand, you could be the voice of experience and help counsel those who need solid advice and direction in their lives.

Libra

Your people skills are your greatest asset as a volunteer, Libra! People tend to trust and open up to you. Any position requiring a calming influence, attentive listening, and good advice is Libra oriented. Answering a hotline requires that kind of Libra skill. You could help mediate or provide legal advice if you're trained in those fields. You're also well matched to volunteer positions that tap into your creative side.

With Saturn in Virgo, you may serve in a hospital, correctional facility, or other institution. You're likely to find your place with this kind of larger organization, where employees, volunteers and those who receive your services all benefit as you share your knowledge and skills. You will find your ability to act intuitively and in the moment grows with this experience.

Scorpio

Scorpio, crisis intervention and hospice work require a strong, confident personality, and with the depth of understanding and strength your sign is known for, you may have what it takes. Ruled by Mars and Pluto, you're more suited to face humanity's shadow side and to confront life and death situations with grace. Suicide, substance abuse, and domestic violence hotlines save lives. If you're a strong, steady Scorpio, maybe you're up for this kind of challenge.

In 2009, volunteer work that can be done with friends or coworkers will be appealing. Notice what causes your friends are devoted to and what organization your boss belongs to. Join a group whose work you feel very strongly about since Saturn favors long-term commitment. Groups you join this year may look to you for leadership, Scorpio.

Sagittarius

Sagittarius, you're known to be independent and worldly. Ruled by benevolent Jupiter, you also have the spirit of generosity. Volunteer work that allows you freedom and an active role will be most rewarding for you. Since you love animals, a shelter is a natural place to devote your time. Your interest in world culture may also lead you to ethnic centers that provide a variety of services and special events.

This year, a volunteer role can bring your business or career more visibility. You get extra kudos at work for the time you give in the community. Let the company know how you're contributing. If you own a business, you may become a sponsor of a worthy cause.

Capricorn

Capricorn, your work ethic and resourcefulness is just what every volunteer organization needs. From the hands on work of Habitat for Humanity to business coaching for young entrepreneurs, you have so many valued skills to share. You could contribute to career-oriented groups that help people get back to work. Aiding the homeless or poor will appeal to you provided you can teach others to help themselves in the long run.

Volunteer work you take on this year really opens your mind and may even lead you to a new opportunity. For some Capricorns, this is the year to join the Peace Corps, Vista, or other internationally known organization. Going to areas that have suffered tragedies and helping rebuild is rewarding since you can see tangible results.

Aquarius

Aquarius, your vision, sense of community, and commitment make you a great volunteer! Your forward thinking and leadership skills make you an initiator, but you're equally happy to join an existing organization with a cause you have a passion for. Either independent or team positions can suit your style. Sharing your knowledge, from tutoring to technology coaching, would be enjoyable for you.

In 2009, Saturn has a spiritual influence on you. This may lead you to volunteer work that requires compassion including hospital or hospice work. A position affiliated with a religious organization could attract you.

Pisces

You have the empathy and generosity to make an excellent volunteer, and work with animals, in community gardens and co-ops, and in the arts matches your natural gifts. You could be suited to work with the sick, homeless, or drug addicted as well, but you are very sensitive and need to set good boundaries if you do.

In 2009, you and your partner or best friend may feel inspired to volunteer together. Dedicating yourselves to common work will forge an even stronger bond between you. Animal rescue work or energy devoted to environmental causes help you tap into the earth energies of Saturn in Virgo.

A Road Map for the World of Criticism

by Bernie Ashman

Several years ago I went on a job interview for a social work position. The supervisor who interviewed me asked me a series of questions. Finally she asked me, "How do you feel about criticism?" I surprised myself and responded with a very serious face, "I hate it!" We both broke into laughter and a real connection was built in that moment. Within a few days I received a phone call from her telling me I was selected for the job.

Being criticized can be downright painful and depressing. It hurts to be told that you haven't done a job right. People sometimes try to soften the blow by saying they are offering constructive criticism. But does that really make you feel any better? Probably not!

One of my favorite sayings is: "Be harder on the problem than on the person." We are all human and therefore will at times be too critical of others. It's important to learn how to later make positive comments about a person you may have hurt with the wrong remarks. You can always say the magic words: "I am sorry." Learning how to help others without tearing down their self-esteem takes a bit of sensitivity and is a learning process.

Each of the twelve astrological signs reacts differently to criticism. What follows is a brief guide pointing to how each sign deals with being criticized. Perhaps this discussion will help you understand yourself or someone you know better.

Twelve Unique Responses to Criticism

Aries

The relentless Warrior, when faced with criticism, will either react spontaneously with anger or hide a hurt ego in dead silence. You can never be quite sure which response you might get. Why? Because this fiery soul isn't exactly sure him or herself which reaction to choose. These fast-paced people tend to act on instinct. The men tend to generally respond more aggressively to confrontation. The women may start slowly, but then warm up to a very direct self-expression to thwart off the opposing opinions.

The path to harmony with these adventurers, is to first say something positive even if you are upset with this dare-devil. Aries is full of raw energy. There is a primaeval sense of survival in their bones. Criticism feels like an immediate threat to their security. It's like a match to gasoline to pounce on their ideas with a frontal attack of displeasure. It's a far better tact to let one of these fireballs down slowly.

If you are an Aries, then remember to be patient and listen carefully to those not agreeing with you. Take from their words what you can incorporate into your life and try not to overreact. But for sure don't give up on a key goal because someone doesn't approve. The key to success in the midst of adversity for your sign is to move forward with poise, and to deepen your ability to stay objective even when your emotions are on fire.

Taurus

The persistent Bull can become downright bullheaded when provoked by criticism. Those critical of a Taurus can be stampeded by a flurry of defensive stands. This sign likes to stake out life on its own terms. The men display a hurt face—a self-portrait, painted with a question, "You aren't really trying to mess with my ideas, are you?" They dig in deeper when fighting off conflict. The women can typically retreat behind a quiet demeanor. What can (and should) worry you is what she is plotting behind the calm smile. After all, she is feeling that surely you are misguided in your negative take of her thinking. Both sexes can stubbornly wait you out until you get tired of seeing that your critical words aren't really putting a deep dent in their plans.

The path to harmony with these smooth operators is to say what you mean, even if it ruffles their feathers. If you don't, they will not get the point. This earthy bunch needs you to talk business.

If you are a Taurus, try to learn a little flexibility and you will run into less resistance to your goals. You don't have to be a doormat when dealing with people not agreeing with you. The key to success in the midst of adversity for your sign is to learn the art of compromise and to adjust your thinking to create more win-win situations.

Gemini

The mental messenger can turn your criticism right back on you faster than the speed of light, and that's real fast! This champion of the mind can fight off your criticism until you forget what you didn't like in the first place! So offer a cool, rational insight into their thinking or behavior if you want to get to first base. The men get very nervous if you state a critique of their ideas. The women can become equally as edgy, especially if you are too abrupt in your delivery. It's better to start with an intellectual spin when dealing with either men or women, one that can be morphed into more emotional feeling later. If you don't follow this tact, then don't be surprised if your words fall on deaf ears.

The path to harmony with these intellectual kings and queens, begins and ends with clear Communication (notice the capital "C"). Speak clearly with factual accurateness and with at least a hint that you are perceiving their need for lots of mental freedom.

If you are a Gemini, try to remember that you think faster than most. When you respond to those not agreeing with you, give them enough time to process your laser- like mind. The key to success in the midst of adversity for your sign is to slow down internally enough to digest the information and stimuli coming at you, so you can keep moving ahead clearly with the vibrant pace you enjoy.

Cancer

The introspective Crab can become moody when confronted by criticism. Deep feelings conceal and protect these security-oriented beings. Retreating into a shell to hide from your critical eye is their natural instinct. Shortly after birth this very emotional sign has a knack for side-stepping direct confrontation. The male version can seem like they are on the run from your verbal attacks and then suddenly make a u-turn right back at you. They are not afraid to defend their ideas if you cross over into their most highly prized ideas. The female representatives are equally difficult to predict. They often are more adept at using their intuition to know just how to make you come around to their way of thinking. You can be fooled into thinking they agree with you only to later see they managed to secretly get their own way.

The path to harmony with these mysterious and sensuous personalities is to tread on their egos lightly. They would rather you just read their minds or not too boldly express displeasure about them. With practice, you may discover how to get a Cancer to hear the real emotion embedded in your words.

If you are a Cancer, try to understand that the rest of us can't read your mind. If you disagree with our opinion, please tell us why. The key to success in the midst of adversity for your sign is to tune into your own emotional undercurrents, and don't forget to reveal the signals to others that will keep them in the know about your real needs.

Leo

The dramatic Lion or Lioness has an ego that is easily bruised by criticism. Although, they may never let you see their pain. Then again, the Lion of this sign can explode if you interfere excessively with his ferocious ideas. Generally speaking, the female ambassadors of Leo accept criticism better than their male counterparts.

However, their feminine power will eventually blow you out of the way if you keep stepping on their freedom-oriented toes.

The path to harmony with these dynamic souls is not to crowd them, yet you have to talk straight and loud enough so they get your message. It's best to let them think they are in control when you are pointing out their flaws. Be sure to keep the fun and seriousness separate if you want to get their best attention.

If you are a Leo, please understand that others can't always dance to your tunes. The key to success in the midst of adversity for your sign is learning how to share center stage.

Virgo

The efficiency expert responds to criticism by inspecting your words to see if they are orderly and logical. This is as important as your displeasure to this sign! It's not a good idea to attack the Virgo's need for routine and perfection. The men tend to turn critical remarks on their heels by accusing you of the same behavior. The women might reframe your questions and accusations to make your words less anxiety-producing.

The path to harmony with these meticulous souls is to carefully point out what you perceive to be bad judgment on their part. Don't talk in a blaming tone as it only serves to escalate any disputes.

If you are a Virgo, try to understand that those of us trying to interact positively with you might need some instructions on the best way to play by your rules. We want to speak your language. The key to success in the midst of adversity for your sign is not to get lost in the details, and to maintain a broad enough vision that allows others to walk the journey with you happily.

Libra

The social diplomat doesn't like much conflict. Don't be surprised if he or she is weighing your remarks on a set of scales to evaluate just how to respond. The men would rather the tension instilled by criticism disappear through compromise. The women might choose to distract you away from your concerns or observations through convincing you to talk over your differences at a restaurant or other pleasurable place. Each of the sexes demands fairness during disputes.

The path to harmony with these gregarious types is to give them plenty of time to reflect over your dislikes. The trick is to be sure to emphasize what you like about them. Better yet, if you talk in a matter-of-fact tone, rather than an accusing one, you are more likely to be heard.

If you are a Libra, learning not to fear disapproval is as important as accepting a little criticism now and then. When you stay cool under pressure you maintain a better sense of balance and inner peace. The key to success in the midst of adversity for your sign is learning to flow with life's ups and downs.

Scorpio

The quiet and resilient Scorpio doesn't show their hand when criticized. They tend to process, reflect, and perhaps brew. Their response varies, depending on how hurt or befuddled they feel. The men definitely can stay silent for long periods of time. The women will usually let you know how they feel, but with a lot of intense emotion. Both sexes may explode if holding their feelings in too long.

The path to harmony with these passionate souls is to not rush them. But then again, it's a good idea to see if you can get them to talk. They might scream at you initially, but if you stay persistent, will get it all out on the table, if that's what you desire. Learning how to get them to open up is a lifetime of practice. It will test your patience. It's a bond of trust the two of you must build.

If you are a Scorpio, then learn to communicate. It might be painful, but it brings those you care about closer. You won't lose your power or wealth by developing openness with others. Honest! The key to success in the midst of adversity for your sign is not fearing self-analysis and to stay in touch with your inner motivation for actions.

Sagittarius

The adventurous and jovial Archer is sensitive about criticism. They hate being told they're wrong. This is a generous sign in many ways. The men can demand to be told the truth, but may react angrily afterwards. It's only when they grow dogmatic or narrow in their thinking that they tend to argue incessantly. The women can be just as strong-minded about their ideals. Both sexes will be more open to criticism if you point out the big picture. Your criticism has to fit into their idealistic and lofty outlook.

The path to harmony with these energetic fireballs is to engage them more so when you are traveling or doing something that is active. Their minds are restless and they listen better when they are in motion. Their saving grace is their ability to eventually adapt to change or to make changes you need to see.

If you are a Sagittarius, remember to keep an open mind when challenged. You can hold onto your ideas. Let others speak freely. The key to success in the midst of adversity for your sign is to agree to disagree and don't lose sight of the trees when exploring the forest. The little things can matter to others, even if not important to you!

Capricorn

The Goat, a champion of pragmatism, can stop in fear when criticized. However, they can stay so focused on an objective that nothing will hold this earthy, solid-as-a-rock sign back. These people don't like failing, so be careful about how you express any disapproval. The men are likely to make concessions if you communicate in a businesslike way. The women will work with you if you respect their point of view, and please don't forget to do that!

The path to harmony with these grounded souls is not to ask too much in the way of change overnight. They need time to snuggle up to the suggestion. You do need to talk directly to get their logical brains to hear you.

If you are a Capricorn, try to bend a little. When you make a concession or two, others will do the same for you. The key to success in the midst of adversity for your sign is to realize that letting others see your faults only serves to strengthen you. It's when you remember to enjoy the journey that the steps to success are filled with joy, allowing those you love to appreciate you more.

Aquarius

The Rebel and Innovator can become aloof in reacting to criticism. The mental filters are huge and quick, making you wonder why you voiced any displeasure in the first place. The men might show great surprise along with a little defensiveness if you attack their ideas or favorite way of operating. The women can react in the same way, and like the male persuasion of this sign, rebel strongly against a critic.

The path to harmony with these unpredictable lightning rods is to state your position swiftly and concisely, and you might try leaving out excessive emotional outbursts. Why? Because they will stop listening if you get too far off the mental highway.

If you are an Aquarian, be patient with those questioning your actions. It's not that others necessarily want to hold back your freedom. They may need you to consider their needs as well. The key to success in the midst of adversity for your sign is not to fear emotional situations and to perceive how to get what you need through utilizing clear negotiation strategies.

Pisces

The Dreamer and Idealist may run for a favorite escape in responding to criticism. These are sensitive souls. The men live in a world of dreams and ideals, and they don't exactly seek out conflict. The women are more apt to listen to critical commentary about themselves, but like the males, they could slip into dead silence and hope you will let them off the hook, whether they change a behavior or not.

The path to harmony with these mysterious people is to first realize you are talking to beings that live in a different inner world than you. They peer out into the outer one wishing not to be inconvenienced by you pointing out their imperfections. So, communicate clearly and be prepared to repeat the same message until heard.

If you are a Pisces, it's important that you do talk when your thinking is questioned. Silence is not responding! People will not be able to read your mind. The key to success in the midst of adversity for your sign is to walk your talk, and then translate your actions so that the rest of the world understands you.

Find Your Passion: A Guide to Finding Work

by Eileen Grimes

Once upon a time there was a young boy who seemed destined to become a doctor, like his father, and his father before him—the entire family expected it of this boy. There was basically no other possibility for this young life: a doctor he would have to be.

From an early age, medical books were thrust into his lap by his father, and his mind was being inundated by an enormous amount of medical data and information all through elementary and high school. When he got to college, he breezed through the courses of study with honors. And when he got to medical school, he excelled there, too. He worked very hard to achieve this goal, much to the pleasure of his father, whom he always tried to please.

Then, just as he started his first practice, his father died, and overnight this man's drive to be a doctor died as well. He could not understand it. He was left with nothing but a hole where his ambition should be, and little or no energy to work at what he worked so hard to achieve. What happened? Why had it all come to a screeching halt?

He had developed his medical talents and was an excellent doctor. All of his patients loved him. Throughout his life he had looked to his father, and the rest of his family, as the measure of his success. But after the father's death, it all meant nothing. A lifetime of study—thousands of dollars and hours of work—down the drain.

The emotional investment in this work was significant; his entire being had been on pointe toward this goal. The man had reached a crisis point of no return, and yet he couldn't go back to what was. It would have literally killed his spirit to do so.

If we were to look back into this man's private moments, we would have seen exactly what was sustaining him throughout all the years of pressure from his father. Behind his closed doors, and under the bed covers, he was looking at the medical books, but he was drawing and sketching what was in those books. Those precious moments brought him complete joy and peace; he absolutely loved to draw and sketch, but because of his father's constant hovering presence, he felt he had to keep that side of himself secret. Making a living as a doctor was the only allowable expectation. The son was left alone to fulfill dreams that weren't his.

His private moments spent working with his art sustained him through the difficult time of having to be what he didn't want to be. The essence of who this man was, was in the artwork he created in private.

. . . .

How many of us hide who we are under a bushel, or in this doctor's case, in his bedroom under a blanket? One of the most difficult things to do through in life is to face who we really are versus who we think we are, and look at what kinds of results have been produced. Our doctor had an expectation of being a doctor his whole life, until his father died, and then he found out that it wasn't what he wanted at all. It is hard to imagine investing an entire lifetime in an image or profession that we really don't want for ourselves. Yet many of us do this. After all we spend a great deal of time investing in that part of us—at least we deserve to be who we're meant to be, and not someone else's expectation of us.

If the time spent at a job is no longer giving us sustenance, or we have lost our passion for it, we need to shift directions and re-find the grains of passion within us. That might include a complete change in direction, but it also might include a repackaging of what has been done before. Passion and enthusiasm for what we do will sustain us in almost any kind of job situation, even if the job doesn't look like something we would have chosen for ourselves.

In my own case, I was looking at my own expectations of myself in my professional life. There have been many twists and turns in my career. I have been an astrological counselor for the past seventeen years. At one time I did very well with it, and was able to sustain myself financially. I had also spent the years between 1994 and 1998 writing my first book.

I had expected that astrology would be my only source of income for the rest of my life and I would become well-known because of the book I wrote. Those were huge expectations! After the first few years, however, the money started to decline. I still loved it, but the tide was turning. I was weary of having to endlessly promote myself. I was pretty much empty of desire and focus. I had no energy left. At that time, too, I had also been diagnosed diabetic, so I had to focus on health issues.

After I got my physical health in reasonably good order, I started to reexamine my purpose and my true motivations. I was still doing astrology, but I had to acknowledge that astrology might not pay the bills. I became depressed and abdicated personal responsibility for making a good living to support myself. I started to rely on my uncle and his family to help me pay the bills. They resented that after a while, I can tell you, and when my family finally pulled their financial support, I had to get with the program. (I must thank, in particular, my uncle, whose "tough love" turned my life around.) Something had started to free up within me, and I began looking at other options.

Part of this rebuilding process involved looking at many of the gifts I had inherited and that I still valued. I realized that I came from a long line of very creative people, and I am here to continue that legacy. Both my parents had had abundant creative abilities. They were both professional artists in the 1950s and 60s. I remember that early in my childhood my parents spent a great deal of time creating their masterpieces (I have over 300 paintings of theirs). I couldn't help but follow in their footsteps in some way; my venue early in life was music, and still is to some extent, but I later found my own avenue of visual creativity.

I also looked back at a few other previous career possibilities. First, at administrative work, which I had never fully enjoyed, but I had developed a keen critical eye, especially when proofreading documents. However, I found the more I looked in this old direction, the less momentum it had. I was applying for clerical jobs, and nothing happened. Clearly, something had changed, because the previous types of employment weren't opening up.

Then, I went back to another time in my life. In the 1980s I had worked as a fashion/image consultant, which was a very popular profession at that time. I remembered that I had been so passionate about it. That was a huge key—the passion. I found that I was very good at assessing the right colors and personal style for my clients. I worked with clients to creatively build their wardrobe; my clients were the "canvases" that I worked on.

I started to think about working in women's retail clothing again. There was no reason I couldn't do the same work I had done twenty years earlier, but from within the framework of working in a retail store. On a whim, I applied online to two major retailers: Nordstrom and Macy's.

Within one hour of submitting the application to Nordstrom, I was called for an interview, and a few days later, I was offered the job. On the same day, I was also called by Macy's to interview in their larger women's department. To make a long story short, I worked at Nordstrom for two days, and quit, but I felt as though Macy's was calling me. And it did—literally!

A Fashionista in Spandex!

I was pacing around my house on the following Sunday morning, wondering if I should bother with working in retail—Nordstrom had not been a good fit, after all—and heard in my head: *Get to Macy's now!* Now, take into consideration that at that moment, I was not dressed for success. I was in spandex work-out clothes, a Superbowl cap, sneakers, and my hair was wet. The thought of going to Macy's dressed like that was more than a little embarrassing. I argued with myself all the way to the store, but when I got there, the manager that had wanted to meet with me before was there. I met with her for a short time before she offered me the job. She also placed me in as a specialist, which usually requires several months of service before promotion to that type of position.

Another major realization hit me at that time: my mother had told me that I'd never be good in sales. I had to confront a belief about myself that I had assumed was true. After a few months on the job, I realized I *was* doing very well in sales. After all, if I could sell myself, I could sell clothing! (Twenty years self-employed had counted for something. Those skills I learned from my own businesses applied wonderfully on the new job).

As my first year at Macy's ended, I had $400,000 in sales. I have submitted a proposal to Macy's to implement special training programs to do the type of work I've been doing with image for over twenty years. I want to teach other sales staff the techniques I've used during my image consulting years, and think that that kind of specialized service will really help spark new business for Macy's. I realize I want to get back into training and teaching, where my heart belongs.

I can tell you this: When the timing is right, and the situation is right, and the job is right, you *can* get a job—even if you're wearing spandex! The doors will naturally open and admit you. You just need to take the step through to the other side.

We have to assess what our version of success looks like because it cannot be compared with anyone else's. Our process in life is our own, and events will play out in their own way, in their own time. The important thing is to pay attention to the direction your life seems to be going in. The manifestation of one's dreams into reality depend on following a course that works for you. Drop what doesn't work, and adopt what does work.

What About You?

Take a look at the following list, and see just what might help you make a new start. Write down the answers so you can see where you've been, and acknowledge the movement you've made in your life.

1. Are you doing things in your life that you bring your God-given talents to?

2. What are those talents? You likely have talents you're not even aware of. What are those things you do with natural ease, that maybe others don't?

3. What do you perceive are your gifts? Where, or whom were they inherited from?

4. What are some skills you've used in the past that you perhaps have forgotten about, that you can bring forward to today? How can you take those skills and perhaps repackage them, so that it creates a demand in today's job market?

5. What do you do that no one else can do as well as you? What makes you indispensable?

6. What things do you do that make you an expert?

7. Who seeks you out for your wisdom? (These are people who might hire you!)

8. Do your talents give you as much joy to they do for others?

9. What do you do that you would pay someone to let you do?

10. What do you have fun doing? Could it be parlayed into a job?

Once you figure out what you've got to work with, you'll be better able to identify something that suits you. If you're at a loss as to what your talents are, here's some more questions. Take a look at each of these fundamental abilities and see which you do best:

1. Do you need to nurture, and soothe others? Does comforting and sheltering others appeal to you?

2. Do you like to inspire others to their own greatness? Do you like to shine, or help others shine?

3. Do you like problem solving with your intellect, using your mind to brainstorm, and share ideas? Writing? Do you have meticulous attention to detail? Do you like to organize?

4. Do you like the creative design process? Are you geared towards esthetics, and beauty?

5. Do you like going it alone, making your own goals, and doing things that haven't been done yet? Would you rather be self-employed? Competitive? Like to be #1?

6. Do you like teaching and uplifting others? Would you like to mentor, or be mentored?

7. Do you like running the show? Do you like to lead and show others the way? Can you step in and help structure a larger working environment?

8. Are you revolutionary? Do you like being a part of new, innovative technology? Do you function best when you're a part of a larger group?

9. Are you a dreamer who can create things?

10. Do you operate naturally, like a psychologist who can cut through layers of pretense? Do you have a deep, laser-like approach to life and relish helping others with deeper problems?

It is indeed possible to find any of these qualities in jobs out there. Identify one or more you really relate to, and go from there to find a job with those qualities. I was lucky to realize I could use the creative principle and teaching and mentoring in my job I do now. And it is infinitely satisfying.

. . . .

And, what about that doctor from my first story? After the dust settled, he parlayed his artwork into a sideline career. His father's death was the catalyst that moved him into his real profession. He didn't give up medicine, but he no longer hides his creative light under a blanket. He allows his creative side to come front and center in his life, so that he can be a better doctor. In fact, one feeds the other; he gets his needs met through the creative work, and he is more able and available to work with those who are sick and need healing. And his pictures now hang in his medical office.

We can reinvent the wheel, or repackage our existing skill-sets into new ones. In fact, it is periodically necessary to keep life fresh and moving forward. If you are going through a professional reassessment right now, shelve all those unfulfilled expectations, and then find out what your passions are. If you do that, you can start to infuse your work with what your true nature is, and perhaps find a place where your talents can be utilized. Your job/career, no matter what it is, will be satisfying to you. This can make an enormous difference in the psyche and the spirit.

Whatever you do, do it with joy and purpose, and passion.

. . . .

Note From the Author

At the time that I went through this change, a massive double Pluto transit—Pluto squaring my Sun/Moon opposition at the same time—was occurring, and I was looking at what I needed to feel emotionally secure and stable, as well as giving my own ego, if you will, some greater definition. This transit really revealed all of those things to me, as well as helping me to let go of past models of myself that were clearly worn out and not functioning anymore. It really had to do with, like I said in the article, going back and revisiting areas of my life where I had some kind of success with something, and perhaps re-finding the gifts that were mine to use.

I think, too, I wanted to see in what areas of my life I could experience joy and passion. Working with color and clothing was a great deal of fun. I even remember the first time I realized I wanted to become an image consultant and finding someone who could mentor me. It was one of the most joyful times in my life, as well as extremely passionate. That joy and passion are what I was looking for again.

Pivotal Moments: The Powerpoints of Your Year

by Gretchen Lawlor

Have you noticed that you are inclined to launch major projects at the same time, year after year? Or that you have met significant loves or great friends in the same month, though years apart?

What if there was a predictable window in your year that could almost guarantee a successful outcome to any venture initiated during that time? What if there was a time when progress would only occur if you collaborated with others, a time when pruning back your efforts in all matters would ensure sturdier and more authentic growth for the rest of the year?

We feel new hopefulness and *joie de vivre* in spring, and we slow down with the inward turn of the wintery months. The power points of equinoxes and solstices are pivotal turns in the cycle of a year and affect our energy and attitude. These shifts remind us that we are part of some greater story, that we too are creatures of this planet, affected and informed by mysterious rhythms beyond our smaller desires, intentions and understanding.

How to Calculate Your Personal Powerpoints

Sign	Awakening	Grounding	Connecting	Celebrating
Aries	April	July	October	January
Taurus	May	August	November	February
Gemini	June	September	December	March
Cancer	July	October	January	April
Leo	August	November	February	May
Virgo	September	December	March	June
Libra	October	January	April	July
Scorpio	November	February	May	August
Sagittarius	December	March	June	September
Capricorn	January	April	July	October
Aquarius	February	May	August	November
Pisces	March	June	September	December

There is another cycle attuned to our own birth season and birth sign that further elaborates upon and refines our interactions and efforts in the world. Astrology, as a highly sophisticated study of cycles, reveals a unique pattern to each person's yearly experience that is based upon the month of birth. What appears random and out of our control can actually be predicted and used to make our lives easier and more gracious.

There are months best suited for those born in a specific sign for all manner of things: launching new ventures, putting work on public display, resting and recharging your energy. Think of this as wise ecology, your personal contribution to the energy crisis. If you are in sync with your own rhythms, you experience less resistance, you use less energy, and you stay healthier and happier.

Each Sun sign has four key power months around which the rest of the year pivots. These powerpoints act together like a compass, allowing you to make incremental steps in a course of action, to pace yourself, and to map your progress. These are months for focused intent—the most important times to check your course.

The other months of the year organize around what happens in these four. It's helpful to remember that you do not need to be pushing hard all the time. A healthy cycle must contain both ebb and flow, action and effort that is nourished and informed by moments of stillness.

Awakening

This is a crucial month in your annual journey, when impulses deep within you are cultivated in your imagination and begin to stir in your veins. Throwing off inertia, you feel compelled to step beyond the rules and expectations that have dictated your efforts in recent months. Now is the time to head for what you want. Create. Take risks. Shrug off forethought and caution and just do it—whatever your impulse leads you to.

There will be time later that is better suited to modifying or clarifying, but for now, new things are being born of you. Life is an act of faith and you do not know where you are going. New life is spilling out of you; let your impulses propel you forward. Take inspiration from the image of the Fool in the tarot cards. The Fool instinctively steps forward, even though the circumstances and the nature of the journey ahead are yet unknown.

It is important to trust that you have already been preparing for this Awakening time, that your instincts have put you in just the right alignment to respond perfectly to this moment. In the last few months, if you think back, you will understand how you have been setting up the perfect circumstances for this time. Whether consciously or unconsciously, you have been thinking about new projects and new interests you wanted to develop. Through dreams or in contacts with inspiring people, exciting possibilities, and fresh goals have appeared upon your horizon.

Don't concern yourself with the details of how you will accomplish anything; this will naturally emerge in the months to come. Trust that *life* is living through you; that you are a perfect conduit just as you are.

Notice the things, interests, projects, or people that used to be important, but no longer spark your enthusiasm, passion, or curiosity.

Notice what has recently dropped down in the list of your priorities for the year ahead, perhaps dissolved, disappeared, been lost or taken away. Notice where you have been saying no, even if this has brought you grief. All of those things and events have prepared you for this moment of Awakening. Appreciate how all of this has helped you make space for something new to emerge in your life.

This making of space is most important, a necessary emptying. Stress and overwhelm come from hanging onto everything, from continually adding more to your schedule, for never letting the old life go. We have forgotten this important truth in our busy lives as we double book our calendars and fill our days with impossible lists, as we forever push and hungry for more.

We have truly forgotten the rich abundance and sweet simplicity of down time. We have forgotten that the lush green growth of the old year naturally decays to provide good nourishing compost for the new year's seedlings.

Grounding and Gathering

This is the month to steady your course, not to expand but rather to stabilize, to gather in energy or even to cut back your efforts. Life is manifesting its fullness, and you can become swamped by so many possibilities that your original intentions are obscured.

This is a month best suited for feeling your way into what is emerging, for making it your own, for reconsidering and reviewing, pruning and marking your efforts with a personal touch.

Allow yourself to rest and to dream. Directions will then be able to well up from deep in your subconscious. Eat slowly, stare out the window, cancel unnecessary meetings, fritter away time just doing nothing. Trust that this is important to the larger scheme of things Trust that this stillness will ultimately make all efforts, projects, and intentions much richer and more truly reflective of your own inner being. There is a regenerative quality in stillness. In Chinese medicine, it is believed that stillness grows strong bones (in this culture we believe bones can only strengthened by plenty of aerobic weight bearing exercise. Hmm).

You'll be happiest in familiar surroundings and feel less inclined to push yourself or your agendas out to the world. This is the time to reconnect with your family, to review your history and acknowledge your roots. In doing so, you will become more aware of motivations that direct (or even sabotage) your efforts. Psychological self-evaluation or even the support of a wise friend or professional counselor in this month can help you identify behavior patterns from your past that are no longer appropriate.

You have been preparing for this time. If you look back at the last couple of months, you will see that you have found ways to support your awakenings, you've shared your dreams with others and made connections that will help things happen you've found your voice and had important conversations about what you are doing and caring about. You've gathered information, made contacts and explored possibilities. Now, in your Gathering and Grounding month, it is time to check whether you like the feel of what is emerging.

We override our feelings and instincts all the time. We don't rest. This is the month when it will seem that attempts to quiet down and go inward will be particularly fruitless. Young children, still in touch with their instincts, tend to get ill in the month around their power points. A pause in their schedule, due to sniffles and fever, allows for integration and reorganization- and is usually followed by some significant developmental leap in the next few months.

In the next few months, this strategic withdrawal during the Grounding and Gathering month will demonstrate its worth over and over. Rooted in yourself, your intuitive knowing of right and wrong strengthens. During the next couple of months, devote yourself to listening to your heart's desires, and to allowing your heart to reveal new ways of living your life. Follow your heart and remember the children's game, where someone yelled "warmer, warmer" if you were closer to your goal and "colder, colder" if you were going in the wrong direction? Listen to your own inner kid when you get close to something or someone, and make sure your heart sings when you are there. Having fun and making sure your personal life is well tended are most important now and in the next couple of months. Doing so will provide energy and effervescence and improve the quality of the whole year!

Connecting

This is your month to make significant connections. Other people are very important to you and to the well being of your wishes and dreams. Be attentive to the electricity between yourself and others; it will be amplified at this time. Progress now absolutely requires that you collaborate.

Spend less time trying to know yourself and more time discovering and knowing the people around you. You need the fresh perspectives of outside sources to let go of doubts about yourself. People will feel inclined to be generous with you and they will feel as though they are getting as much out of the contact as you do.

Connecting doesn't just refer to lovers. People you meet during this month are more likely to continue being your good friends, important allies, or even professional partners in the year ahead, and perhaps beyond. Obviously, you are less able to benefit from the Connecting window if you stay at home, so get out there and mingle. Connecting time is excellent for seeking consultations on projects and personal issues, from finances to legal issues, to health and home repair. Mentors for your spiritual growth may also appear at this time.

Look for ways to expand your interactions, from the elevator to the grocery line. Get out and walk around your neighborhood. Hang out in a local gathering place, such as a coffee shop, the library, or the post office. Smile and say hello to people, your evolution is particularly dependent upon contact at this time. Be willing, as well, to scrutinize the one-to-one relationships you are part of, and be willing to release the ones that no longer spark, support, or inspire you. Review your expectations and the understandings you have with those who really matter in your life, and recommit to them. Find the courage to speak out loud your promises. Review and rewrite job descriptions.

Notice the ways in which each important relationship supports the wishes for your year. As a culture we tend to feel that we are wasting time hanging out with people, that we could be more productive. Actually, your personal connections, or "social capital," will serve you better in hard times than any amount of money in the bank.

Celebrating

This is the month when your efforts ripen. Now you can most clearly see what it is you have been tending in the past year. This is also the time that recognition for your efforts comes most easily, and your reputation for the year ahead is formed. I have a number of clients who now make sure they have a gallery show booked for their Celebrating month. Instinctively, people will look to you at this time to see what you have created (even though they don't consciously know this is your Celebrating time).

I like to describe this month as similar to being at the top of a ferris wheel; the time when you come up the over the crest and from that vantage point you can see everything in perspective. This time doesn't last, though; you will drop back into the cycle, so take the time to appreciate this glimpse. It's very important for you to see the whole year, the full cycle, in context.

Celebrate your accomplishments! Instead of constantly wishing and longing for more, take this time to see whether you have made full use of what you already have. Acknowledge the good here, in the present time of your life. Celebrate the richness of the world around you, revel in your senses, and take in the abundance. This will make it easier to accept the abundance within yourself, which is the richest gift of the Celebration period.

Throw yourself a party! Give yourself credit for what you've been and what you've done. Share your abundance with others; let it flow out of you. Be aware of what you can give easily at this time. In the northwest Native American tradition, a truly powerful member of the tribe can give away everything. The underlying intention of the Potlatch ceremony, in which someone will give away most of their wealth and belongings, is to model that true strength comes from an inner spiritual abundance. Throw a party, have a show of your work, pass on what you have discovered or created, take on an apprentice, get your book out.

Review your efforts. The failures as well as the successes give you information upon which you will set your next year's intentions. Ask yourself who you have become and what you've really been trying to do during this year past. Be sensitive regarding authenticity and integrity. This is the month when who you are and what you do with your gifts will be most on stage. This time can amplify the shortcuts or incongruities just as readily as the radiance.

From the clarity and perspective of this month, you will very soon be choosing the seeds of your next annual cycle. There may be things you would like to do better, and you will choose to once again commit to their progress. Others will clearly have been taken as far as you are able or willing, and it is time to pass them on or let them go.

In the month following your Celebration month, be especially vigilant of your dreams. They will be particularly inspiring, pointing you toward the future, introducing possibilities through metaphor or through images. Write down your dreams, they are full of information. Consult the tarot, visit an astrologer, read your tea leaves, consider the lines on your palm. Be a dreamer in your waking hours, let yourself dream those impossible dreams—they are the seeds of the future. You do not need to know, at this time, how they will come into being, just dream.

Be prepared to let things go, especially in the month just before you Awakening month. This may require supreme trust, faith, and surrender. You are likely to doubt yourself, and the abundance of life. Let go anyway. Prayer is most fruitful now.

Honing and Fine-tuning

Within each of these pivotal power months there will be specific times that particularly amplify the month's intention. Over time, and through your reflections of past years, you will begin to identify these days. One in particular—the day of that month's New Moon—is extremely potent for gathering and focusing your intentions.

Life is generous and there are other potent windows that occur during your four power months. Another day to watch for is when the Moon is in the same sign as your Sun. For example, Librans would use the Moon in Libra (two-plus days) every month. These alone give you three days a month for focusing your intention and efforts. And perhaps this is all you can do, and it will be enough.

Remember also how important it is to be still, not to push but to gather energy. We tend to forget this in these pushing, striving, and driving times, and our lives are full to overwhelmed as a result. Sometimes the best way to attune to the magic of a new Moon is just to sit still.

Surrender to Chaos and to Order

The original meaning of the word *chaos* was "the essential unity of all things beyond surface appearance." This art of *being* human requires that we become more conscious participants in a hidden harmony, a higher order where everything and everyone is in its right place.

Once you begin to organize yourself around these potent months, your life will begin to flow more smoothly. Conscious of these rhythms, you can settle into your place in the mysterious wholeness and inter-connectedness of life.

Seeing each year as a series of steps, with its significant pivotal moments, makes life more manageable. Being as present as you can in the moment help. Applying hindsight and foresight that puts everything in perspective helps.

Give yourself reasonable goals, get to know your strengths and be gentle with you weaknesses. The more you know about your own annual cycles, the more present you become to all the possibilities and richness of the moment, the simpler it all becomes. You don't need to invent yourself over and over; you don't need to do everything alone, you don't even need to figure it all out by yourself. Conserve energy, tap into your own personal source of power during your power months.

All In The Family

by Donna Cunningham

You are responsible, conscientious, organized, perfectionistic, and highly motivated to succeed. You're a Capricorn, right? Maybe, but you probably are the first-born in your family. Your mate is too independent for his own good, a maverick, and rebel who doesn't fit into his family but devotes much of his energy to his groups or friends. He's an Aquarian, right? Maybe, but he's probably the middle child. Then there's your adorable but exasperating little brother—the show-off, the class clown, with charm out the kazoo, but not someone to rely on in a crisis. A Gemini/Leo mix? Perhaps, but these traits are also typical for the youngest in the family.

Psychologists have studied the effects of birth position for decades, and their results are consistent and fascinating. A very readable exposition of their findings is Dr. Kevin Leman's entertaining and helpful paperback, *The Birth Order Book* (Dell, 1992). Although it pooh-poohed astrology, it moved me to consider how astrology can modify or even increase the effects of birth order.

Check out some thoughts on your chart's most important facets—
the Sun sign, Moon sign, and Ascendant. (If you don't have a copy
of your birch chart, you can obtain one free of charge by going to
www.astro.com and entering your birth information—the time,
date, and place of birth.)

Analyzing Your Natal Chart

The positions of the Sun, Moon, and Ascendant in your natal chart
are important clues to your astrological makeup. To follow these
directions, look for the positions of these celestial bodies in your
natal chart. Your Ascendant was on the eastern horizon when your
horoscope was calculated and drawn.

One qualification—you may identify as strongly with the reading for your Ascendant as with the one for your Sun sign. The
Ascendant and any first-house planets describe the tap dance you
learned as a child to get along in your family. Rather than the real
you, it represents the role you were assigned by family members.
Capricorn rising is often "the responsible one," who had to grow
up fast and take on many family responsibilities. Doesn't that echo
Leman's description of the first-born? The Moon, which shows a
mother's influence, can also be relevant.

Let's take a look, then, at how birth order modifies the nature of
the twelve signs. If you don't identify with the description of your
Sun, Moon, or Ascendant, perhaps one of the outer planets in the
solar system makes an important angle (aspect) to your Sun or sits
on your Ascendant. For instance, Neptune aspects give a Piscean
flavor, while Pluto imparts a Scorpionic intensity, and a strong Saturn can make you seem like a Capricorn.

As Dr. Leman's book explains, there are many modifications
in birth order characteristics, especially with gaps of five years or
longer between siblings. The first-born male in a long line of sisters
may have a special place. A disabled or otherwise unusual child
may make a difference in the lineup, as may step siblings and half
siblings. Onlies are a breed of their own, part oldest, part baby. Still,
you will undoubtedly see facets of yourself and your siblings in these
descriptions.

Aries Sun, Moon, or Ascendant

First-Born

Except where planetary aspects interfere, the leadership qualities of your sign are enhanced by the steadying effects and strong motivation to succeed of your birth position. An Aries thrives on being first, and you were the ground-breaker for your siblings and now for your set or workplace. Just don't take your followers' compliance for granted, for a good leader is also a good listener.

Middle Child

The rebel or maverick side of the middle position would be even stronger in an Aries native, who fumes at criticism or being told what to do. You are ill-suited for mediation, so you are apt to strike out on your own with even more independence than most middle children. Just be sure the groups you so naturally lead don't wind up leading you astray.

Last-Born

Aries thrives on attention—indeed, demands it—and so does the youngest of the family. When you don't get your way, temper tantrums are a temptation. Don't indulge in such ploys too often, as they won't make people love you any more than they already do for your freshness, zest for living, and razor-sharp wit.

Taurus Sun, Moon, or Ascendant

First-Born

Except where planetary aspects interfere, adding the self-discipline and success potential of the first-born to the solid business sense and perseverance of a Taurus can result in a steady climb to the top and a healthy bottom line. As both first-borns and Taureans can be conservative, you are likely to stick to the tried and true path to success.

Middle Child

You are the least conservative natives of the sign, for you're enough of a free spirit to stray from the tried and true. The family business is not for you, because you want to make it on your own—and you probably will, but you'll complain that you get no respect or recognition from your loved ones. In your quest to belong somewhere, you may have to learn the lesson of not mixing money and friendship more than once.

Last-Born

It's tempting for the Taurean "youngest of the family" to equate money and lavish gifts with the unconditional love your birth position craves. Conspicuous consumption can also be used as an attention-getter, but don't equate possessions with self-worth. You are one of the best-grounded last-borns in the zodiac and thus are likely to do well for yourself.

Gemini Sun, Moon, or Ascendant

First-Born

More focused and disciplined than the average Gemini, you are likely to excel in scholarly pursuits or communication. Siblings being a major concern, you may well take on more responsibility or worry about them more than is healthy. If there is a family newsletter or round-robin letter, you're doubtlessly the editor.

Middle Child

It's hard enough for Geminis to keep their identities separate from relatives without being caught between elder and younger siblings, so figuring out who you are and where you fit into life is a long-term project. The middle child's propensity for mediation added to that Gemini flair for words could result in professional excellence as a family or marriage counselor, deal negotiator, or mediator of disputes.

Last-Born

The youngest in the family is often the class clown, and who can play the role better than verbal, witty Gemini? You show off, but with such charm and flair! Still, in crisis times when you need to relinquish center stage and get serious, these usually appealing traits can prove disappointing to loved ones who want you to shoulder your share of the burden.

Cancer Sun, Moon, or Ascendant

First-Born

You were undoubtedly put in the position of being mommy's little helper—the responsible big sis or big brother—and you may still be playing the indulgent parent to all the waifs and strays you meet. Though you may well have come far professionally, you haven't forgotten your roots and still can be counted on to nurture your loved ones. There's just that distressing tendency to overeat to make up for the energy you burn taking care of others.

Middle Child

The middle child's tendency to feel betwixt and between, not fitting anywhere, is so difficult for Cancers, to whom roots are everything. Though family feuds can prove distressing to your sensitive nature, you can provide a nurturing environment for the disputes to be resolved. Where family ties prove too hard to maintain, you are likely to make a second family among friends.

Last-Born

Sorry to say it, but you can be the baby of all babies, looking to find mommies and daddies everywhere, and feeling aggrieved and deprived when the T.L.C. you were brought up thinking you had to have isn't forthcoming. Still, you'll do anything to keep the family alive and to make family times a memorable delight.

Leo Sun, Moon, or Ascendant

First-Born

Talk about the heir apparent—you were born to rule and unless other aspects work against you, your birth position makes your ascension virtually a certainty. Coming first in the family, you doubtlessly soaked up tons of attention and came to see it as your due. Still, your sense of responsibility and keen motivation for accomplishment make you anything but a lazy Leo.

Middle Child

What a tough thing for a Leo—to always share the spotlight with older and younger sibs, not to mention dad, when you really want the starring role. Still, as family mediator in that pride of lions, you carved out a memorable niche. You may well seek out community groups where you'd shine due to your capacity to create a small universe around you.

Last-Born

The Leo's Leo, Lucille Ball, has nothing on you—you were born to perform and hold court. Seriously, you should find some outlet—even a local theater group—for that charm, flair for drama, and star quality. Otherwise, the perpetual propensity for drama can come out in door-slamming domestic tiffs.

Virgo Sun, Moon, or Ascendant

First-Born

Virgo is known for being reliable, trustworthy, serious, hardworking, perfectionistic, and critical—and so are the first-borns! Thus, unless there is a serious interference from a planetary aspect, the first-born Virgo is a paragon, the rock for family and employer. However, unlike the usual striving, success-oriented first-born, modest, self-effacing Virgos are worker bees by nature rather than queen bees, uncomfortable at the helm and likely to be the real but unrecognized center of productivity.

Middle Child

Rebel? Maverick? Doesn't sound like conservative, careful Virgo at all, does it? Maybe you just every now and then neglect to change your underwear. Bu independent, for sure. Perhaps you are a natural for the alternative health fields, where non-traditional but sound approaches and attention to detail are an asset.

Last-Born

We'd hardly know you were the youngest of the family at all, as those conscientious and hard-working Virgos shun the center stage and feel love has to be earned. Could you be the exception to the birth-order rule? Or do you unconsciously arrange for the attention your birth position craves by suffering from a variety of psychosomatic ailments?

Libra Sun, Moon, and Ascendant

First-Born

The first-born seeks to please and thus can be too placating—as can Libras, so be sure you aren't taking on too much responsibility and overdoing in an effort to keep everyone happy all the time. Too much stress comes from the impossible striving to be perfect—looking perfect, always socially correct, considering everyone's needs and point of view. You have more leadership ability and drive for success than the average Libra, but are likely to lead in a gracious, diplomatic manner.

Middle Child

You are sure to seek love outside your family, since it's hard to compete with siblings for the short supply. Middle children are born mediators and so are Librans, so you will doubtlessly find yourself in this position often. You're gifted at reaching compromises between warring parties, so maybe you should do it professionally. Just don't become too committed to peace at any price!

Last-Born

The Libra need for unconditional love can become an obsession for the youngest of the family. "Love me, love me, love me," is your plea to the world, and you can be so delightfully charming, engaging, and winsome, that this demand is almost—but not quite—fulfilled. It's just that people want such tedious and unglamorous things in return for all that love and attention.

Scorpio Sun, Moon, or Ascendant

First-Born

Combine Scorpio's political savvy and understanding of the dynamics of power and wealth with the first-born's dogged determination to succeed, and you have an unstoppable combination, unless there are other planets interfering. It's up to you whether that power to make things happen is self-serving or dedicated to transforming or reforming parts of our world that need to be healed.

Middle Child

The alienation many Scorpios feel in a society that lives on the surface can be intensified by this birth position, where you are betwixt and between and seldom first in your family's considerations. Still, your keen understanding of underlying motivations and dynamics could make you a natural mediator or healer of family or group conflicts, even as a profession.

Last-Born

Last-borns are often manipulative in their quest to get people to take care of them and can be aggrieved if they don't get the attention they feel they are entitled to. Scorpios have a genius for "psyching out" other people and knowing what buttons to push to get the results they want. The combination of last-born and Scorpio could be a bit much, until you learn to appreciate other people's unspoken needs and motivations as only Scorpio can. As last-born, you can be more easy-going, light-hearted, and fun to be around than the intense and murky type of Scorpio.

Sagittarius Sun, Moon, and Ascendant

First-Born

Academia may well be your forte, for you are a scholar at heart. Even if self-educated, you are a serious thinker, a spiritual seeker. More likely than most of your sign to stay focused on a long-term goal, your natural desire for growth and expansion can make you a success.

Middle Child

Your roots may not hold you, and you may become the traveling type of Sag. If you're sports-minded, your team commitment and loyalty can make you a valuable player. In scholarly pursuits or your quest to answer the great questions of the ages, you are likely to strike out on your own and take the road less traveled.

Last-Born

What enthusiasm, what pizzazz, what *joie de vivre*—no wonder people seek you out! Unless other planets dampen your spark, you're like the Fourth of July every day. The Fourth of July has its place—but every day? When they expect you to pitch in and clean up after the picnic, you can be long gone.

Capricorn Sun, Moon, or Ascendant

First-Born

As we noted earlier, traits attributed to Capricorn and to the first-born are virtually identical, so the combination doubles the perfectionism, drive, and success potential. You doubtlessly had heavy family responsibilities growing up, and the result is a highly capable, reliable individual born to be a CEO, unless other planetary aspects undermine you.

Middle Child

With Capricorn's innate desire to rise to the top, you are stuck in a position with older siblings always being ahead of you in learning and younger siblings needing more attention and caretaking. You'll probably find your niche in middle management, for you have a sure sense of how to juggle the demands of those above and below you.

Last-Born

If you read the description of your position, you probably think it's hogwash, for Capricorns never get to be babies anyway. They emerge from the womb with lunchbox in hand, headed for prep school. If there are any last-born Capricorns, they were probably born seven years or more after their older siblings, so they're more like only children—that is, like first-borns in spades.

Aquarius Sun, Moon, or Ascendant

First-Born

You're more conservative than most Aquarians—based on your experience, you may even be convinced that the old rulership of your sign by Saturn is true. Sill, even though you probably organize as well as any Capricorn and are prone to success, your point of view is original and inventive, and you're in the vanguard of your line of work.

Middle Child

One of the first observations I made about birth order was how many middle children are Aquarians. Rebel, maverick, and loyal to your homies? Your special destiny—and most Aquarians want to believe they have one—may well rest in your contributions to groups, and that may have been why you chose a birth position that gave you distance from your family.

Last-Born

Would the word zany describe you, by any chance? At the very least, you could march to an entirely different drummer than anyone in your family—part of what gives you that pied-piper charisma. Just be sure, when you shock for shock's sake, that you're not shooting yourself in the foot at the same time.

Pisces Sun, Moon, and Ascendant

First-Born

Mother Theresa has nothing on you—you probably adopt every stray dog or human that crosses your path and then wonder why you can't keep all your promises. And guilt? You are not single-handedly responsible for the burgeoning national debt or the shrinking rainforests, no matter what you think. Work on loving yourself as a human and fallible, and you won't be so overwhelmed.

Middle Child

You feel for those above you, you feel for those below you. You can identify and empathize with all their woes, but who are you and where do you belong in the universal scheme of things? Sorting out spiritual and ethical questions like these can keep you busy for the next several lifetimes, but at least you'll probably remember enough about the last few to give you a head start.

Last-Born

They doubtlessly call you fey, whimsical, and charming. You're a soulful performer even if you never get on stage, with the heart of a poet or musician, but all too many of you are the type mother warned us against. You know, the type portrayed in the song, "Don't Fall in Love with a Dreamer." Ah, well, the rules don't apply to you anyway, because you're not here to run the savings and loan.

Remember the suggestion that you include your Ascendant sign and your Moon sign, if you know them, or that you obtain a computer chart if you did not. Which did you relate to most? My money is on your Ascendant sign!

Note: This article was reprinted with Donna Cunningham's permission. It first appeared in *Llewellyn's 1998 Sun Sign Book*.

About the Contributors

Bernie Ashman has practiced a humanistic approach to astrology since 1974. He has more than twenty-five years of vintage experience, and he's authored books, including *Sign Mates* (Llewellyn) and the *Astrological Games People Play* (ACS). He consults from his office in Dunham, NC, and you can contact Bernie by going to his Web site at http://www.bernieashman.com/

Donna Cunningham MSW, is an internationally-known astrologer and the author of nineteen books and thousands of articles and columns about astrology and flower essences in which she combines her forty years of metaphysical studies with her master's degree in social work. Her new online seminars are designed to support people who wish to write about astrological, metaphysical, and self-help topics. See her books, writing tips booklet, and more about her seminars at www.moonmavenpublications.com/

Alice DeVille is an internationally known astrologer, writer, and consultant. In her busy northern Virginia practice, she specializes in relationships, government affairs, career and change management, feng shui, real estate, and business management. She has worked under contract with the federal government as an executive coach and management consultant. Alice is also a licensed realtor, with a number of real estate specialties including credentials as a Seniors Real Estate Specialist (SRES). She has developed and presented over 160 workshops and seminars related to astrological, metaphysical, motivational, feng shui, real estate, and business themes. Alice's writing appears on the StarIQ.com Web site and other nationally known venues, including Learning Escapes. Alice's Llewellyn material on relationships has been cited by Sarah Ban Breathnach in *Something More*, Oprah's Web site, and in material used by The Federal Executive Institute and The Franklin Planner. Alice focuses on helping clients discover the spiritual, psychological, and practical tools that support their life purpose. Contact her at DeVilleAA@aol.com/

Lesley Francis is a professional astrologer, writer, journalist, and teacher, whose five planets in Aquarius have led her on a fascinat-

journey through life. Her study of astrology began thirty-four years ago after interviewing her future astrology mentor for a story in the local daily newspaper. It proved to be a passion and an avocation until ten years ago, when her journalistic career gave way to her new life as a professional astrologer, psychic, and teacher. Lesley has lectured across Canada and at 2007 NORWAC in Seattle. She can be contacted at lesley_francis@hotmail.com/, or by going to www.andnow.ca/

Eileen Grimes, a practicing astrologer and registered counselor since 1990, is part of a growing number of professional astrologers who approach their role as psychological facilitators for their clients. Grimes is a familiar face and voice in the Pacific Northwest media, having appeared on numerous television and radio talk shows. She is the author of *Titanic Astrology: A Grand Design of a Famous Shipwreck*. Grimes' investigative approach to the astrology of the Titanic disaster has placed her at the forefront of her field, and her work is touted by some of the most influential astrologers in the world. Eileen Grimes has served on the Board of the Washington State Astrological Association, and teaches a popular series of astrology courses and workshops. To contact Eileen Grimes, please visit www.titanicastrology.com/

Elizabeth Hazel is an astrologer, tarotist, and author. She writes various horoscope columns. Elizabeth's Web site can be found at http://www.kozmickitchen.com/

Robin Ivy is a radio personality, educator, and astrologer in Portland, Maine. She fuses her passion for music and the metaphysical in Robin's Zodiac Zone, a feature on her morning show on 94 WCYY, Portland's new rock alternative. Visit Robin's Web site at www.robinszodiaczone.com/

Gretchen Lawlor has been an astrologer for nearly forty years. She writes the predictions for We'moon Almanac, that encourage, teach, and counsel people all over the world. She has a particular passion for making astrological wisdom accessible and exciting, especially to teens and people in transition. She creates Lifemaps and uses Astroplay for this purpose. For more information, see her Web site: www.gretchenlawlor.com/